W9-BGM-120

GETTING FUNDED

THE COMPLETE GUIDE TO WRITING GRANT PROPOSALS

To my friends
at BGI –
Keep up the good work!
Susan Howlett

GETTING FUNDED

THE COMPLETE GUIDE TO WRITING GRANT PROPOSALS

by Susan Howlett & Renee Bourque, M.Ed., GPC

5th Edition

Copyright © 1977, 1988, by Mary S. Hall, Ph.D.;
2003 by Mary S. Hall, Ph. D., and Susan Howlett;
2009 by Susan Howlett; 2011 by Susan Howlett
and Renee Bourque. All rights reserved.

First edition, *Developing Skills in Proposal Writing*, published 1971. Second edition 1977.
Third edition, *Getting Funded, A Complete Guide to Proposal Writing*, 1988.
Fourth edition, *Getting Funded, The Complete Guide to Writing Grant Proposals*, 2003.
Fourth edition, 2nd printing, *Getting Funded, The Complete Guide to Writing Grant Proposals*, 2010.
Fifth edition, *Getting Funded, The Complete Guide to Writing Grant Proposals*, 2011.

ISBN 978-0-9842772-8-5

Library of Congress Control Number 2011934942

Printed in the United States of America

10 09 08 07 06 05 04 03 02 01

Word & Raby Publishing, Seattle, Washington

Designed by Zach Hooker
iamabookdesigner.com

Publisher's Cataloging-in-Publication
  Howlett, Susan, 1951-
    Getting funded : the complete guide to writing
    grant proposals / by Susan Howlett & Renee
    Bourque. -- 5th ed., completely rev. and
    updated.
       p. cm.
    Includes bibliographical references and index.
    LCCN 2011934942
    ISBN-13: 978-0-9842772-8-5 (softcover)
    ISBN-10: 0-9842772-8-5 (softcover)
    1. Proposal writing for grants--United States.
  2. Grants-in-aid--United States. 3. Proposal
  writing for grants. 4. Grants-in-aid. I. Bourque,
  Renee, 1968-   II. Title.
  HG177.5.U6H355 2011   658.15'224
  QBI11-600176

Copies available from:
Word & Raby Publishing
260 NE 43rd Street
Seattle, WA 98105-6549
www.wordandraby.com

Every effort has been made to provide current
website information. All website URLs were current at the time of publication. Due to the nature
of the World Wide Web, URLs may change at any
time and some pages may no longer be available.
For updated links and additional resources, see
www.gettingfundedbook.com.

CONTENTS

FIGURES

PREFACE

This fifth edition of **Getting Funded** reflects the experience of three authors: Dr. Mary Stewart Hall, author of the first three editions and co-author of the fourth edition; Susan Howlett, co-author of the fourth edition and of this fifth edition; and new co-author Renee Bourque. The combined experience of these three authors represents eighty years of making grants, writing proposals, consulting to private foundations, participating in federal and state review committees, leading professional grantmaking and grantseeking associations, and teaching proposal writing.

New to This Edition

With each edition, the authors have tried to make the content more accessible to readers while remaining rigorous. In this edition, you will find much more emphasis on organizational readiness for grantseeking and on the importance of clearly defining the need, situation, or problem that you intend to address in your proposed project.

This edition also includes new content suggested by many of the valued instructors who use *Getting Funded* regularly as a textbook. You will find expanded sections on government funding and on how to respond to funder requests for electronic submission of proposals. Look for updated and user-friendly worksheets for planning various portions of the grantseeking process, and refreshed syllabi for one-day and nine-session classes. In addition to the selected list of resources included at the back of the book, an expanded list of resources for grantseekers will be maintained on a website, which will be updated regularly with links and information that emerge after publication. That website is www.gettingfundedbook.com.

The book has been written to meet the needs of both beginning and experienced grantseekers, from organizations as large as the Red Cross and as small as your neighborhood association. Readers from a broad spectrum of disciplines—from scientific researchers to arts presenters to social justice activists and beyond—will find valuable information on getting their projects funded.

How to Use This Book

This book is organized into three parts. **Part I** offers suggestions for how to prepare your organization and your proposal idea so that when it's time to write, you'll have the answers you need and the process will unfold swiftly. **Part II** describes the different types of funders, the various kinds of support you can ask for, and ways to determine which are a good match for your organization and project. It also advises you how to approach funders prior to submitting a proposal. **Part III** begins with information about project management for grant proposals and also details the standard elements of proposals, what funders are looking for in each section, and how to make your answers as competitive as possible. The chapters in Part III are designed to help you craft a tight, compelling document. The final chapter, "Investing in Ongoing Relationships," covers what happens after your proposal is submitted and after you get funded. The **Appendixes** include helpful checklists for those who teach courses or workshops on proposal writing, as well as tips for working with freelance grantwriters.

Throughout the book you'll find quotes and tips from funders and seasoned grantwriters as well as stories and case studies to bring concepts to life and illustrate their relevance to the real world. The stories and case studies are drawn from the authors' experience working with actual grantseeking organizations; names, places, and events have been omitted, changed, or combined to maintain confidentiality.

You'll also find a series of excerpted advice from Ken Ristine, senior program officer for the Ben B. Cheney Foundation since 1989; author of the blog Ken's Corner, hosted by the Puget Sound Grantwriters Association; and longtime contributor to CharityChannel online forums on grantwriting, fundraising, legal issues, and organizational development. He routinely consults with nonprofits throughout the Pacific Northwest, and is a valued source of wisdom on how grantmakers think and what they expect from grant proposals.

KEY TERMS and their definitions are included at the ends of chapters, and a glossary has been added at the back of the book to help clarify terms and concepts.

We trust this book will help you think about, prepare, and produce a compelling, persuasive proposal that demonstrates that your project is worth funding. And we hope you enjoy the process.

ABOUT THE AUTHORS

Susan Howlett has been helping nonprofits raise money joyfully since 1975, as a board member, development director, executive director, freelance grantwriter, and consultant. For the last twenty-five years, she has consulted with over one thousand nonprofit organizations throughout the United States on fundraising, leadership development, and organizational development.

From 1991 to 2001, Susan led the Seattle-based Puget Sound Grantwriters Association, bringing thousands of grantseekers and grantmakers together through presentations, conferences, workshops, and joint projects. Under Susan's leadership, the organization grew into the largest association of grantwriters in the country. She also worked closely with the regional association of grantmakers, which often had her train new funders on how to work with nonprofits. Most of Susan's current clients are funders, who engage her to strengthen the organizations they fund.

Susan has served as a grant reviewer with private and public foundations as well as with local, state, and federal government agencies. She served as a subject matter expert in the early development of the national Grant Professionals Certification program.

For over twenty years, Susan has been core faculty in the yearlong Certificate in Fundraising Management program at the University of Washington, where she earned their Award for Teaching Excellence in 2004. She has taught grantwriting to faculty, staff, and students in several departments at the University of Washington and a dozen other colleges. She developed the Non-Profit Management certificate program at Bellevue College, in which she taught for twenty years.

Her most recent book—*Boards on Fire! Inspiring Leaders to Raise Money Joyfully*—helps nonprofit organizations remove the barriers that keep board members from participating fully in leadership and fundraising.

Susan has served on many boards, including the Northwest Development Officers Association, which awarded her their lifetime Professional Achievement Award for a career of service to philanthropy and the development profession. She speaks, trains, and consults nationally, and is known for simplifying complicated subjects with practical tips, stories, and humor.

Renee Bourque graduated summa cum laude with a Master's degree in Education, Curriculum, and Instruction. She is Grant Professional Certified and recognized as a subject matter expert by the University of South Florida and the Grant Professionals Certification Institute. She is president and principal consultant of Bright Star Grant Consultants, Inc., and a passionate advocate for social justice.

In her roles as Bright Star principal consultant and strategy expert, she has led local, statewide, and international initiatives that integrate constituency, program, policy, and infrastructure objectives. She has led multicountry community assessment and development plans, diversified fund and program development, and managed international organizational scale-ups. Renee's projects have taken her into the African bushlands, Central American rain forests, and American boardrooms. She has worked on issues ranging from economic development to cancer, from water development to education and human rights.

Renee's work to enable people and communities to rise to their greatest potential has advanced on many fronts. Renee is president of the Puget Sound Grantwriters Association and volunteers for numerous causes in her Whidbey Island community. She engages in philanthropic work as a grantmaker for Pangea Giving and through her family's foundation. Teaching is a great passion for Renee, applied in her "Finance, Prospect Research, and Grant Writing" class for the Certificate in Fundraising Management program at the University of Washington as well as in classes at the University of Idaho and the regular workshops that she presents. As part of a team, Renee helped develop the Grant Professionals Certification exam to help bring standards and a high level of professionalism and recognition to the field of grantwriting. She has taught grantwriting at the University of Idaho to support community-powered rural economic development. You can read her articles every month in *The FundBook*, an online magazine devoted to information and strategy on government funding.

Some of Renee's commissioned publications include *Cool Tools for Grant Writers: Fund Development Resources to Reach Your Financial Goals* as well as *Grant Writing for Law Enforcement* and *Grant Writing for Neighborhood Network Centers* for the Department of Housing and Urban Development.

Bright Star Grant Consultants is a full-service fund development and organizational development firm serving government, nonprofits, and universities. Services include organizational development, grant research and writing, program and evaluation development, strategy and initiative consulting, facilitation and coaching, and training and conference presentations. Find out more about Bright Star at www.brightstarconsultants.com.

ACKNOWLEDGMENTS

Susan and Renee appreciate the many people who helped them produce this fifth edition of *Getting Funded:*

- Dr. Mary Stewart Hall, an icon in the philanthropic world, who set a high bar for grantwriting texts in this country with her earlier editions
- Peers in the field who offered early ideas and perspectives that were useful in creating a book that reflects the wide grantmaking world: Dr. Kris Mayer of KL Mayer Consulting Group, Dr. Todd Johnson of the Center for Research and Data Analysis, Sylvie McGee of All for a Good Cause Consulting, Kathleen Warren of the Washington State University Foundation, Goodwin Deacon, PhD, of Deacon Consulting, and Ken Ristine, Senior Program Officer of the Ben B. Cheney Foundation
- Jeannette Privat, supervisor of the Nonprofit & Philanthropy Resource Center of the King County Library System, a generous and zealous reference librarian who tirelessly supported our efforts to create a robust resources section for this book
- Former students Rebecca Kelley, Katrina Freeburg, and Tavia Kachel, who helped us understand how to make this edition even more useful for readers and students
- Colleagues Parke Nietfeld and Shelley Milne, who checked final drafts for professional accuracy
- Michael Wells, author of the Grantwriting Beyond the Basics series, who encouraged and promoted this book among his national contacts
- Kyra Freestar, Connie Chaplan, and Anne Moreau of Tandem Editing LLC, who edited this edition, and Zach Hooker, who designed it
- All the instructors who have invited students to embrace these lessons by suggesting it as a textbook for the last forty years

Susan acknowledges Eileen Allen and Tom and Linda Dacon, who offered beautiful places to write. And she offers deep gratitude to David Bauman, a calm and affirming husband as well as a wise and supportive publishing partner, whose skills and personality traits were the perfect complement.

Renee thanks her parents, Janet and Fred Bourque, for acting as her cheering section, sympathetic ear, and role models in life. Milo offered regular comic relief and reminders to put down the book project and go smell the roses. Renee is also deeply indebted to Doris Buffett and Candace Spitzer for providing long-standing faith and support.

DIAGRAM OF THE PROPOSAL DEVELOPMENT PROCESS

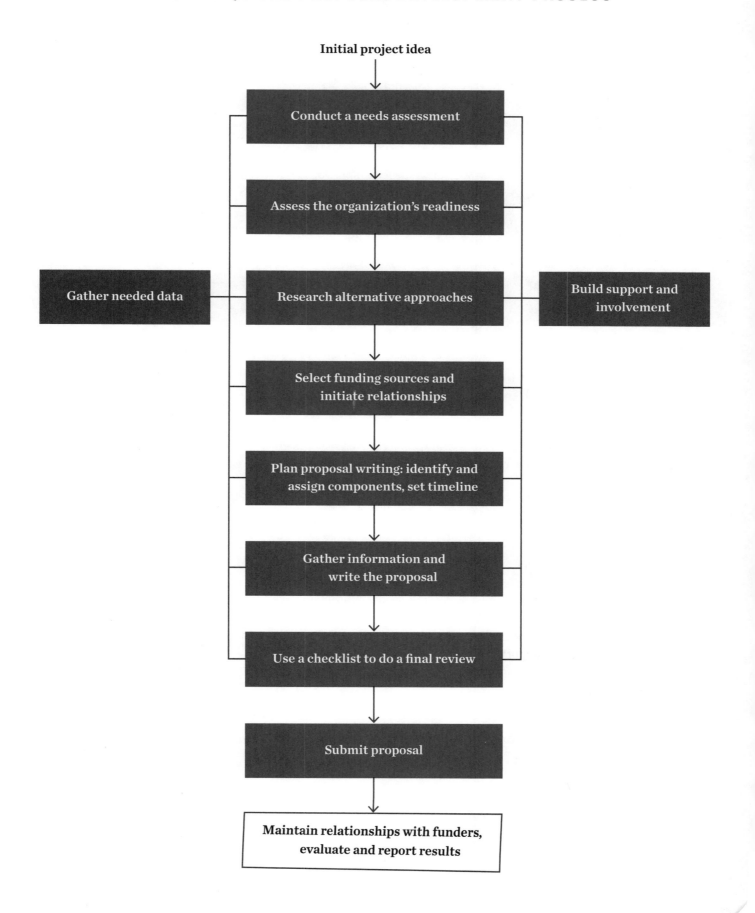

Initial project idea

Conduct a needs assessment

Assess the organization's readiness

Gather needed data

Research alternative approaches

Build support and involvement

Select funding sources and initiate relationships

Plan proposal writing: identify and assign components, set timeline

Gather information and write the proposal

Use a checklist to do a final review

Submit proposal

Maintain relationships with funders, evaluate and report results

PRINCIPLES OF SUCCESSFUL GRANTSEEKING

Imagine this common scenario:

The board of directors of a nonprofit is engaged in an animated discussion of a new initiative they hope to launch. At the end of the meeting, they agree it's time to get started on it, and task the staff member who would implement the project with writing some grants to fund it. The next day, the staff person starts looking online for grants, eager to start filling out the application forms.

This scene takes place daily in grantseeking organizations throughout the land, whether in nonprofit organizations, government departments, or major universities. There's a common perception that there's a lot of money "out there" and that all you have to do is fill out some forms to get it.

The reality is that grantseeking is a complex process that takes time, effort, strategy, and the cooperation of many players to be successful. The process of becoming an organization that gets funded—that understands from experience how getting funded really happens—is often transformative to the organization. Starting in Part I, we provide step-by-step directions for getting funded, and at each step we've offered specific details from our own experience working in this field.

In this introduction, we present a few key principles and concepts that should drive how you engage in the grantseeking process.

Plan Before You Write

As the scenario above illustrates, many GRANTSEEKERS are tempted to jump directly into writing the proposal. We recommend, instead, that you first take the time to work carefully through the planning process, and we've written the early chapters of this book to help you with that. Writing the proposal is one of the last steps in a sound grantwriting process. Good planning and preparation result in the proposal practically writing itself, because the hard part—the thinking—has been done. Starting in Part I, we offer guidance on how to prepare your organization and your project, and then we provide a road map, with details from our own experiences, for how to get your project funded. But before you get started, here are some things to keep in mind.

Grants Are Not the Answer

Many organizations go into grantwriting with the mistaken impression that if they just get a grant, everything will be okay. What they fail to understand is that GRANT-MAKERS seldom offer money for an organization to keep on doing what it has been doing. And even if they did, once one grant runs out, another has to replace it.

GRANTS are meant to be just one element of a larger funding plan that includes multiple sources of income and that uses many methods. That's because healthy organizations have diverse funding streams so they don't become reliant on one source, which could evaporate. Historically, nonprofits have gotten the preponderance of their funding from contributions from individual donors, while the donors are alive and through bequests upon their death. Those contributions may result from events, from mailed or online appeals, or through earned income from fees for services, memberships, or workshop registrations. Colleges and universities generate income from tuition and fees, while public entities can levy taxes or charge fees. Regardless what type of organization you serve, you'll need to have more than grants to sustain your work.

Grantmakers Prefer to Fund Healthy Organizations

Funders don't want to be your main source of support, and they don't want you to rely on them year after year. You'll need income from other sources to look attractive to them, because they want to know others value your work. Desperate appeals to save your organization will only lead grantmakers to believe that you didn't plan ahead or didn't maintain the organizational infrastructure along the way. Although there may be good reasons for the situation your organization is in—the economy, a leadership change, or a disaster—funders will be looking at what your organization can do to positively influence the future.

Grantmakers Operate on Their Own Schedules

Grants are not a short-term solution, and grantmakers seldom respond to the urgent need or time frame of grantseekers. Funders usually have from one to four deadlines during the course of a year, and after a deadline, it usually takes weeks to months for them to decide whom to fund. It's rare to get a swift response and not likely to be worth your time to write a proposal if your organization is looking for money in the near term. That's why it's important for you to have a reliable funding stream that doesn't depend on any single source. A good grant strategy looks out a year or two at a time.

> *"If you're calling me about an emergency grant, I figure it's already too late."*
>
> —Vice President, Community Affairs for a regional bank

You Have a Lot of Competition

Funders routinely get twice as many proposals as they can fund, so understand that you're part of a very large pool of grantseekers competing for support. There are over a million nonprofits in the United States who are in a position to apply for grants. And it's not just nonprofits who can apply. Schools—from preschools to universities—are competing for grant money, as are cities, counties, public/private entities, quasi-governmental agencies, and even for-profit companies.

A lot of organizations and agencies that used to be funded by tax money, such as parks (both local and national), are now seeking grants, and even university professors are being forced to find funding for their own salaries through grants.

The Internet has altered the circumstances for those seeking funding as well. Because funders are more visible online, more grantseekers can locate them, increasing the number of competitors. And because more data about each topic are available online, there are no excuses for not understanding your field more holistically and explaining your anticipated results more compellingly. Also, as funders offer online tutorials on how to plan and write stronger proposals, the playing field among grantseeking organizations has been leveled.

Collaboration Is the Name of the Game

Grantmakers have grown weary of funding stand-alone organizations, ideas, or individuals. They have realized after decades of experience that the only way systemic problems in a community or a field get resolved is for many disparate entities to work together. Rogue organizations aren't as appealing as those who are willing to make the effort to cooperate with others to address something that one organization by itself could not solve.

The president of a family foundation was speaking at a meeting of non-profit leaders about a collaboration she had participated in. She apologized to the leaders, saying, "I've been insisting that you collaborate all these years, but I didn't understand how incredibly difficult that is. Now that I've been part of a collaborative effort, I'll appreciate more fully what it takes. I'll also know from my own experience that it's the only way real change takes place."

You Need an Exit Strategy

Almost every funder will ask the question, How will you support this work after this grant is spent? They're investing in your project, so they want to know that you have a plan for sustaining it without simply coming back to them with your hand out again. Even if all you intend to do is buy something, such as a building or a piece of equipment, they want to know how you plan to insure and maintain it in the short term and replace it in the long term. If you're asking for a new staff position, they expect you to suggest how that position will be funded in years to come. That plan may be to ask other grantmakers, but they'll want to see what types or which sources you intend to approach to keep their investment thriving.

Even the Best Proposals May Not Get Funded

There could be all sorts of circumstances that lead the decision makers to fund another organization. There may be political maneuvering behind the scenes that you have no knowledge of. There could be a deep relationship between one of the decision makers and another organization's cause or leaders. Decision makers could have a negative impression of your organization

A group of academic researchers were taking a class on grantwriting, hoping to get their work funded. After seeing some drafts, the instructor pointed out that they might not want to use the word "I" in their narratives. Hearing her suggestion that they use "we" instead, one scientist protested that it was *his* research. But the instructor pointed out that funders prefer to support an individual who is working with a team, within a department, within a university that is cooperating with other researchers on other teams at other universities to view the problem from a more global perspective.

from twenty-five years ago that colors their opinion. Or something especially urgent or timely might be happening with one of the other applicants that you have no control over. These are just some of the reasons why you mustn't use a grant to plug a budgetary hole.

Recognize the Distinctions Among Funders

There are many types of funders, and each one views its role distinctly. While Chapter 4 goes into great detail on the various categories of funders, here's a brief overview.

Government (public) funders make grants to carry out purposes established by their respective legislative bodies (federal, state, county or borough, municipality, etc.) and generally support projects that help a large number of individuals. The funds they grant are derived from taxes and reflect the priorities of governmental leaders or bodies. These priorities shift in relationship to new census data, disasters, political aspirations, and the ideology of the party in power. (For example, there was a huge fluctuation in availability of funds for faith-based organizations during and following George W. Bush's presidency.) The goals usually address a need for research or delivery of services that will improve the current situation in the nation or community (such as research on the latest epidemic, or job creation following the recession). There are thousands of separate grant programs supported through the federal government and managed by myriad departments, bureaus and offices. Organizations new to grantseeking should be cautious about approaching federal funders, as the process is elaborate, complicated, and time-consuming.

Foundations are nonprofit corporations that offer grant money emanating from interest earned on their investments. There are many kinds of foundations (community, family, public, etc.) and each one has a unique purpose, determined by the source of the funds. The 2010 edition of *Foundation Giving Trends* reported that over the past thirty years, the number of U.S. foundations grew from around 20,000 to nearly 80,000. In the same thirty years, these foundations' assets grew from under $50 billion to nearly $600 billion. And the amount of money awarded increased from $3.5 billion to nearly $50 billion. See the Getting Funded website, www.gettingfundedbook.com, for more information on general funding trends, patterns, and priorities.

Corporations offer support through many vehicles, one among them being grants. They also provide financial support through sponsorship or underwriting, through matching the charitable gifts of time and money their employees give to nonprofits, and through participation in public/private partnerships. Companies can also support groups by offering in-kind gifts of goods—such as equipment, products, or the use of space—or services of their staff in the form of printing, consulting, transportation, and so forth. Who makes the decision within the business varies from company to company, as does the motivation for giving. But the primary reason corporations contribute money or services is to further the goals of the company and its owners or stockholders.

Other funders, described in detail in Chapter 4, include service clubs, fraternal organizations, professional associations, faith communities, and many other types of organizations that share their resources to improve a community or further their own goals.

Know Where You Fit in the Big Picture

Funders will expect you to understand the larger environment within which you're operating: general economic and political trends, general funding trends, and effective funding strategies for your type of organization. For example, after the 2008 economic downturn, many foundations, who make grants based on the interest they've earned on invested funds, were forced to halt or curtail their giving because no interest had accrued. They expected savvy GRANTWRITERS to adjust their requests accordingly.

The big picture also includes lots of fields of interest, and it behooves you to learn about how your field relates to others in terms of percentages of grants awarded. There are countless topics and issues, but some broad-brush categories are religion, education, human services, health, public benefit (such as parks and civic efforts), arts/culture/humanities, environment, animals, and international affairs. There is no single definitive source that captures and reports for all fields which groups get how much money, as some sources don't include government grants, while others don't include religious giving.

Every year, the Giving USA Foundation and Indiana University's Center on Philanthropy produce a report with statistics on the previous year's giving from private sources. While it does not include government funding, the report is considered the definitive source of information on private funding in the United States. Government funding is tracked and reported in the *Consolidated Federal Funds Report,* an annual report from the U.S. Census Bureau. Check the Getting Funded website, www.gettingfundedbook.com, for links to the most recent statistics from this and other sources.

Be Aware of Changes in Funding Patterns

In the past couple of decades, across the grantmaking landscape, some things have remained unchanged, while other aspects reflect new realities about where the money is coming from, how the process is unfolding, and what criteria decision makers are using to determine whom to fund.

Among the things that have stayed the same is that certain fields consistently get more money than others. For example, for decades, funding patterns for nonprofit organizations, universities, and hospitals have remained higher than for other fields—such as the arts and the environment.

Here are some things that have fluctuated in recent years:

- Government grants have been drastically reduced in some sectors as others grew exponentially.
- Foundations that had historically made their grants from the interest earned on amassed capital discovered in 2009 that they had little or nothing to give.
- Where foundations seldom used to offer grants for operating support or multi-year funding, both types of support are now increasing.
- As individuals earned or inherited large amounts of money, they created unprecedented numbers of new private foundations.
- Many of the newer foundation donors are getting more engaged in the work of the GRANTEES, viewing themselves as "venture philanthropists" as they infuse nonprofits with their own financial and intellectual capital, resources, and contacts.

- Corporate giving, which used to be dominated by banks and power companies, is now coming from much more diverse types of companies, though often in lower amounts.
- People not traditionally engaged in philanthropy joined together with like-minded individuals to form new public foundations and giving circles (social investment clubs), where their pooled resources created enough money to give to particular causes, communities, or countries, making impacts much larger than they could have made as individuals.
- International funding has grown exponentially as our worlds have expanded, Internet access has increased, and major international foundations have started to affect policies and priorities.
- More and more funders have moved away from traditional paper proposals toward electronic submission of applications, altering the way grantseekers frame proposals.

Build a Proposal-Writing Team

As a grantwriter, you will participate in the process from one of three perspectives: (1) as a staff person whose primary role (programmatic, administrative, fundraising, etc.) is something other than grantwriting; (2) as a staff person whose primary role is grantwriting; or (3) as a freelance grantwriter, hired on an hourly or contract basis. Regardless of your role, part of your job will be to build a team of disparate players, each of whom adds unique value to the final document.

You will do well if you possess the following skills:

- **Research:** for identifying and researching funding sources as well as data about your community, your field, and your own organization's background
- **Cultivation:** for building win-win relationships with funders and other allies
- **Collaboration:** for gathering input from program staff, finance staff, board leaders, and other nonprofits and government agencies to answer grantmakers' questions
- **Writing, editing and, formatting:** for creating concise, compelling, readable documents that make the best case for supporting your project
- **Stewardship:** for crafting follow-up reports, invitations, acknowledgment communications, and contacts that will strengthen the organization's reputation and facilitate future funding
- **Storytelling:** for sharing your story powerfully in documentation of need, acknowledgments, and reports
- **Equanimity:** to remain calm under pressure

See Chapter 8, Preparing to Write, for more on working with a committee or team and finding a supportive community. Refer to Appendix B for more on working with a freelance grantwriter.

The key value grantwriters can offer is the quality and persuasiveness of the proposal. But even the most beautifully written proposal will fail if other factors—at the organization and funder level—are not taken into account. That's why it's so important to pay attention to all the steps covered in Part I, which are all the steps that come before you begin to write. Proposals succeed or fail for a number of reasons, most of which are out of your control as the grantwriter. Among these are:

- How strong the project is: whether it's feasible, whether it meets a clear community need, and whether it has a well-planned budget

- How well the project fits the funder's interests, both implicit and explicit
- What the grantseeking organization's reputation is, including track record, and financial history
- How well the funder knows and trusts the grantseeker's leaders
- How many other requests the funder has received, and from whom
- How much money the funder has available in this funding cycle

Whether you are a novice or an experienced proposal writer, you will be more successful if you follow the guidance offered in this book. And whether you get funded or not, your organization will be stronger as a result of the planning, preparation, and clarification that happens during the process.

Conclusion

Despite dramatic shifts in the economy since the fourth edition of this book in 2003, grants remain a powerful source of revenue for organizations and institutions seeking support.

You and the organization you are affiliated with will be more successful with grantseeking if you view the process in a larger context. Keep in mind that you're trying to fund one idea in one organization among many in your field or community who are all approaching similar funders who care about the issue on a larger scale. And imagine that the particular proposal you're developing is one piece among many in your organization's overall financial picture.

Terminology

Because this field includes so many types of grantseekers and so many types of funders, words take on different meanings in different contexts. For the purpose of this book, we have chosen the following definitions.

Those organizations, agencies, institutions, or government agencies *seeking funding* will be referred to as grantseekers, organizations, nonprofits, or institutions.

Those entities *offering money* to grantseekers will be referred to as grantmakers, funders, or funding sources. Government agencies may also be grantmakers and in those cases may be referred to in that way.

Those individuals responsible for *preparing the document* to be submitted to the grantmaker will be referred to as grantwriters, grant professionals, proposal developers, or investigators (in the case of research grants).

The *document* submitted to the funder will be called an application or proposal. (Some use the word "grant" to refer to the proposal that is written and submitted, but technically, the grant is the support awarded to the grantseeker. We've retained the technical usage to avoid confusion.)

Key Terms

GRANT: An award of financial support, equipment, or other assistance, based on a proposal written in the format and to the guidelines required by the funder. A grant does not have to be paid back to the funder.

GRANTEE: The agency or organization that receives the award or grant.

GRANTMAKER or FUNDER: The agency, foundation, or individual that gives the award or grant.

GRANTSEEKER: The agency or organization that is looking for funding or grants of any type.

GRANTWRITER: The person who writes and assembles the proposal on behalf of a grantseeking organization.

PART ONE
Know Your Organization and Field

The most successful grant proposals manifest the thinking and planning that led to the proposed project. So while it can be tempting to jump into the process and start filling in answers to a funder's questions, your proposals will be much more competitive if you first take the time you need to ensure that your organization is prepared to participate in grantseeking. This book opens with three chapters that will help you understand what makes one organization more competitive than another, fully evaluate the need that you hope to address, and ensure that your proposed project has been developed carefully and thoroughly. This preparation will increase your chances of getting funded and meeting the need you wish to address. Thinking and planning in advance will also save you precious time when you're scrambling to meet a funder's deadline.

Part I of this book introduces and explores ways to get your organization "grant-ready," determine the true nature of the need for your project, and design a project that promises to make a difference.

1 ENSURING ORGANIZATIONAL READINESS

This chapter explores what it means to be "grant-ready" and how you can prepare your organization to be more competitive among other grantseekers. Writing a grant proposal is a time- and resource-intensive endeavor. While it may seem like it will take even more time to prepare your organization before you begin writing, doing so will lead to better results.

Writing proposals is a great way for your organization to get its act together. Because preparing an application requires thinking and planning, the process can be beneficial whether you submit the request or not. The preparation gets your colleagues to talk to one another, prioritize their work, and take the pulse of the community. And along the way, internal problems, such as a vague mission statement or unrefined strategy, get identified and worked out, and systems get put in place.

All proposals have costs for the applicant organization. Staff time is the biggest one, as the process always takes more time than anyone anticipated. Sometimes matching funds are necessary, meaning your organization will be required to contribute or raise as much as the funder promises. And often the staff or supervisors who are to be assigned to the newly funded work are already overloaded, so the new project might compromise their current work. It may cost your organization money to even become eligible for a grant. You may be required to make your building more accessible or to buy a certain type of tracking software, for example. There may also be costs incurred in acknowledging new funders, such as creating new signage or reprinting materials that must have the new funder's logo on them.

When grantwriters start to seek money from external sources, often they discover balls that have been dropped. Perhaps they realize there is no definitive list of who the organization has gotten funding from in the past. And once they cobble that list together, they realize that the organization neglected to send final reports to some prior funders, the database is out of date, and no one has kept track of when donors or clients were last communicated with. Or possibly, they find out the organization's tax determination letter from the IRS has been misplaced, the mission statement is boring, the budget doesn't reflect reality, or pivotal relationships necessary to be competitive have been left to languish. Asking others for support always strengthens the infrastructure of an organization, so whether one decides to apply or not, the process is worth it!

So you and your organization's leaders will have to answer honestly whether you have the time, expertise, and resources necessary to do a creditable job on each application, whether the proposed project is the best use of your resources, and whether it will help propel your organization's mission, vision, and strategic goals.

Be it a grassroots nonprofit or a large university, your organization will need to prepare in order to compete. Writing a proposal requires much from a grantseeking organization: planning, teamwork, commitment, communication, and expense. So, early in the process, you will want to thoroughly review the factors of organizational readiness reviewed in this chapter, as each plays an important role in funders' decision making. Discuss them with your internal stakeholders, such as those who govern your organization, those who manage it, those who volunteer or contribute to your work, and those who benefit from it. After considering each factor carefully in the context of your own organization, you'll be ready to answer the questions in Figure 1.1, "Checklist for Assessing Organizational Readiness." Considering these factors will help you discern whether you are ready to apply for a grant and how your organization can become sufficiently competitive to warrant the investment of time, effort, and money to apply.

Too often, organizations hear about available money and enlist a grantwriter to write the proposal. In no time, the grantwriter discovers that not only does she not know the answers to some of the questions, but no one else knows them either. Getting others together to discuss and agree on the answers can take time and bring up other issues.

Mission

Grantmakers want to see a clear mission statement that articulates the reasons you engage in your work and the difference you're trying to make. Before you apply, be sure your mission and goals align with those of the funder and that the purpose of the proposal is consistent with the overall mission of your organization. Your mission statement is often the first thing funders read, and they use it as a measuring stick to assess whether your idea reflects your mission. Funders dislike "mission creep," where organizations shift their own priorities to look more suitable to a funder. Funders prefer to see an explicit tie between the purpose of the proposal and that of the organization submitting the proposal.

A freelance grantwriter once admitted that she used to craft new mission statements for organizations while she was developing their proposals, because the organizations had none, or because the official mission statements were uninspiring or didn't suit the funder's guidelines. But the mission statement really does need to be written and adopted by the board. And it really should be shaping the organization's work.

Need

Clearly articulating the problem or opportunity that needs to be addressed is the most important part of any grant proposal. Consider honestly: How well can you describe the need for the project you propose to implement? Many grantseekers undertake work simply because it interests them or because it's what their organization has always done. But your proposal will suffer if you cannot make a compelling case for why the need at the heart of your project should receive attention, even above and beyond other important needs in the community. The more compelling the need, the more competitive the proposal. See also Chapter 2, which offers more detail on how to assess the need; Chapter 3, which addresses sound project design; and Chapter 9, which helps you describe the need effectively.

Beneficiaries

Your organization needs to be able to describe who or what will benefit from your work and in what way. This will help you, when you write your proposal, to make your case for the project very clear. Think about who benefits directly from your work—those are your primary beneficiaries—as well as who might benefit indirectly. Think about how your work affects people who live and work with your primary beneficiaries. What ripple effects do you foresee? Consider how the larger community is improved by the work you do. Chapter 2, on assessing the need, will help you clarify this in terms of your proposed project, and Chapter 3, on design, provides tools to help you further refine your ideas.

Two nonprofit organizations realized, as they clarified who benefited from their work, that it was a much narrower pool than they had thought. One organization decided that when they mapped the flora and fauna of a city's green spaces, the primary beneficiaries were the people responsible for the stewardship of those properties, and the secondary beneficiaries were the people who used the parks. The other organization realized that when they were presenting information in court about child custody cases, their primary beneficiaries were the judges, who needed the information to make sound decisions, and the secondary beneficiaries were the children involved in the cases. Being crystal clear about who or what your organization serves will focus your project's activities and outcomes, making your proposal more credible.

Strategic Plan

Funders want to know that an applicant organization has a strategic plan that outlines a vision and direction for the future, including goals that will guide the work of both board and staff. A competitive grant proposal shows the funder how the work you propose to do will propel your organization toward its strategic priorities. Be prepared to document realistic strategies for funding and implementing the proposed project within your organization's overall activities. Strategic planning documents give funders one piece of evidence that a grantseeker is thoughtful and practical about its work and has the plans and capability to make the project happen.

A grantwriting consultant got a phone call one Friday night from a nonprofit volunteer, who said: "I just heard that the Arts Commission has a grant deadline tonight at midnight, and I thought I'd write a quick proposal and submit it. I was hoping you could help me figure out how to answer a couple of the questions." Turning in a first draft proposal that hasn't been planned well or approved by others wastes grantmakers' time, insults their intelligence, and can suppress philanthropy for us all.

Leadership

Organizations that apply for grants are expected to have strong leaders at both governance and administrative levels. This expectation holds for all funding organizations, from foundations to corporations to government agencies. Funders want to see that you have experienced individuals at the helm. They'll also want assurance that leaders are held accountable for the organization's mission and values, and that board members have made their own financial contributions to support the proposed work. (See the Resources section for more about organizational leadership.)

At a meeting of foundation executives, the funders acknowledged that the questions they ask in their application forms often drive behavior in grantseeking organizations. So all the funders agreed that from then on, they would include questions about what percentage of board members attend meetings, what percentage make their own charitable gifts to the applicant organization, and how the board and executive staff determined that this project was a priority, knowing that some nonprofits would likely change their behavior to be better candidates for funding.

Budget

Your budget is a powerful storyteller. Ideally, it conveys that your organization is competent and healthy, with diverse funding streams and realistic goals. Funders are less likely to fund an organization that is seeking grant money just to survive. If you plan to request money for a particular project or program within your organization, you'll need to show how the project budget relates to the overall budget, and how your organization plans to participate in the project with its own finances. Be prepared to assure funders that you have adequate accounting and reporting procedures in place to separate grant monies from other funding streams. Those accounting procedures will need to include internal controls (checks and balances) to protect the organization and its leaders from liability. Chapter 12 provides more details on how to present budget information in your proposal.

Buy-in

The grantseeking process requires many people to cooperate. To succeed in writing a competitive proposal, you will need commitment and buy-in from those who are essential for success:

- The leaders who must sign the proposal, e.g., the dean or board president
- The people who will be carrying out the funded work
- The people who will be evaluating the work, e.g., program staff or auditors
- The people who will be budgeting and managing the money
- The people responsible for minimizing organizational risk, e.g., legal or financial staff
- The people in charge of communications
- Those in your organization who have received funds from the same source
- The people who will be accountable for the success of whatever work gets funded

Collaborators

Funders know that they are more likely to achieve long-term success with a systemic approach in which organizations partner with other nonprofits, educational institutions, government agencies, and policy makers. Collaborative projects can be an effective way to make the most of funders' resources, and thus help funders extend their reach. Collaborations reassure funders that grantees aren't duplicating efforts. Collaborations also improve an organization's ability to sustain a program in the future when support from the original funders is discontinued, and funders view this as a significant advantage. An organization that has already built cooperative relationships is in a more competitive position than one that hasn't. Chapter 3 further discusses working collaboratively as you refine the project proposal.

> The director of programs of a private foundation that grants over $20 million a year told an audience of grantwriters, "We don't award grants to fund organizations. We award grants to solve community problems. We expect you to be working with other entities to effect change, not be lone rangers."

Strengths

All organizations have strengths and weaknesses. Proposals are most competitive when they describe projects that build on an organization's strengths. To do this, you will need to know who else is doing similar work and how your work is distinct from theirs—or how it will supplement, build on, or improve their efforts. Factors such as your location, history, prior experience, clientele or beneficiaries, and staff or volunteer knowledge or qualifications can set you apart from fellow applicants.

Reputation

Assess how your organization's reputation might affect your grantseeking. Think about who has supported your work in the past and whether those funders have been pleased with the results. Think about any recent media attention, both positive and negative, your organization may have received. If the attention was negative, consider what has been done or can be done to overcome those negative perceptions. Also review your organization's politics: has the organization aligned politically with groups your potential funders might disagree with, or whose market position might be too close to theirs? If you are aware of how your organization is viewed by others, you will be able to address any issues as you choose which funders to approach (see Chapter 4 and Chapter 6) and as you write the proposal (see Part III).

Responsiveness

To be competitive among other grantseekers, an organization needs experienced leaders who can make decisions quickly enough to compete in a timely manner. At some universities and large agencies, it may take weeks or months to get a written proposal through all the necessary review processes. You'll want to find out how decisions are made so you know what needs to happen in order to meet a funder's deadline. You'll also look better to funders if you have a disaster preparedness plan and a crisis communications plan in place. And you'll want to show that your organization is stable enough to respond to unanticipated changes that could upset a project once it's funded. Proof may come in the form of financial reserves or predetermined protocols for managing unexpected situations.

Infrastructure

Before you begin to apply for grants, make sure you have the space, the time, the equipment, and the systems necessary to succeed. Government grants often require grantees to use particular hiring practices or to use sophisticated financial accounting systems to track expenditures. A funder may expect rigorous evaluation processes or stringent adherence to building codes, a certain level of technology, or established processes for dealing with conflicts of interest or crisis communication along the way. Another aspect of infrastructure readiness is staffing—do you have or can you get the right staff for this project? A final factor concerns your financial accounting system and whether it is able to manage or spend the funds within the allotted time.

Eligibility

You must have the proper legal status to receive funds. Very few funders will award grants or contracts directly to individuals (with the exception of individual artists). Most grantmakers insist that the applicant be a public (governmental) agency or a private nonprofit organization that has received 501(c)(3) status from the Internal Revenue Service. (This IRS status is separate from and not the same as state-issued designation as a nonprofit.) Note that federal funders do issue contracts and grants to for-profit businesses.

Depending on the project and the organization, funders may also require licenses, accreditation, insurance policies, or permits to do whatever you propose. Many funders also stipulate that an audited financial statement must accompany the proposal (see Chapter 12 for more on preparing financial documents for a proposal).

If you do not qualify for an award from a particular funder, consider teaming up with other organizations that do qualify and collaborating with them on a proposal. Otherwise, you will need to take the steps to get the necessary legal status before you write and submit your proposals.

Figure 1.1 provides a list of questions to consider when deciding whether your organization should submit a proposal.

FIGURE 1.1 CHECKLIST FOR ASSESSING ORGANIZATIONAL READINESS

- ❑ Can you describe what problem or opportunity needs to be addressed?

- ❑ Is your organization eligible to receive funds from government funders, private foundations, or corporations?

- ❑ Does your organization have a good governing structure or board? Are the leaders experienced and committed?

- ❑ Is the purpose of the proposal consistent with the mission of your organization?

- ❑ Does your organization have a strategic plan that effectively guides your work?

- ❑ Can you clearly articulate who or what will benefit from your proposed project?

- ❑ Do you have a clearly laid out strategy to accomplish what you intend to do?

- ❑ Can you measure the outcomes of your work?

- ❑ Do you know who else is doing similar work on this issue and can you explain how your work is distinct from theirs? Do you understand your organization's competitive advantage for this particular proposal?

- ❑ Do you have collaborative relationships with others doing similar work?

- ❑ Do you know how the reputation of your organization will affect this proposal?

- ❑ Do you have a project budget that fits within your overall organizational budget?

- ❑ Can your organization respond to deadlines and benchmarks in a timely manner?

- ❑ Does your organization have the required commitment on the part of all those who could affect the success or failure of the proposal?

- ❑ Do you have the appropriate infrastructure to support the project and to ensure that you can spend the funds within the required time frame?

Summary

Grantseeking requires commitment on the part of the entire grantseeking organization, whether it is a nonprofit, university department, for-profit company, or government agency. Before you decide to apply for a grant, it's important to affirm that your organization is prepared or that the leaders are willing to do what it takes to become prepared. If everyone views the grantseeking process as an opportunity to strengthen the organization, rather than just an opportunity to get money, the experience will be a win-win for everyone, whether your proposal is funded or not. The work you do to prepare will make your organization more sustainable and more appealing to all types of funders, including individual donors.

Key Terms

COLLABORATOR: One of the people or groups with common goals, and shared or complementary interests, assets, and professional skills, that work cooperatively for the community's benefit.

INFRASTRUCTURE: The buildings, equipment, systems, and policies that make an organizational functional.

STAKEHOLDER: One of the people or organizations touched by the situation you hope to affect. Internal stakeholders might include staff, board members, and volunteers, as well as the people or groups you serve, such as clients, audiences, or students. External stakeholders might include cooperating agencies and organizations, elected officials, local planners and policy makers, individual donors, and people and groups tangentially affected by the issue.

Find more terms in the Glossary. For further resources, see the Resources and References section at the end of this book or visit the Getting Funded website, www.gettingfundedbook.com.

2 DEFINING THE NEED

This chapter clarifies why the best proposals are shaped by need. When you can identify and describe precisely what situation needs attention and why, you will be able to convince others that it is urgent and important.

Grantseekers are so eager to share *what* they want to do that sometimes they neglect to explain *why* they're doing it. It is easy to assume that everyone understands the problem and agrees that it needs attention.

But the clearer you are about precisely what is at stake, the clearer you can be about every other element of your proposal. Your articulation of the need will shape your articulation of the solution, and will affect everything else in your grantseeking process.

Some people call a proposal's need statement the problem statement. However, not every proposal claims to solve a problem. Arts organizations, museums, zoos, civic groups, and people involved in preservation don't necessarily view what they're doing as solving a problem so much as creating or responding to an opportunity, or simply adding something valuable to their community. The words NEED, PROBLEM, and OPPORTUNITY will be used interchangeably in this chapter. The essential question is, What situation are you hoping to affect? Paint a picture for the funder of something that merits attention.

Here are some concepts to consider as you begin to clarify the need for your proposed work.

Assessing the Need

One way or another, you're going to have to determine the need for what you propose to do. There are many ways to conduct a needs assessment and this chapter provides a number of topics to consider. You'll want to start by looking for research that others have done about the situation. Here are some sources for statistics regarding a need, problem, or opportunity:

- The local United Way, as well as their regional and national associations
- The local college or university, including academics or researchers in your field
- Government departments, commissions, and agencies, e.g., the City Planning and Community Development Department, the County Public Health Department, the State Department of Wildlife, or the Federal Department of Labor

- Elected officials, local, regional, and national
- Lobbyists for other organizations concerned about the problem
- Census data from the Department of Commerce
- School districts, police departments, health departments, hospitals, and court systems
- Alliances or coalitions of groups that have coalesced around the problem
- Funders, government and private, who may have conducted research on the topic, especially funders familiar with the affected community and statewide associations of funders who can see broad patterns
- Journalists or investigative reporters
- For-profit companies whose products or services relate to the issue
- Individuals who are affected by the issue

If you discover that there simply are no relevant data you can cite, it will be up to you to do your own needs assessment. You can start by using your direct experience with the problem. Perhaps you get more requests for shelter beds or to take in unwanted animals than you can accommodate. You can also try to get someone else (such as one of the organizations or agencies listed above) to conduct a survey on your behalf, or you can conduct a survey of your own. Consider holding one or more focus groups or roundtable discussions to ask others about their experience with the need you are interested in. For more information on finding statistics or conducting a needs assessment, see the "Statistics and Facts" section of the Resources at the back of this book, or go to the online resource list available on the Getting Funded website, www.gettingfundedbook.com.

A sexual assault center planned to launch a new program to serve very young children who had been molested. Realizing that no statistics existed to prove to what extent child sexual assault was a problem in their geographic area, the staff at the center put together a focus group. They invited representatives from the police department, the state child protective service, the hospital emergency room, the public health department, the child care providers association, a group of local clergy, and the association of school counselors. They asked the people who attended to share their own perspectives on the scope of the problem in the area, as well as what they thought should be done about it. Responses from the focus group became the basis for several successful grant proposals.

Clarifying Who Is Affected

There are layers of people or things that are affected by any need or opportunity, and it will strengthen your proposal to first list the groups that are affected separately and then show how they are interrelated. Take for example a community whose historic downtown is full of rundown empty buildings. A downtown revitalization organization could list the following layers of people and groups affected by the problem:

- The owners of the buildings, who can't attract good tenants
- The surrounding businesses, who have trouble attracting customers
- The city, which is not getting optimal tax revenue from the downtown core
- Community members, who have to do business farther away, which may be inconvenient or inaccessible
- Unemployed community members, who have fewer opportunities for employment because there are fewer businesses in those buildings

- Children, who grow up in an uninspiring downtown with no natural gathering place and a less-than-robust sense of community
- Parents, whose children may leave town as soon as they can
- Law enforcement officers, who may need to handle an increase in crime in the area of the rundown or vacant buildings
- Public health officials, who deal with increased problems with garbage, pests, and other sanitation issues

As you list the many groups of people and organizations affected by the problem, you may also see more types of potential funders emerge. In the downtown revitalization example above, in addition to government funders and foundations, the following sources of funding come to light:

- An association of commercial property owners
- The chamber of commerce
- Various city departments, e.g., utilities, transportation, public safety, or the visitors bureau
- Private employment agencies
- Environmental groups that discourage extensive driving
- The police guild or police union
- Health promotion groups or the regional hospital

See Part II, "Know the Funders," for more about researching funders and identifying appropriate funders for your organization and project.

Before you begin to write your proposal, ask key people in your organization to name all the groups affected by the problem and describe how each is affected. Narrow your list to those groups you think you can affect. Then describe the need or problem you see primarily in terms of these groups, but also show how the needs of these groups fit into the larger scheme of things.

Reviewers who scored proposals for a county commission noted that almost every proposal asserted that "all citizens of the county" would be served. But the reviewers wanted to know, in priority order, which citizens would be most directly and deeply touched by the work, which would be less directly affected, and which would be affected tangentially. A common mistake made in grant proposals is defining too broadly who or what will be served. Larger numbers are not always more impressive.

Seeking Out the Root Cause of the Problem

Describing the current problem well is important, but you must also be able to explain what factors led to it, as those factors will inform how you define and approach the problem.

Let's look at low-income housing. A first draft might describe the problem this way: "There's not enough housing for low-income people." But there are many other ways to characterize this need, depending on your organization's perspective. For example, these are just some of the reasons that people could be without housing:

- Laws affecting minimum wage were relaxed, so breadwinners are earning less.
- Banks tightened their lending practices in particular neighborhoods.
- Developers were given more enticing incentives to create high-end housing.
- Governments, to save money, released from jails or mental health institutions people whose housing was formerly covered by the state, increasing demand.
- Housing vouchers for people with disabilities were cut from the state budget.
- The homes of older adults who have difficulty performing maintenance tasks are deteriorating beyond repair, which reduces affordable housing stock.
- Low-income housing is being destroyed because the land it's on is worth more if developed as commercial or upscale residential property.

You can see that the way you characterize the problem will dictate your response to it. One description might direct you to mobilize volunteers to fix up older adults' homes, while another description might send you to the state capitol to change laws. And regardless of the specific action you propose to take, you must describe the problem in a way that lets funders see the context within which you operate. The more sophisticated your understanding of the problem, the more favorably funders will view your proposal.

Measuring the Scope of the Problem

Think about the situation you hope to affect as existing on a continuum from the global level down to the tiniest manifestation. Take hunger. Hunger exists around the world, and some organizations work on a *global* basis to address it. But there are also *national* or *regional* issues of hunger that might stem from a geographic barrier, a political conflict, a transportation issue, or an environmental situation such as toxic waste or land mines near farmland. On a more *local* level, there may be hunger in a particular community because a major employer closed, leaving thousands of breadwinners unemployed. And within that community, there may be *pockets* of people who are suffering more than others, such as new immigrants or people living on very low incomes or those experiencing mental health challenges.

As you define the problem you will address, visualize a funnel: begin with statistics on a macro basis, then offer some data about national or regional hunger, then describe the larger local picture, until you have narrowed the scope of the problem to the level where you could actually affect it with a funder's support. This should help you grasp what you can reasonably hope to achieve. Align your description of the need, which will become a first draft of the proposal's need statement, within the scope that you can actually affect. (See Chapter 9 for a more detailed discussion of writing the need statement. For sources of data, see the "Statistics and Facts" section of the Resources.)

> *"Describe the need in such a way that I feel like my support could have an impact. I don't want to feel like the problem is so huge, my contribution will only be one drop in a vast deep bucket."*
>
> —CEO of a community foundation

Exploring Who Else Is Doing Similar Work

Many grantseekers are quick to claim they are the only ones working on a particular issue, but this is seldom the case. If, as you assert, there is truly a problem, someone else must be concerned as well. You can turn this to your advantage in your proposal. Perhaps there's a church that has a less formal program than yours, or perhaps a statewide advocacy organization does work that touches on your topic tangentially. Maybe another organization is dealing with the same topic but with a different constituency.

It's essential that you identify these other parties and illustrate how they all fit into the larger description of the problem. You will look more appealing to funders if you do not claim that you are the only organization working on the problem, but instead you say, "This problem is so big that it requires the attention of many parties. This is the aspect of it we think *we* can affect."

Explaining Long-Term Implications

As you assess the need, consider the implications of not addressing it, as well as how the situation may change if not addressed soon. If the problem will grow and affect more people, affect the same people more deeply, or lead to other associated problems, this information can help you provide a more complete, compelling picture of the situation. If other aspects of the community will be affected or the results of doing nothing are serious, the urgency of your project proposal will be clearer to funders.

An assessment of need will provide you with answers to all the questions listed in Figure 2.1, which will help you design a project based on need (see Chapter 3) and then write a compelling need statement (see Chapter 9).

Naming Opportunities, Not Needs

Arts organizations, museums, professional associations, and similar groups must think creatively about the need for their projects. One place to begin is to point to what would be missing from your community if your project were not to happen. If you didn't challenge or entertain citizens with art and music and drama, what critical community conversations might not happen and whose lives would be affected in what way? If you didn't preserve and showcase the history of your town, what would be lost, among whom? It's up to you to paint a vivid picture of how your community would be different if you were unable to do your proposed work. Make the links as clear as possible between the work you want funded and the changes you can actually bring about. And make sure you can measure and prove the results of your project after the grant is over. (See Chapter 11 for more detailed discussion of project evaluation.)

Even if your organization seeks funding to meet an internal need, such as strategic planning or fundraising training or technology improvements, you will still have to find a way to describe the need in terms of others. Try to capture how your organization's lack of these things affects its ability to accomplish its mission. Chapters 9 and 10 discuss how to write a proposal's need statement and project description in terms of external needs. Chapter 5 discusses types of grants that fund organizational costs. For more resources on these topics, see the Resources section at the end of this book or visit the Getting Funded website, www.gettingfundedbook.com.

Ensuring that Need Drives Everything

How you define the need will dictate every other aspect of your grantseeking process:

- Which funders you approach for support
- What type of grant you ask for
- What activities you suggest as the solution to the need
- Whom you choose as partners in the process
- What scale of work you propose to accomplish
- What outcomes you promise to achieve
- How you measure success

"Never say the need is your own. No one will give you money because you need it. Funders give you money because they have their own goals. And if what you propose will further their goals, they might consider supporting your work. But they don't really care if your organization has needs. Your role is not to have needs—it's to meet needs. The need belongs to those you benefit directly, and ultimately to the community at large."

—Executive Director of a regional association of grantmakers

Savvy arts organizations quantify the economic benefits of the arts to their community. By demonstrating arts-related increases in employment, retail activity, and tax revenue, these organizations can frame the need in terms of the loss or absence of these benefits.

FIGURE 2.1 CHECKLIST FOR COMPLETING A NEEDS ASSESSMENT

❑ Have you examined previous literature, research, or work that addressed the same issue?

❑ Have you gathered both hard and soft data from several sources in several ways as you conducted your needs assessment?

❑ Have you identified precisely who is affected by the issue and in what way?

❑ Have you explored the root causes of the issue so that you understand the best ways to approach it?

❑ Have you clarified the scope within which you could reasonably affect change?

❑ Have you researched who else is working on the issue and what they have learned about the need?

❑ Have you predicted the long-term implications of the issue and what might happen if you don't address it?

Summary

You will find that as you clarify the need, whether problem or opportunity, you will be building a framework for the rest of your grantseeking process. The details of your project—including the specific groups of people you'll serve, the quantifiable results you can expect to achieve, and the organizations or agencies with whom you'll collaborate—will be defined and refined as you do your needs assessment. And the way you define the need will shape all the elements of your written proposal as well. While it's tempting to sit down and start writing before the need has been completely determined, your proposal will unfold with greater ease and look more appealing to funders if your description of the need is complete, thorough, and targeted. The need described in your proposal, which must always be attributed to some external group and not to your own organization's needs, is the basis for everything else in your proposal.

Key Terms

NEED or PROBLEM or OPPORTUNITY: The situation your work will affect, or the reason you plan to undertake the proposed project.

3 DESIGNING YOUR PROJECT

This chapter offers a framework for designing a project that convinces funders that you have a plan, that you've determined the best way to implement it, and that you're capable of achieving your goals.

Making the effort and taking the time to refine your approach and methods will make your project design more effective and more likely to be funded. Chapter 1 explored whether your organization was ready to apply for grants. This chapter will help you make sure your idea or project is grant-ready as well.

Framing the Project Design

Once you've clarified the need, your project design will begin to unfold. The first step is to align the project design with the need. The second step is to align the project design with other aspects of your organization and the community where the project will be implemented.

Relevance to the Community

While the significance of your project will likely be obvious to you, your project plan should show that you understand how the community views the proposed plan and its benefit to society. The more clear it is that your project addresses something that really matters, the simpler it will be to make your case for funding. You'll want to show that the project will make enough impact to justify the resources spent on it, and that the problem is actually solvable. (See Chapter 9 for more about framing the need.) And finally, remember to research and examine the possible reasons the problem has not been solved before now.

Mission Alignment

As discussed in Chapter 2, every need is multifaceted and can be viewed and addressed from many different angles. Ask yourself what part of that overarching problem your organization is most suited to take on, considering your mission, vision, and goals. A common complaint among funders is "mission drift," in which organizations, looking for money wherever they can find it, shift their aims to meet a funder's guidelines. To make your project most appealing to funders, make sure the connection between your organization's mission and the proposed project idea is clear.

Relevance to Your Organization's Other Work

Consider how well your project idea ties into or enhances the other important work you're doing, or whether it detracts instead. Of all the things you could be doing, would this project be the best use of your organization's staff time and resources? Find out how others who work for or are served by your organization view the relative importance of this project. Consider whether taking on this work might alter the structure or culture of your organization, such as by adding new staff members or changing established METHODS.

Timeliness

Your proposal will be more compelling if you can show that the situation your project is designed to address calls for immediate attention. Consider how you might shape your project to address recent community concerns. Perhaps the local political climate favors change right now; newly released research results naturally support your premise; the topic has been in the news lately, making the subject seem timely; or the population to be served has been particularly visible or vocal lately. Another way to look at it is to ask what will happen if this particular idea *isn't* implemented right now.

Capacity

Project planning includes accurately assessing your organization's capacity to take on the work in question in light of all the other things currently in play. Think about constraints that could affect your organization's ability to implement the project, such as cash flow issues that would make it difficult to pay for reimbursable expenses up front; hiring freezes or union rules that might prevent your organization from hiring the right people on time; or changes in the economic climate that might make it more difficult to get a loan or acquire matching funds from individual donors. Every project has associated costs, and you want to be sure that the benefits outweigh those costs.

Commitment

The commitment your organization makes to its funders needs to be supported by the people who carry out the work. Funders know that sometimes organizational will depends greatly on whose idea the project was in the first place, and they want to know that staff members and volunteer leaders are willing to make the project a priority. As you proceed with planning and learn more about which of your colleagues believe the project is worth pursuing, identify the people who will ultimately own the project and hold others accountable to your organization's commitments to funders. Many organizations have found, even after getting a proposal funded, that the staff who were expected to implement the project were unwilling to do so. Your ability to assure the funder that your co-workers are committed to the idea will make your idea more viable.

Collaboration

As mentioned in Chapter 1, collaborations can make your proposal much more attractive to funders. Consider how healthy the relationships are among the current collaborators, and whether the project aim is sufficiently important to all of them that they will make the effort to work cooperatively on it. Who else might you need to collaborate with to make your project successful? Before you approach a potential PARTNER, take into account whether your relationship with that organization or agency is strong enough both to ask for support and to implement a project plan together.

A science-oriented nonprofit could not figure out why their sound idea, presented in a well-crafted proposal to the National Science Foundation, got rejected three times in a row. Then they spoke to an insider and discovered that if they partnered with the local research university and submitted the proposal jointly, their idea would be more competitive. Once they did that, they got funded almost immediately.

Choosing Your Approach

There are many ways to address a particular need, and your organization will need to choose an approach and justify that choice.

Take, for example, the problem of a disease that threatens public health: one group might choose to conduct research on how to cure the disease, while another group educates the public about lifestyle changes that will prevent people from getting it, while a third group offers support to individuals who already have it, and a fourth group meets with policy makers to change laws that affect the disease's treatment and transmission. And even within each of those approaches, there are numerous ways to do research (on human or animal subjects), educate people (via ad campaigns or workshops), offer support (individually or in groups, using professionals or peers), or change laws (via lawsuits, initiatives, regulations, or statutes).

You'll need to defend your approach by citing research, presenting what others in the field are experiencing, and describing your own experience with various approaches.

Use the following hierarchy to plan and describe your project design.

Goals

Based on the need, your organization will define one or more goals it hopes the project will achieve. GOALS are the overarching targets you are aiming to achieve through your proposed work.

Example: To reduce the number of homeless refugees in Seaside County.

Example: To reduce the incidence of childhood obesity among students in Pine County School District.

Approach or Strategy

To meet the goals, your organization will choose one among the many ways to tackle the problem or need. This is called the APPROACH or STRATEGY.

Example: Draw refugees into county food banks to connect them with resources.

Example: Expose students to healthy food options at school.

Methods or Tactics

As you put the approach into play, you will need to select which processes or means to employ. These are called METHODS or TACTICS.

Example: Use culturally appropriate outreach and case management staff to introduce refugees to resources for food, clothing, temporary housing, health care, and child care.

Example: Incorporate lessons about healthy food into classroom curricula and school-based activities.

Over the years, behavioral health specialists have gotten better results when keeping troubled families together than when separating them. Sexual assault specialists have figured out that treatment of sex offenders doesn't really "stick." Building nursing homes in rural communities has proven too expensive to sustain. Helping babies with disabilities learn to move about in "natural environments" works better than bringing them into a centralized facility.

Activities

Finally, your project design must indicate the specific steps you will take for your methods or tactics to work. These are called ACTIVITIES.

Example: Send bilingual outreach workers to homeless encampments with information about how to find culturally familiar food at the food banks and where to find bilingual case managers who can help identify needs and how they can be met.

Example: Engage third-, fourth-, and fifth-graders in planning, planting, and managing cafeteria gardens, while teachers weave food choices into classroom activities and assignments related to math, science, reading, geography, social studies, and art.

Outputs

OUTPUTS are quantifiable items or units of service resulting from the activities you engage in to accomplish your work.

Example: Outputs for the homeless refugee project could include the number of refugees who were contacted in person by outreach staff, the number of refugees who arrived at the food bank within a given time frame, the number of contacts refugees made with case workers, or the number of refugees who took advantage of other resources offered through the food bank.

Example: Outputs for the childhood obesity project could include the number of students who participated in planning and planting the garden, the number of hours students worked in the garden or in the cafeteria with the food produced by the garden, the number of classroom activities or assignments in which teachers incorporated healthy food, or the number of assignments students turned in regarding the topic.

Outcomes

The outputs don't matter unless they make an impact, such as a measurable change in attitude or behavior among participants, more acres of protected wetlands, or decreased incidents of death from a disease. If they truly make a difference, the resulting change is called an OUTCOME. Outcomes measure the amount behavior or attitudes increased, decreased, or stayed the same, compared to a measurement taken before the project took place.

Example: The outcomes of the homeless refugee project could be that refugees reported less hunger, more access to resources, an increased sense of connection or hope or possibility, and fewer nights spent in the homeless encampment.

Example: The outcomes of the childhood obesity project could be that children reported an increased interest in what they ate, a greater awareness of the impact of food on their health, increased enthusiasm for gardening or food preparation, or an actual reduction in weight among participants.

You see that the outcomes have taken you full circle back to the original goals!

As you decide precisely how you will go about your work, consider not only your organization's strengths and experience but also how your proposed approach relates to what others have tried in the past and what they learned in the process. Think about what you have learned from your own work, and find out what the latest research says about best practices. Are you in a position to adopt those practices? If there's more than one way to deal with this issue, how will you decide which option to go with? As you develop your project, make sure you can place your approach and methodology in the historical context of your field and show funders

FIGURE 3.1 WORKSHEET FOR SELECTING A PROJECT APPROACH

When selecting among possible approaches and strategies and weighing their merits, consider the following criteria:

Feasibility and Effectiveness

- What has been the experience of other organizations or individuals in launching similar projects? Who else in the region or the field is doing this type of work and what has been learned from their experiences?

- What does the research or existing literature show about the success or failure of similar approaches in the past?

- How do your collaborators view the different approaches? Would they cooperate more readily if you chose one over another?

- What do public policy makers see as potential barriers and benefits to each type of approach?

- What are the anticipated costs versus benefits for each approach?

Suitability

- Which approach is most suited to your organization's capabilities and interests?

- Does the potential approach fit the priorities and preferences of the potential funders? Is one approach clearly of more interest to them than another (e.g., prevention rather than crisis intervention or preservation rather than new construction)?

- How does each approach complement or further other work done on the issue?

Uniqueness

- How is each approach innovative or distinct?

- Is there anything to be gained from a dramatic or unusual approach?

Anticipated Impact

- What will be the anticipated short-term and long-term effects of each approach in solving the particular problem?

- If a particular population or group of people is involved in the project, how will it be affected?

Utility and Sustainability

- Which approach will be easiest to sustain with contributed or earned income after the grant ends?

- Which approach will be easiest for other organizations to replicate?

that your strategy is based on research and experience and is the best choice your organization can make to meet the need.

Figure 3.1 can help you clarify the approach you want to take. If you'd like more help designing your project, look for a beloved resource called *Program Planning & Proposal Writing*. This brief and readable booklet was first published by The Grantsmanship Center in Los Angeles in 1972 and is still the most widely used guide on the subject in the world, helping tens of thousands of organizations design powerful programs and projects.

Anticipating Results

One of the most essential aspects of your project design is the description of what difference your work will make in the world. Many grantseeking organizations struggle to articulate the results of their work. In your organization, have you collectively agreed on what change in attitude or behavior you are aiming for? Think about what experience your organization has in effecting the desired change and how you know that it's *your* work that's responsible for the change, and not a combination of other factors in the community. You can start by learning what your organization measures consistently and what systematized procedures are in place to track and report findings. Think about what difference you can claim this project will make, and why you believe that your efforts could be of lasting value.

As you design your project, aim for results that can safely be attributed to your own work. For example, you don't want to promise that your project will result in young people refusing to join gangs, because funders know there are far too many factors influencing that decision for you to affect it with a single project. But you may be able to claim that your project will improve young people's school attendance, increase their participation in healthy after-school activities, and change what they say about the desirability of joining gangs.

Also plan out how you'll measure what difference you made. Funders want to know that you're promising something you can actually measure and evaluate. Figure out what you will be able to track and make sure you'll have access to relevant data both before you begin and at the end of the project. Many a grantwriter has struggled to describe the degree of change resulting from the funded work because there was no baseline data gathered to create a reference point. You can't claim a change if you don't know what you're measuring yourself against.

A grantwriter in a social service agency discovered that she would not be able to promise the outcome evaluation necessary to apply for a particular grant because the social workers at the agency were so protective of their clients that no one was allowed to ask them if they were better off as a result of the organization's work. Similarly, health clinic regulations protected the confidentiality of patient records, so no one but medical staff had access to the results.

Find out whether you will have permission to share collected data with analysts. If not, make sure your organization's staff have the capacity to analyze the data well enough to prove results.

Using Logic Models in Project Design

One way to think through project design is to create a LOGIC MODEL diagram that shows the relationships between your proposed actions and the expected results. There are many frameworks for logic models. Figure 3.2 is an example of a simple logic model presented as a matrix with five columns.

Funders who require that proposals include logic models usually stipulate what columns to use, but the five columns described here are common to most models.

FIGURE 3.2 ELEMENTS OF A FIVE-COLUMN LOGIC MODEL

RESOURCES	ACTIVITIES	OUTPUTS	OUTCOMES	GOALS
The assets you need to succeed with this project	The broad-brush type of activities you will engage in	The quantifiable units of value that you will deliver	The desired change in knowledge, behavior, or attitude resulting from the outputs	The ultimate reason why you hope to attain your outcomes

Resources: In the resources column, include all the assets necessary to be successful at the activity you propose. Assets may be things like buildings, vehicles, and computers, but can also be things like knowledge, experience, skills, relationships, and reputation. Note which assets you already have access to, as these will make your organization and your proposal more appealing to funders than a competitor who doesn't have access to these resources. Your resource list could include the following:

- A facility with a long-term lease and improvements made to accommodate the project
- A curriculum already developed and tested
- A ready base of clients, students, audience members, or participants
- Transportation available to participants
- Physical equipment necessary to do the work
- Trained and experienced staff
- Committed and trained volunteers
- An engaged and experienced board
- Relationships developed with potential collaborators
- Connections to elected officials or other influential people
- A diverse funding base that indicates you aren't relying too heavily on one source
- Money in reserves that indicates you're not operating hand to mouth
- Experience managing grants
- Established administrative systems, e.g., accounting, data management, and internal and external communications
- A reputation or track record

Activities: In the activities column, list the activities you will need to engage in to accomplish your goals. One grantseeking group might choose to provide prevention education or do research, another might focus on legislative solutions, one might engage in community organizing to enlist community members to solve their own problems, while another uses professional staff to solve the problem on behalf of the constituents. In the logic model for your project, this column should effectively outline the activities you have chosen to do.

Outputs: The outputs column is where you'll list the quantifiable items or units of service that will be produced by the project's activities. For example, a literacy organization might indicate that they'll offer fifty students five hours of after-school tutoring each week, or that each student will receive twenty new books over the course of the project. An advocacy organization might say they will provide three two-hour trainings for people to learn how to identify and communicate with lawmakers. An organization that serves youth could state that five hundred teenagers will receive training, resources, supplies, and support to help them prevent unwanted pregnancies. An environmental organization might promise to preserve one hundred acres of wetlands. The outputs you list in this column must be countable. Often, these outputs are what you want the grant money to pay for.

Outcomes: In the outcomes column, you'll describe the difference you expect the outputs to make. While the outputs column answers the question, What?, this column answers the question, So what? The difference must be captured in terms of a measurable change in a situation. (For further reading on measurable outcomes, see "Evaluations and Outcomes" in the Resources section.) The change is often in behavior, knowledge, or attitude. In the case of the literacy organization above, the outcome might be that 80 percent of the third-graders in the program will be at a third-grade reading level by the end of the school year. In the case of the advocacy organization, the change might be that one hundred citizens reported feeling more confident about talking with a lawmaker about their concerns. For the youth-serving group, the promise could be that the pregnancy rate among the teens who received training and support will be reduced by 20 percent compared to the rate among the same age group the year before. And the environmental organization could call out the species of plants and animals whose habitat will be retained, or quantify how much erosion or air or water pollution will be prevented due to conservation of the property. The outcomes must show how behavior or attitudes will increase, decrease, or remain the same as a result of the outputs listed in the previous column.

Goals: The goals column describes the desired effect of the outcomes. How will people's lives be different? What will success look like in the community?

Often the goals are prescribed by the funder, and the grantseeker must shape the project to meet the funder's goals. For example, a United Way chapter serving a particular geographic area named forty developmental assets that, based on the results of widespread research, were considered the building blocks for healthy child development. The list of assets included factors like the presence of caring adults who are not the children's parents, the opportunity for children to serve others, and a sense of safety at school. The United Way then tied their funding to those assets to encourage nonprofits to create the desired environment for children in their community. Organizations with mentors, coaches, or scout leaders could easily point to how their work would help develop one of those assets. In their goals column, they could write, "Children will have access to caring adults who will be role models and offer a support system beyond the family." Remember, what you put in the goals column should reflect not only the funder's goals but also the goals in your organization's mission statement and strategic plan.

Filling out a logic model early in the design process will help you pinpoint new ways to strengthen your project design. When identifying the resources for a project, you may realize you have assets that could set you apart from other groups that may have an idea but perhaps no infrastructure yet, or no established relationships with potential collaborators. As you detail the logical flow of the project's activities, outputs, and results (outcomes), you might discover missing elements or figure out how to state something more clearly. Developing a logic model helps create a clear road map for project implementation.

So-That Chains

Logic models can be challenging at first. An exercise called a SO-THAT CHAIN can help get you started. A so-that chain helps you create a sequential description of what you're planning to do and why. Write down the activity you plan to engage in, followed by the words "so that," and repeat the pattern until you feel like you're done. Here's an example:

> We train parents how to use checklists   SO THAT
>
> Parents will get more involved in monitoring their children's reading performance   SO THAT
>
> Parents will encourage their children to become proficient readers   SO THAT
>
> Children will reach third-grade reading level by the end of third grade   SO THAT
>
> Children will be more likely to stay in school and graduate   SO THAT
>
> Children can become responsible, independent citizens in the community.

You might consider having several of the people involved in the project write their own so-that chains independently and then share them with one another. Each person may include a step that others left out, or say something in a way that triggers other ideas. To make it a group exercise, give each person a pad of sticky notes and have them write one "so that" on each sticky. Then have each person first arrange their notes sequentially on a table or window, and then move them around to integrate them with others' notes. The early sticky notes usually describe the project's outputs, and later notes generally reflect outcomes and goals. If you're lucky, everyone's last sticky note will be similar in concept. That goal should be what you ultimately hope to achieve by doing the proposed work.

You'll find further discussion about using logic models in the chapters on project description (Chapter 10) and evaluation (Chapter 11). See also the Resources at the end of this book and the Getting Funded website, www.gettingfundedbook.com.

Summary

Your project will be more sustainable and the grant proposal you write to fund it will be more competitive if you take time to carefully frame the concept and clarify what you hope to accomplish. Ensuring that your idea is soundly aligned with your organization's goals, relevant to an important community need, and designed with attention to current knowledge and anticipated results will make it easier to write the rest of your proposal. It will also make it more likely that you will get funded.

Key Terms

ACTIVITY: A specific step that will be taken so that an organization's methods or tactics work.

APPROACH or STRATEGY: The course of action you engage in to effect change.

GOAL: One of the overarching targets you hope to achieve through the proposed work.

LOGIC MODEL: A graphic representation of a project that shows the relationships between what you propose to do and the results you will achieve.

METHOD or TACTIC: The way that an organization implements a project and/or evaluates the results of a project, including the steps taken to achieve project outcomes.

OUTCOME: A specific, measurable change in decision making, knowledge, attitude, or behavior resulting from your project's outputs.

OUTPUT: A quantifiable item or unit of service resulting from the activities you propose.

PARTNER: A contractually bound party that works closely with another party with specified rights and responsibilities.

SO-THAT CHAIN: An exercise that helps identify project outputs and outcomes. Either individually or in groups, participants write down a series of phrases describing what activity will be undertaken and why, followed by the prompt "so that." Participants continue this pattern to home in on definable objectives and a clear goal for the proposed activity.

PART TWO
Know the Funders

Not all funders are alike, and not all grants are alike. The more you know about what types of funders exist and what types of things they can do to support your work, the more you will be able to target your approach. Finding and discerning which types and sources of funding are most suitable for your organization and your project will make the overwhelming number of options seem more manageable. And learning the rules for approaching funders will improve your chances of a positive relationship with them.

Part II of this book introduces the different types of funders and how they operate and explores ways to locate appropriate funders for your project and determine which ones to approach, for what, and how.

To review, before you begin to identify funders, you'll want to have completed the following steps:

- Reviewed your organization's capability, secured the basic systems needed to develop the project and the grant proposal, and determined that the project design is compatible with your organization's mission and priorities (see Chapter 1, "Ensuring Organizational Readiness")
- Completed a needs assessment, including appropriate statistical data and research, to justify your proposed work (see Chapter 2, "Defining the Need")
- Brainstormed several options for meeting the need and implementing the project; evaluated the pros and cons of each in light of related research, local interest and capabilities, your organization's prior experience with similar project designs, potential benefits, feasibility, and degree of innovation; and chosen the most promising approach (see Chapter 3, "Designing Your Project")
- Secured the preliminary buy-in of any cooperating agencies or departments necessary for implementation (see Chapter 1, "Ensuring Organizational Readiness")

4 IDENTIFYING POTENTIAL FUNDERS

This chapter examines the types of funders that exist and the characteristics that differentiate one type of funder from another. This comprehensive look at funding organizations will help you begin to determine potential funders for your project. Identifying the appropriate funders for your organization and for your project depends on having a thorough understanding of the three subjects explored in Part I: your organization, the need you hope to address, and the strategy you'll implement in your proposed project.

As you proceed toward finding and contacting potential funders, you'll find that the effort you made getting your organization ready for grantseeking and the time you spent designing your project will pay off: your respect for the grantseeking process, as well as for specific funders and philanthropy itself, will be apparent to the grantmakers you approach. Not only is this a gracious approach, but your proposal will be more likely to meet with success.

Many grantseekers want to jump directly into finding out who might fund their project. But before you can identify which funders are appropriate to approach, make sure that you have first taken the steps mentioned in the previous chapters. Failure to do so doesn't just jeopardize your own possibility of success—it discourages philanthropy for all grantseekers, as it shows a lack of respect for the grantmaking process and the grantmakers, and reflects badly on the whole grantseeking community.

Types of Funders

All funders fall into one of two categories: public (government) and private. The government category includes federal, state, and local granting agencies. The private category includes foundations, corporations, and organizations. This chapter describes the various types of funders and what distinguishes them from one another. To begin, Figure 4.1 summarizes major differences between public and private funding sources.

Public Funding Sources

GOVERNMENT FUNDERS make grants that reflect the priorities of their respective legislative bodies: federal, state, county or borough, or municipality. Government grants generally support projects that help a large number of individuals. They are called public funders because the funds distributed are derived from taxes. Each level of government has its own set of funding characteristics. Organizations new to grantseeking are likely to be more successful if they begin by approaching local government funders and work their way up to applying for federal support. Figure 4.2 lists things to consider before deciding to apply for government funds.

FIGURE 4.1 COMPARISON OF PUBLIC AND PRIVATE FUNDING SOURCES

PUBLIC

Federal government

State government

Local government (e.g., city, county, borough, municipality)

PRIVATE

Foundations

Corporations

Service clubs

Professional associations

Trade associations

Unions

Special interest groups

Faith communities

WAYS THEY DIFFER

Where the money comes from

Why they're giving money away

Who's involved in the decision-making process

What the decisions are based on

When and how they want to initiate contact

What timelines are followed

What they want reported and how

How they like to be acknowledged

How much money they will award

How long they will fund a project

ADVANTAGES

PUBLIC

Large, multiyear grants that can include operating costs

Purpose set by legislation; transparent decision making

Aim is to affect significant groups in society

Many funding opportunities available (e.g., grants, contracts, appropriations, dedicated funds)

Prescribed processes and formats for proposals

Policies may allow renewal

Lots of staff; resources for technical assistance

Funds available to wider array of organizations (e.g., for-profit, nonprofit, other public entities)

Accountable to elected officials if bias suspected

PRIVATE

Large and small grants

Guidelines determined by founder or board

Competition may be less intense

Proposals usually less complex and lengthy

Can be much more flexible in responding to unique needs, circumstances, and time frames

Seldom have complex tracking and reporting requirements

Can help open the door to large public grants and other types of funding

Can often provide forms of help other than just cash

Can be much more informal

Often better for local needs and smaller organizations

DISADVANTAGES

PUBLIC

Complex applications and reporting requirements

Proposals are longer and require assurances of nondiscrimination and fair practices

May require matching funds or cost-sharing

Many more organizational requirements once funds are received

Tend to favor proposals from established organizations

May be reluctant to fund new or high-risk approaches

Higher cost to organization for securing such funds and carrying out projects

Changing political trends affect security of some programs and continued availability of funds

PRIVATE

Average grant size usually smaller

Priorities can change rapidly, making continued support harder to predict

Grantseekers have limited influence on decision-making process

Information on policies, procedures, and preferences can be harder to identify, requiring more lead time for research

May be unwilling to pay all project costs or indirect costs

Smaller staff size may limit opportunity for preliminary discussion or site visits

Decision-making process is not always transparent

May not explain a rejection, making it harder to compete more effectively next time

Government Funders: Federal

There are thousands of separate grant programs supported through the federal government, managed by myriad departments, bureaus, and offices.

The federal government is the largest grantmaker in the world by all definitions, including number of dollars granted, number of grant programs, and geographic reach.

Applying for federal funds is an elaborate, complicated, and time-consuming process. When you're ready to approach a federal funder, start by gathering the necessary information listed in Figure 4.3 which may also help you determine which government funding sources may be most appropriate for your proposal.

Government Funders: State and Local

State and local government agencies serve as sources of grant or contract funds in at least four ways:

- They receive federal or state funds and are responsible for redistributing those funds to local applicants. These are often referred to as flow-through or pass-through monies.
- They receive a federal grant or contract for their own projects, distinct from flow-through money, and want either to use the funds within their agency or to identify others who will subcontract or partner with them for part of the project's requirements.
- They are designated as the administrator of a grant program established by the state legislature or county, borough, or city council, and must then choose recipients for these funds.
- They use their own budget to purchase (through a contract, not a grant; see Chapter 5) a particular product or service that will help them implement some part of their responsibilities.

State and local governments have two distinct advantages over federal agencies. Although the availability and size of state and local government grant awards may not match those of federal funders, local government staff are usually more accessible, and the competition for funds is likely to be less intense.

If you are seeking state support for research, note that state and local agencies routinely fund studies on issues appropriate to their jurisdictions. While they may not offer the same type of research grants that federal funders do, they frequently arrange for consulting contracts, personal services agreements, and internships, with some internships tied to doctoral dissertations.

Characteristics of Government Funders

Availability: All federal government funding opportunities and resources can now be found online through Grants.gov (see "Researching Funders" in the Resources section), though individual departments may also make announcements about funding opportunities through RSS feeds from their websites, grant announcements, Facebook, Twitter, and other electronic means. State funding opportunities can be found on the state government website, usually organized by government department. Researchers may find that their universities or institutions have internal departments that research and present new funding opportunities.

Accessibility: Because the money given away by the government is garnered through taxes, and because government staff are paid with tax revenue, government funders must be accessible and transparent to the public. Don't hesitate to contact their staff to ask about the suitability of your project idea. You can ask about the best time to apply, a reasonable amount to request, or what aspect of your work might appeal most to reviewers. Connect early in the process.

Priorities: Government grants reflect the priorities of governmental leaders or bodies. These priorities shift in relationship to new census data, recent disasters, leaders' political aspirations, and the ideology of the party in power. The goals are usually to meet a need for research (for example, research on the latest health epidemic) or for delivery of services that will improve the current situation in the nation or community (for example, affordable housing in a post-recession economy).

Decision makers: Who makes the funding decisions varies. Some government funders have permanent, full-time program officers whose job it is to issue RFPs (requests for proposals; see Chapter 5), review proposals, determine who gets funding, and maintain relationships with the funded organizations throughout the course of each grant. Other departments hire outside reviewers, usually professionals from the field, and pay the reviewers a stipend for their efforts. Still other agencies seat a panel of volunteer peer reviewers with expertise in various aspects of the topic.

Criteria: Government funders must maintain a transparent review process that helps keep them accountable to taxpayers. Thus the review criteria for government funding are clearly articulated and have explicit scoring procedures. A matrix with mathematical values scores aspects of ideas, execution, cost, population served, innovation, and benefit to the greater population. This makes the selection process highly measurable. Grantseekers can request their scores and a summary of the review, and then use that information to retool for the next time they apply.

Amounts: Federal grants and contracts constitute the largest amounts of money being awarded in the nation. The *Consolidated Federal Funds Report* quoted $744 billion for 2009. See www.census.gov/govs/cffr/ on the U.S. Census Bu-

> Sometimes government funding comes from unlikely sources, so don't write off a department because it doesn't sound like it would fit. Major research grants concerning breast cancer have been made by the Department of Defense, and a city's utilities division funded tree-planting projects.

FIGURE 4.2 CHECKLIST FOR PREPARING TO COMPETE FOR PUBLIC DOLLARS

❑ Do you and your colleagues have the time to do the research, preparation, writing, and gathering of attachments that will make you competitive?

❑ Does this government grant opportunity fit your organization and project?

❑ Is your organization the right scale for the grant—large enough to handle audits and complex reporting and accounting requirements?

❑ Do you have at least a 50 percent funding match? That is, can your project already count on money or other resources that equal 50 percent of the government request, and do not come from another federal agency unless specifically allowed?

❑ If the grant money will arrive at the end of the project to reimburse you, can you front the expenses? It's permissible to use a line of credit from a bank or a program-related investment as a bridge.

reau website for their most recent report. State and local government funding can range from the low thousands of dollars to millions.

Accountability: Government funding often requires complex and detailed reports from funded organizations. Government officials need to match project results against specific mandates, such as reducing illiteracy by 20 percent in a given census block within a given time frame and budget. They must prove to the public that outcomes were achieved and public dollars were well spent.

Private Funding Sources

Private funding sources are those that are not supported by taxes. The money they give away may have been earned, inherited, or collected from people or groups affiliated with the funding organization, or it may be the interest generated from capital that has been invested or saved. There are three major categories of private funding sources: foundations, corporations, and organizations.

FIGURE 4.3 CHECKLIST FOR GATHERING INFORMATION ABOUT POTENTIAL GOVERNMENT FUNDERS

Do you know:

- ❑ the correct name of the grant program or program category?

- ❑ the correct name and contact information of the administering agency?

- ❑ the name, title, and contact information of the key administrator of the funding agency?

- ❑ the relevant names and contact information for decision makers in state and local government selection processes or grantmaking programs?

- ❑ the names and affiliations of recent proposal reviewers, so you can learn more about their affiliations, backgrounds, and interests?

- ❑ the major purpose of the legislation that authorized the program?

- ❑ the eligibility requirements for applicant organizations?

- ❑ of any restrictions placed on use of the program's funds?

- ❑ whether any geographic regions may be a higher priority for this funder?

- ❑ the requirements for matching funds or cost-sharing?

- ❑ the latest regulations governing the funding program, and whether they may change?

- ❑ the current priorities of the funding program, and whether they may change?

- ❑ the appropriations for the current fiscal year and amount projected for the following year?

- ❑ the amount of money already appropriated for continuation of prior awards?

- ❑ the pertinent compliance requirements (if any) of the funding agency, or of Office of Management and Budget (OMB) policies?

- ❑ the steps required to gain permission to submit a full proposal?

- ❑ the required proposal format and what accompanying forms are needed?

- ❑ the application deadline(s)? If there is more than one deadline per year, the anticipated review and notification dates?

- ❑ the application and review process, including the selection criteria and rating form?

- ❑ what grants or contracts the funder has awarded recently, including award amounts?

- ❑ the typical award ranges for your type and scale of project?

- ❑ if the funder has an indirect costs rate, and whether or not they fund indirect costs?

- ❑ the percentage of the total project cost the funder is likely to cover?

- ❑ the funder's policies about offering renewal grants?

- ❑ what obligations (e.g., reports, administrative requirements) follow the grant or contract?

Foundations

Foundations (also called charitable foundations) are legal entities designated by the Internal Revenue Service. As such, they must award an amount equal to a specific percentage of the interest earned from their principal (the money they have invested), and they must file reports on their activities annually with the IRS. They work toward goals established by their founders or their trustees, and they generally support efforts in a specific field, issue area, or community. There are several types of foundations, each with distinct characteristics, and you will want to know precisely what kind you are approaching, as funders will expect you to understand their place in the philanthropic landscape.

Private Foundations

PRIVATE FOUNDATIONS are usually endowed by a single source, such as an individual, a family, or a business. This individual or group shapes the priorities of the foundation. The category, also called INDEPENDENT FOUNDATIONS, includes FAMILY FOUNDATIONS and company-sponsored CORPORATE FOUNDATIONS. See Figure 4.4 for a summary of the characteristics of each type.

Public Foundations

PUBLIC FOUNDATIONS, not to be confused with government funders, may or may not have a single source of money, as private foundations do, but rather raise money from the public to be granted to worthy recipients. This category takes several shapes. OPERATING FOUNDATIONS are usually aligned with an institution, such as a university or hospital, and were created to sustain that institution. They might, however, fund external organizations as well. For example, a hospital foundation might eagerly support groups that promote health. COMMUNITY FOUNDATIONS are tied to a geographic community. They encourage people in their community to contribute to a pooled fund, through cash, appreciated stocks, real estate, or other assets. The interest generated by a pooled fund is what a community foundation gives away. Other public foundations simply raise money through charitable contributions from those who share their priorities, and award grants from the proceeds. They usually emerge to address unmet needs in a particular constituency, such as a specific school district, gays and lesbians, women and girls, African Americans, or people living with AIDS.

Characteristics of Foundations

Accessibility: Established foundations with staff are relatively easy to find and connect with. They are listed in directories and can be located online or by phone. But some smaller family foundations may be more difficult to locate or contact. In fact, they often don't want to be accessible: they may give primarily to organizations the family is involved with and not welcome requests from others. These foundations may not have a website, and may choose not to be listed in directories.

Priorities: The monies awarded by private foundations usually come from the interest income generated by amassed capital, and the priorities for grant awards are set by those who donated that capital. Look at where that money came from, as the source of the money has an enormous bearing on the funder's goals and procedures. For example, a foundation created by a company that makes its money in resource extraction, such as mining or logging, may not look favorably on proposals from environmental organizations.

FIGURE 4.4 COMPARISON OF TYPES OF FOUNDATIONS

PRIVATE FOUNDATIONS

PUBLIC FOUNDATIONS

Independent or family foundations	Corporate foundations	TYPE	Operating foundations	Community foundations	Other public foundations
Independent grantmaking organizations established to aid social, educational, religious, or other activities chosen by founder	Legally independent grantmaking organizations with close ties to corporation providing the funds	DESCRIPTION	Organizations that fund the programs, research, or services of an institution, such as a university or hospital	Organizations that make grants to address the needs of a specific community or region	Organizations often formed to serve specific populations or specific fields or issues
Endowments from a single source such as an individual, a family, or a group	Endowment and/ or annual contributions from a profit-making corporation	SOURCE OF FUNDS	Endowment from the sponsoring institution, also eligible to receive tax-deductible gifts from the public	Contributions from many donors or an endowment	Contributions raised from a large number of individuals who share the organization's goals
Donor or donors, donor's family, an independent board, or a bank/ trust officer acting on the donor's behalf	Board composed of officials from corporate headquarters or local office, or employees who are assigned or elected	DECISION-MAKING BODY	Usually an independent board of directors, often with ties to the sponsoring institution	Board of directors representing the community	Peer review panels representing donors and constituents; panels sometimes include grantees
Broad discretion allowed, but may have specific guidelines and give grants in only a few specific fields; most specify particular communities where they will make grants.	Grants given in fields related to corporate activities and/or in communities where corporation operates, usually give more grants, for smaller amounts, than do other private foundations	GRANTMAKING ACTIVITY	Grants given directly to the institution's program, but occasionally fund outside organizations with mutual goals	Grants given are generally limited to charitable organizations in the local community	Grants often made in conjunction with training or technical assistance, sometimes for multiple years

An insurance company foundation director proudly announced a shift in their guidelines by saying the foundation would now fund only organizations whose work would help strengthen their company's bottom line. He mentioned the foundation was interested in supporting groups that encouraged healthy eating, exercise, helmet use, safe play areas, and swimming and boating safety, or that discouraged smoking, drug use, drinking and driving, and crime. "We owe it to our stockholders to grow their investment by funding organizations who help us decrease claims."

Independent foundations must carry out the specified intent of the original founder, whether the current leaders agree with those wishes or not. The board members of one foundation, charged with giving away the fortune of a timber baron, found themselves at odds with the founder's mandate to promote logging. Armed with recent research, they honored the founder's wishes by supporting groups engaged in sustainable forestry practices.

Family foundations may be established to create a shared family activity, to garner tax benefits, or to facilitate giving to groups with whom they are already involved. Public foundations reflect the values and aspirations of their myriad donors.

Decision makers: Large private foundations may have professional program officers who are instrumental in the selection process for grant awards, but leave the final decision to the trustees. Depending on size, some family foundations employ staff who are pivotal in the decision-making process, but in many of these foundations, unpaid family members make the determinations. Since operating foundations exist primarily to fund an institution, the decision-making body is usually made up of individuals from the board and staff of the institution. Community and public foundations want their proposal reviewers to reflect the community or population they serve.

Criteria: Foundations may base their decisions on more subjective criteria than do government funders, though the trend is toward careful measurement and high accountability. Foundations may put more emphasis on the people serving on the board of a nonprofit, on how the alliance between organization and foundation might reflect on them in terms of marketing or politics, and on whether leaders or volunteers in the applicant organization are also part of the foundation. Reputation, clarity of purpose and presentation, and a sense of capability all affect reviewers' opinions. Ultimately, all decisions hinge on whether the proposal furthers the funder's goals, whether those goals are clearly stated or not.

Amounts: The size of foundation awards varies greatly, from low hundreds to hundreds of thousands or millions of dollars. *Giving USA 2011* quoted $304.5 billion for the total amount of funding distributed by private American foundations in 2010. See the Giving USA Foundation website, at www.givingusareports.org for the most recent report. Private foundations must distribute a minimum of 5 percent of their annual asset value.

Accountability: Foundations have lower expectations about reporting and acknowledgment than do government funders, but they do expect to hear how their grant monies were spent and to be acknowledged in print or online. The larger the gift, the more rigorous they will be about accountability, asking for receipts, audits, professional evaluations, frequent communication, and reports.

Eligibility: Foundations mostly limit their grants to tax-exempt organizations that have been certified by the Internal Revenue Service as qualifying under Sec-

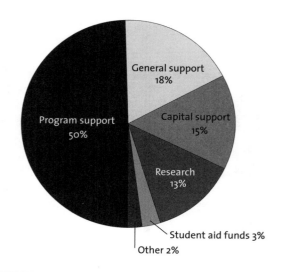

FIGURE 4.5 FOUNDATION GRANTS AWARDED BY PROJECT TYPE, 2010

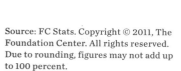

% of dollars

General support 18%

Capital support 15%

Program support 50%

Research 13%

Student aid funds 3%

Other 2%

Source: FC Stats. Copyright © 2011, The Foundation Center. All rights reserved. Due to rounding, figures may not add up to 100 percent.

tion 501(c)(3) of the Internal Revenue Code. Some foundations will make grants to public entities as defined under Section 170(c) of the Internal Revenue Code. A small number of foundations will also make grants directly to individuals.

If a foundation wishes to support an organization that has not yet earned the appropriate designation from the IRS, it may offer a grant pending designation or ask the organization to find a fiscal sponsor, an entity to which the grant can be awarded on behalf of the organization. IRS rules prohibit foundations from making grants to for-profit businesses.

Emerging Developments in Foundations

The world of foundations has changed dramatically in the last two decades, resulting in expansions, contractions, and shifting priorities. Enormous amounts of wealth have changed hands as baby boomers inherited their parents' fortunes and created foundations with their recently acquired resources. Many corporations, and their employees and stockholders, benefited from unprecedented gains in the stock market in the 1990s and invested their assets in new foundations. And many fortunes were tested and lost in the economic crisis of 2008, which led to some foundations simply suspending operations until their reserves were rebuilt.

According to the Foundation Center's *Foundation Giving Trends 2010*, in the last thirty years, the number of foundations grew from around 20,000 to nearly 80,000. In the same thirty years, foundations' assets (the capital from which they receive and distribute interest income) grew from under $50 billion to nearly $600 billion. And the amount of money awarded by foundations grew from $3.5 billion to nearly $50 billion. While the actual amounts vary from year to year, the pattern of the types of organizations and types of support funded by foundations has been relatively consistent, as can be seen in Figure 4.5 and 4.6.

These huge shifts have altered how foundations behave. Emerging trends reflect the attitudes and interests of a new wave of funders. Where foundations seldom used to offer grants for operating support or multiyear funding, there has been an increase in both. And many of the newer foundation donors are getting more engaged in the work of their grantees, viewing themselves as "venture philanthropists" as they infuse nonprofits with their own financial and intellectual capital,

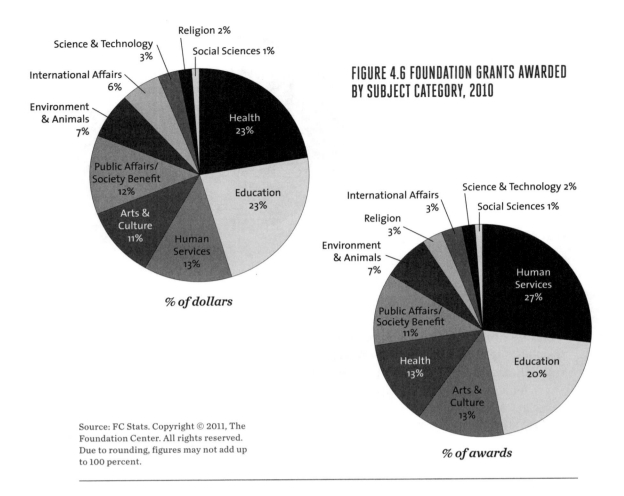

FIGURE 4.6 FOUNDATION GRANTS AWARDED BY SUBJECT CATEGORY, 2010

Religion 2%
Social Sciences 1%
Science & Technology 3%
International Affairs 6%
Environment & Animals 7%
Public Affairs/Society Benefit 12%
Arts & Culture 11%
Human Services 13%
Health 23%
Education 23%

% of dollars

International Affairs 3%
Religion 3%
Environment & Animals 7%
Science & Technology 2%
Social Sciences 1%
Public Affairs/Society Benefit 11%
Health 13%
Arts & Culture 13%
Human Services 27%
Education 20%

% of awards

Source: FC Stats. Copyright © 2011, The Foundation Center. All rights reserved. Due to rounding, figures may not add up to 100 percent.

resources, and contacts. Public foundations have also grown in number and size as people who have not traditionally been part of the grantmaking community pool their resources to award sizeable grants.

In addition, GIVING CIRCLES (new versions of social investment clubs) have emerged throughout the country. Groups of individuals pool their financial resources to make a joint contribution that will have greater effect than a single gift could. While thousands of giving circles choose to operate without paid staff and limit their accessibility to protect their privacy, others have taken steps to become bona fide foundations with offices and staff.

For more information on general funding trends, patterns, and priorities, go to the Getting Funded website, www.gettingfundedbook.com.

Figure 4.5 illustrates the percentage of foundation grants given to various types of projects.

Figure 4.6 illustrates the percentage of foundation grants given to various types of organizations. While these percentages change slightly each year, the patterns represented in these two figures have been similar for decades.

Figure 4.7 offers a checklist of kinds of information to gather on potential private funders.

In recent years, dozens of women's funds have sprung up across the nation and throughout the world, allowing women to leverage their own gifts (often in the $1,000 to $5,000 range) to make a larger impact through collective philanthropy.

Do you know:

- ❏ the correct name and contact information for the foundation?
- ❏ the name and contact information for the primary contact person?
- ❏ the name and address to which the application should be submitted?
- ❏ who reviews proposals (e.g., staff, family members, community members)?
- ❏ the names and backgrounds of donors, trustees, and officers?
- ❏ the names, titles, contact information, and background of staff, if any?
- ❏ which local or regional representative you could contact and that person's role?
- ❏ any contacts who could help influence the funder's opinion of your proposal?
- ❏ anyone who has received funding from the foundation who could offer advice?
- ❏ what relationship-building and communication strategy might be appropriate with this funder?
- ❏ the primary stated purposes of the foundation?
- ❏ the foundation's priorities and core values?
- ❏ the subject areas in which the funder makes awards (e.g., education, health, arts)?
- ❏ the eligibility requirements for applicant organizations?
- ❏ if there are any restrictions that might eliminate your organization (e.g., geography, affiliations, prior funding)?
- ❏ the foundation's program categories and current priorities (e.g., prevention, direct service, advocacy, research)
- ❏ what types of organizations have been funded by this foundation (e.g., grassroots, institutional, emerging)?
- ❏ what types of awards the foundation seems to prefer (e.g., challenge, seed, capital, capacity building)?
- ❏ what types of grants or purposes will not be funded (e.g., religion, publicly funded organizations)?
- ❏ the low, average, and high amounts of grants awarded in previous cycles?
- ❏ the minimum or maximum amounts that are typically awarded?
- ❏ what percentage of a project budget the funder will consider?
- ❏ whether this funder will pay indirect costs and, if so, at what percentage?
- ❏ the total amount of the funder's assets?
- ❏ the total amount the funder granted last year?
- ❏ what portion of last year's grants went to previous grantees?
- ❏ the foundation's application process, including how to initiate contact?
- ❏ when the funder's fiscal year ends (so you can apply early when reviewers have more discretion)?
- ❏ when the funder's deadlines are, and if there is more than one per year?
- ❏ whether the funder requests a letter of inquiry prior to submission of a full proposal?
- ❏ whether the funder has an application form, or accepts proposals electronically?
- ❏ whether the funder wants attachments, and if so, which ones?
- ❏ whether there are known selection criteria and, if so, what they are?
- ❏ the funder's policy on grant renewal, and how many years a project might be supported?
- ❏ whether the funder will support a project that also receives federal or other public monies?

From the Funder's Corner

A private foundation's minimum distribution is tied to its annual asset value. An organization may use a multiyear rolling average to informally figure a giving budget, which can soften declines. But a private foundation using that approach to inform its decision making will likely have to adjust the formula in an up market. A multiyear rolling average will also lessen the increases in an up market.

Some foundations use a rolling average of accumulated interest over three years to determine their grants budgets. Community foundations often use this approach as a way to relate their assets to their grants. As public charities, community foundations are not subject to the 5 percent payout rule that governs private foundations. —*Ken Ristine*

Corporations

Corporations, which are owned by and accountable to their stockholders, support organizations as a way to further the interests of the company. Corporations can provide that support through many channels:

A corporate foundation: A corporate foundation is a legally independent grantmaking organization with close ties to the corporation that provides its funds. A corporate foundation must publicly disclose its grantmaking activities and grant a certain percentage of its assets each year.

A corporate giving program: A CORPORATE GIVING PROGRAM is similar to a corporate foundation; however, it is not required to publicly disclose its grantmaking activities or grant a certain percentage of its assets each year. Giving programs are usually affiliated with a company's marketing, community relations, or public relations department. This form of funding is greatly increasing, and many corporate foundations have changed their funding processes to this type of giving. Companies prefer corporate giving programs over corporate foundations because corporate giving programs allow companies more flexibility, are subject to less scrutiny, and have the ability to base decisions on how much exposure the company can get in conjunction with the support it provides.

> Publicly held corporate funders are ultimately accountable to their stockholders, and their primary goal is to make money. Look for ways to create mutual benefit for your organization and their bottom line, image, or employees.

Contributions in kind: IN-KIND CONTRIBUTIONS are nonmonetary donations of goods or services. Examples include the donation of services of executives and other employees, such as graphic designers, computer experts, printers, planners, or other staff, whose salaries are covered by the corporation. Companies also make gifts in kind of equipment or supplies, often whatever the company makes, sells, or has in abundance. Grantseekers should keep in mind that their budget requests could be significantly reduced if they first asked manufacturers and sellers of products and services for in-kind gifts. This would also provide evidence to other funders of other organizational support, something that most funders want to see in a budget request. As you identify your budget line items, look for opportunities to ask for contributions in kind rather than cash support. Asking for goods and services is an excellent way to cultivate a relationship with a potential funder.

Employee giving groups: Groups of employees at a company collect contributions from their co-workers, and then determine among themselves whom to fund. Sometimes companies provide free office space and support staff to their EMPLOYEE GIVING GROUPS so all money collected can be given to grantees, without any administrative costs incurred. The giving group decision makers, who are usually full-time employees, are often given paid time off to go to meetings and site visits.

A high school science teacher had all her classroom equipment and supplies donated by the companies who wanted the aspiring young scientists to be familiar with their brands.

Employee gift matching: Employee gift matching occurs when a company matches (often dollar-for-dollar, up to a maximum amount) the contributions employees make to nonprofits of their own choice; sometimes the corporation restricts matching to nonprofit organizations in particular fields. Some companies make contributions only to those nonprofits where company employees are engaged as volunteers. Sometimes the amount of company support reflects the number of hours volunteered by employees.

Historically, corporate support has constituted a very small percentage of charitable giving, consistently less than 10 percent of all nongovernmental money received by grantseekers. When your organization creates its funding strategy, keep in mind that corporate funding is an excellent option for certain types of programs and projects, but will probably be a small percentage of your organization's overall budget.

The types of characteristics corporations look for in a successful partnership with a nonprofit organization are listed in Figure 4.8.

Characteristics of Corporate Funders

Corporate giving is generally aligned with three sets of goals:

- **The company's marketing and public relations goals,** e.g., a company sponsoring an event where the audience mirrors the company's target market
- **The company's financial goals,** e.g., an insurance company supporting efforts to reduce accidents and thefts, thereby affecting their bottom line
- **The company's human resource goals,** e.g., a company engaging its employees in charitable causes to build loyalty to the company and camaraderie among employees

Decision makers: In corporate foundations, funding decisions might be made by upper-level managers, by professional foundation administrators, or by a group of employees who serve on a review panel for one- to two-year terms. What these foundations' decisions are based on varies depending on the decision makers and their goals. Sometimes grants are awarded to organizations for which company leaders serve as board members or volunteers. Sometimes grants are made primarily to customers of the company. Some corporate support aims to gain new customers or to appease a constituency that is unhappy with the company. And some funding supports organizations whose work aligns with the company's mission and values. For example, a global airline company might support international disaster relief, and a green building supply firm might support construction of affordable housing.

FIGURE 4.8 CHARACTERISTICS OF A CORPORATE/NONPROFIT PARTNERSHIP

- Promotes internal pride within the company

- Involves participation by employees, thereby promoting a feeling of ownership

- Offers organic growth potential—a built-in ability to develop in unanticipated and unplanned directions because it is flexible and adaptable

- Relates to the commercial interests of the corporation

- Can become part of the corporate culture and last beyond the duration of the first grant

- Can be positioned as a logical extension of the corporation's accepted belief system

- Reinforces values and beliefs that corporate leaders want to have, think they have, or want the public to think they have

- Benefits the nonprofit organization beyond money, extending to enhanced image, expanded management capacity, strengthened skills, etc.

- Can involve the nonprofit constituency (e.g., members, donors, beneficiaries) in promoting the program

- Allows for benchmarks during the decision-making process so the company can see how plans are unfolding and influence their direction

- Can last over time

As decision makers weigh which proposals to fund, they may also consult certain staff members:

- **Risk management staff,** to make sure the project doesn't expose the company to risk. For example, a company might not fund a kids' camp if the counselors are not screened rigorously.
- **Government relations staff,** to make sure the project doesn't jeopardize the company's legislative relationships and goals. For example, a company might not fund an organization that has taken a divergent position from the company's lobbyist on a political issue.
- **Union leaders,** to make sure the grantseeking organization doesn't behave disrespectfully toward labor. For example, a company might not fund an organization that uses nonunion venues or products.
- **Trustees or key stockholders,** to make sure the organization's goals aren't dissonant with those of the company's leaders and financiers. For example, a nonprofit that organizes citizens around tax reform may not be appealing to a company whose stockholders or leaders oppose tax increases.
- **Key management staff,** to make sure that the company supports organizations that have key personnel from the company involved as board members or advisors.

If it is possible, find out who at the company will review your proposal. With this information, you might present your case differently, depending on the reviewers' level of professionalism, knowledge of the field, or personal perspectives. For example, a representative from an employee giving group in a manufacturing firm once told a group of grantwriters, "Your proposal may impress a foundation officer, but our factory workers aren't going to contribute their hard-earned pay to a nonprofit whose top staff earn more than they do and enjoy offices with views."

One former corporate funder divulged that any requests from organizations where the CEO's wife served on the board were to be funded without question.

Generally, corporate contributions staff are also responsible for many other functions, such as coordinating public relations and government relations, leading employee giving campaigns, overseeing in-kind contributions, and managing corporate volunteers, so it may be hard to reach them in person. However, grantseekers should always try to make contact with the staff of corporate funders before submitting any kind of proposal.

Amounts: Corporate funding can range from the low thousands of dollars to hundreds of thousands of dollars. Corporations generally want maximum visibility for their support, especially logo placement on printed materials, clothing, your website; banners or more permanent signs; and acknowledgment at gatherings, including public recognition by the organization at an event or the opportunity to address the audience at an event or offer product sampling.

Accountability: Corporate funders have a variety of philanthropic approaches, many of which are determined by where the corporate foundation or corporate giving program is housed in the company and who determines the funding goals. Corporate foundations tend to have more autonomy and the funding goals might be more philanthropic, whereas if corporate giving is a part of marketing, the funding goals might focus more on promoting the corporate brand. Regardless of how funding decisions are made, the company must justify its giving as a benefit to the owners or stockholders.

Many grantseekers approach corporate funders with a sense of entitlement: "You make money in our community. Therefore you owe it to the community to support its charitable organizations and institutions." This attitude will not strengthen your chances of receiving an award. Successful applicants articulate how their organization can help benefit the company, as well as how the company can benefit them.

The checklist in Figure 4.9 shows the types of information you should gather about potential corporate funders.

Organizations

In addition to private foundations and corporate funders, there are other private entities in the community that can be a great source for funding, both for grants and for contributions in kind. Some of these types of funders have an established funding process, while others are more informal. Discovering which groups might be a good match for your organization could involve Internet research as well as in-person networking. Often groups have regularly scheduled meetings where organizations can learn about philanthropic goals and begin to cultivate relationships.

Service organizations: Regardless of their location or particular interests, service organizations share a common goal: to serve their communities by offering volunteer time, skills, contacts, and expertise, and by raising and contributing funds.

FIGURE 4.9 CHECKLIST FOR GATHERING INFORMATION ABOUT POTENTIAL CORPORATE FUNDERS

Do you know:

- ❏ the full name and address of the company?
- ❏ the name, title, and contact information for the person in charge of corporate giving?
- ❏ the name, title, and contact information for marketing and public or community relations?
- ❏ the company's philanthropic interests and priorities?
- ❏ the company's annual contributions budget?
- ❏ the company's average gift amount and range?
- ❏ the company's fiscal year, so you'll know when it has the most discretionary funds?
- ❏ which type of grants they prefer to offer?
- ❏ whether the company has published guidelines and an annual report?
- ❏ if there are restrictions that might make your organization ineligible (e.g., geography, type of organization)?
- ❏ the best way to approach the company (e.g., phone call, email, letter of inquiry, through an employee)?
- ❏ whether the company has a formal application process, a required form, or preset deadlines?
- ❏ whether the initial approach should be made through local management or headquarters?
- ❏ the role of local management in the process if the company is headquartered elsewhere?
- ❏ what type of decision-making body exists (e.g., management, foundation staff, employee committee)?
- ❏ the criteria upon which decisions are based?
- ❏ the kinds of resources other organizations have been given (e.g., product, in-kind goods or services, employee volunteers, potential board members)?

- ❏ whether the company offers corporate sponsorships, and if so, whom it has sponsored in the past?
- ❏ the types of acknowledgments the company might prefer and whether you could offer them?
- ❏ whether awards are given to organizations receiving annual support from federated campaigns the company supports (like United Way)?
- ❏ who the major competitors in the community are and how the company distinguishes itself?
- ❏ whether the demographic profile of the company's customers or employees also reflects your constituents?
- ❏ whether the company has a significant presence in the vicinity (e.g., a facility, employees, customers)?
- ❏ whether the nature of the company's business is related in any way to the proposed project?
- ❏ whether the company's business is related in any way to research your organization produces?
- ❏ whether issues that are of unique importance to this company or its industry have ties to the work your organization does?
- ❏ whether significant numbers of people employed by the company receive training or education through your organization?
- ❏ whether the company sells substantial products or services to your primary constituency?
- ❏ whether the company would gain any unique benefit by association with your project?
- ❏ whether the company's corporate giving goals would be furthered by your project?

A partial list of such organizations includes Rotary, Kiwanis, Lions, Junior League, Soroptimist, Optimist, Altrusa, Civitan, Zonta, the American Association of University Women, P.E.O., The Links, Sertoma, and Exchange Club.

Some service clubs have chosen a particular area of interest to fund throughout the United States and beyond, focusing on issues such as child abuse and neglect, technology in developing countries, or the loss of sight. Their priority focus does not preclude other issues, so many clubs welcome unsolicited proposals as well. Depending on the size and sophistication of the group, awards can range from a few hundred dollars to hundreds of thousands of dollars, and from one-time gifts to long-term partnerships.

Professional associations: These are groups made up of individuals in the same profession. They number in the thousands and range from large, well-known organizations, such as bar associations for lawyers, to more specialized fields, such as the International Telework Association or the International Society of Certified Employee Benefit Specialists. These associations offer grants, scholarships, and fellowships, using money they generate by collecting dues or donations from their members or by creating earned income through products or services.

Professional associations often invest in programs that will enhance their own field, such as women engineers funding programs that engage girls in science, or in programs that will serve their own constituency. For example, organizations serving people living with AIDS have been generously supported by associations in fields such as landscape design, interior design, and fashion design, in part because those professions have lost so many colleagues to the disease. Organizations that serve a particular ethnic population have gotten support from professionals in that same population, such as Blacks in Technology.

Trade associations: These associations are composed of groups of businesses in the same industry or who produce similar product lines. Some trade associations form their own foundations, while others make cash or in-kind gifts to organizations doing related work. For example, a trade association of contractors supported groups that build playgrounds for child care centers, make home repairs for older people who cannot leave their homes, or provide low-income housing.

Labor unions: An often forgotten but important source of project support, labor unions are particularly interested in projects for services or issues that directly relate to their membership. One union funded independent policy studies on the effect of imports on their employment, while another union funded medical research on the health effects of exposure to coal and asbestos, something that was pervasive among their workers.

Fraternal organizations: While primarily social clubs, these organizations often have a philanthropic motive, contributing millions of dollars to children's health care and community projects. Examples include Elks, Eagles, Moose, Odd Fellows, Masons, Shriners, and the Grange.

Greek-letter societies: These organizations exist in particular fields, such as journalism or social work, and fund mostly education.

Heritage organizations: This category includes groups like Colonial Dames of America and Daughters of the American Revolution that are particularly interest-

An international manufacturing giant had traditionally focused its giving to make an impression on potential customers from around the globe, influential lawmakers, and other industry leaders. But leaders realized that what they supported affected their employees' perception of the company, and if they wanted to retain world-class employees, they needed to support things that made their community an attractive, safe, interesting place to live and work.

ed in history and culture and often fund historic preservation efforts. The Jewish Federations support organizations that benefit Jewish communities, just as Sons of Norway supports Nordic heritage museums, and Sons of Italy or the Caledonian Society foster their respective cultural heritages.

Native American tribes: Native American tribes offer two different types of funding. Because tribes are sovereign nations, the grants they make are technically government funding. But tribes that have formed corporations or that have revenue-generating businesses such as casinos or smoke shops are technically corporate funders. Some states have stipulated that the tribal casinos must give a designated percentage of profits to first responders (that is, emergency-service providers) and to nonprofit organizations.

Military organizations: Groups such as the American Legion or Veterans of Foreign Wars, military wives groups, or retired officers clubs have funded aircraft and naval museums or organizations concerned about veterans returning from conflicts overseas.

Hobby groups: These groups of people contribute to organizations that could benefit from their partnership. For example, quilters have offered assistance to abused children and bird-watchers have invested in habitat restoration. Classic car groups have given millions to children's hospitals, and motorcycle clubs are notoriously generous. One Harley-Davidson Owners Group (HOG) made a large gift to a Humane Society, calling themselves Hogs For Dogs.

Student-based groups: Students contribute money, volunteer time, and in-kind gifts.

- High school or college service clubs may raise money for foster children or cancer research.
- Groups studying a particular profession or industry give to nonprofit organizations working on issues that affect those professions, such as Junior Grange funding a group working on water rights, or Future Teachers supporting curriculum design or education policy efforts.
- Clubs of foreign students might support world affairs work or immigrant rights efforts.
- Members of Panhellenic sororities and fraternities often make significant grants to organizations locally and nationally. Most of these groups have alumni associations that also contribute. This is a particularly important resource among some cultural communities, especially African American and Hispanic communities.

Faith communities: Synagogues, temples, mosques, churches, and other spiritual groups frequently support food banks, family services, homeless shelters, and other social services that enhance the quality of life in their community and abroad. Many churches have built or bought housing for people living on low incomes or those with mental illness, supported policy advocacy, and given generously through special collections, gifts from their own operating budgets, and grants from their regional or national foundations.

Characteristics of Organization Funders

Accessibility: Some of these funding sources will be easy to locate and approach. Other groups prefer to support their own communities. Remaining relatively invisible to the general public, they usually prefer to accept inquiries only from their own members. Before approaching a group, ask your organization's leaders, colleagues, or members if they belong to it. Ask these inside contacts to champion your proposal among their peers.

Priorities: Some of these private funding sources will be focused on serving their own members, while others address a broader constituency. Their funding will almost always reflect the values and interests of their members, who are usually responsible for having generated the grant money through dues or contributions, fees, continuing education tuition, product sales, conference registration, or fundraising events.

Decision makers: In some cases, those who choose which projects get support may be volunteers without much experience with philanthropy or the nonprofit sector, and their decisions may reflect that. Other groups may have very sophisticated decision-making processes.

Amounts: Gifts from these groups may range from low hundreds of dollars to hundreds of thousands of dollars. These types of funders can be a safe place to learn about and practice grantseeking.

Summary

All funders fall into one of two categories: public (government), or private (corporations, foundations, service clubs, unions, trade and professional associations, faith communities, and special interest groups). Generally speaking, public grantmakers exercise a higher level of due diligence with their funding, and their funding requires more complex proposals and reporting. Except for large, formal private foundations, private grantmakers may make more subjective decisions and require less complex proposals and reporting.

A good funding strategy for newer grantseeking organizations is to begin by applying to more local sources for smaller grant amounts, in order to gain experience and credibility with both program and grant management before requesting more significant grants from larger or national sources. Many grantseekers automatically aim for large sums, but big grants can cripple organizations that are not equipped to manage them.

For more resources on the topics in this chapter, see the Resources section at the end of this book or visit the Getting Funded website, www.gettingfundedbook.com.

Key Terms

COMMUNITY FOUNDATION: A foundation formed to encourage people from a particular geographic community to contribute cash, appreciated stocks, real estate, or other assets to a pooled fund. Community foundations use the interest generated by the pooled assets to provide grants to organizations in their community; they also administer donor-advised funds, in which contributions to the foundation can be directed to organizations of the donor's choice.

CONTRIBUTION IN KIND or IN-KIND CONTRIBUTION: A nonmonetary donation of goods or services instead of dollars. Examples include volunteer time, donated space or transportation, or donations of goods, such as a copy machine, or services, such as the pro bono services of graphic designers.

CORPORATE FOUNDATION or COMPANY-SPONSORED CORPORATE FOUNDATION: A legally independent grantmaking organization with close ties to the corporation that provides its funds. Corporate foundations must publicly disclose grantmaking activities and grant a certain percentage of assets each year.

CORPORATE GIVING PROGRAM: A program that makes corporate gifts, derived from corporate profits, outside the construct of a corporate foundation. Corporate giving programs may also be called corporate social responsibility departments; they usually work closely with the company's marketing, community relations, and public relations departments.

EMPLOYEE GIFT MATCHING: A program in which a company matches, often dollar for dollar up to a maximum amount, the contributions its employees make to non-profits of their own choice.

EMPLOYEE GIVING GROUP: A group of company employees that collects contributions from co-workers and then determines among the group whom to fund. While the money being granted is not corporate funds, companies often encourage employee giving by supporting the process with space and staff.

FAMILY FOUNDATION: A private foundation funded by a family. Usually, family members set the grantmaking priorities and make the funding decisions.

GIVING CIRCLE: A group of individuals who pool their financial resources to make a joint contribution that will have greater impact than one person's gift could.

GOVERNMENT FUNDER or **GOVERNMENT GRANTMAKER:** A funder that makes grants, derived from taxes, to support the priorities of its jurisdiction, whether that be federal, state, or local.

OPERATING FOUNDATION: A type of public foundation that is usually aligned with an institution, such as a university or hospital, and was created to sustain that institution.

PRIVATE FOUNDATION or **INDEPENDENT FOUNDATION:** A private grantmaking organization that is usually funded by a single source, such as an individual, a family, or a business. This category includes family foundations and company-sponsored corporate foundations.

PUBLIC FOUNDATION: A charitable foundation that raises money from the public to be granted to worthy applicants. Public foundations should not be confused with government funders, which are public funding sources. This category includes operating foundations, community foundations, and other public foundations.

5 DECIDING HOW TO FUND YOUR PROJECT

This chapter lists the types of support organizations can ask for from funders and the various ways in which funders can respond. In grantseeking, there is a big difference between submitting a proposal for a project or idea your organization has initiated and responding to a proposal that a funder has requested. These two types of grantseeking require different strategies, timelines, and types of information.

Grants are one way to make your organization's ideas come to life. But most funders want to make sure that they are not the only means of support for an idea or project. They want to see broad-based support for your organization's concept, and a healthy, diverse revenue stream. The more diversified and robust your organizational funding strategy, the more appealing your organization will be to funders. Here are some ways to think about funding your organization's idea.

Your organization could generate EARNED INCOME, by charging for a product or service such as tuition, fees, concert tickets, conference registration, a book or how-to video, adventure travel to habitat you preserved, contracted transportation for your clients with disabilities—the possibilities are endless. Your organization could also attract CONTRIBUTED INCOME, by asking individuals, organizations, or small businesses to make a charitable gift.

As you will learn in Chapter 12, on budgets, funders want to see your organization maximize all its options, viewing grants as one piece of a larger funding pie. A grant might be the right solution for one idea—or a specific component of an idea—while earned or contributed income might be more suitable for others.

Types of Grants to Ask For

Grants can support many aspects of your organization or project. You will need to choose the appropriate type of funds for the items in your budget that are appropriate for grant funding. The following list shows common categories of funding awards.

- START-UP or SEED MONEY is funding that helps launch a new initiative or new organization.
- OPERATING or GENERAL PURPOSE FUNDS will financially support the costs of doing business, such as rent, salaries, and other basic needs, with no expectation that the money will be used for a specific activity.

- **PILOT** or **DEMONSTRATION GRANTS** provide support to help show the effectiveness of a model or approach that could later be replicated by the grantee or others using funds from elsewhere.
- **PROJECT** or **PROGRAM GRANTS** fund the costs of a particular activity. If the activity is a fairly limited initiative, it is usually called a *project*. An activity with a wider scope or a longer duration is referred to as a *program*.
- **CHALLENGE** or **MATCHING GRANTS** indicate money that is provided by a funder as an incentive for others to contribute. *Challenge* usually implies that the grantseeking organization must meet a specified goal before the grant money is awarded, while *matching* usually means the grant will match other contributions dollar for dollar up to a particular amount.
- **CAPITAL CONTRIBUTIONS** provide funding to help secure land, build or remodel facilities, or acquire equipment.
- **CAPACITY-BUILDING** or **TECHNICAL ASSISTANCE GRANTS** invest in an organization's ability to function more effectively, scale up, or become more self-sustaining. These grants often pay for strategic planning, leadership development or training, fundraising training, or development of an earned income stream. Sometimes capacity-building grants pay for new staff or new systems, such as a donor database.
- **FELLOWSHIPS, SCHOLARSHIPS,** and **INTERNSHIPS** are given to organizations or institutions who offer them to students.
- **ENDOWMENT** refers to money that grantseekers put into restricted, conservative investments so that the interest earned can pay for program or operating expenses.
- **PROGRAM-RELATED INVESTMENTS** are very low-interest loans from funders for program-specific purposes, such as economic development, low-income housing, or minority enterprise encouragement.
- **LOAN GUARANTEES** allow grantmakers to use their good reputations to help organizations secure a loan. The grantmaker must record a loan guarantee as if the money were actually granted.

> A rural hospital may apply for a *capital* purchase of equipment, say, an MRI machine, but apply for a *capacity-building* purchase of a phone system that will increase the numbers of calls staff can process and decrease call wait times for patients.

Most funding sources give only a few of these types of awards. Check foundation guidelines and funders' websites to determine what type of funding is possible.

Types of Agreements Funders Can Offer

There are three ways funders can respond to organizations' requests: contracts, grants, and sponsored projects. The terms *contract* and *grant* are often used interchangeably, but legally they are two completely different methods for awarding funds. Funders determine which type of award will be made. However, grantseekers should know the characteristics of each type of award and the type most likely to be selected.

A **CONTRACT** is generally awarded for a project solicited through an RFP (REQUEST

> While grantseekers are often eager to ask for support for general operating expenses, there are few private funders who fund those types of requests. Historically, funders have wanted to fund specific items that would allow them to see whether their support had made a difference—such as a capital expenditure or a project with a beginning and end—and they expected organizations to raise their operating money from charitable contributions or earned income. But ongoing conversations between funders and seasoned grantseekers have resulted in more foundations funding operating costs.

FOR PROPOSAL). In this case the funder has already identified the need and the expected outcomes for a project, selected an acceptable cost range, and estimated the time required to complete the project. The object of an RFP is for funders to find eligible organizations and choose the best possible one to carry out the project. The choice is based on factors such as previous experience, location, staff qualifications, and cost.

Cities and states will often award contracts to nonprofits to meet particular needs in their community, such as counseling mental health patients, retraining people coming out of incarceration, or managing waste recycling. Thus community needs are met without the city or state having to create and maintain a government department or agency.

Funders who award contracts also expect to exert fairly strict management control over the contract and may require frequent reports to or visits by the funder's contracting officer. This amount of control is one of the distinguishing characteristics of a contract. The types of contracts commonly used are fixed price, straight cost reimbursement, cost plus fixed fee, and shared cost. The type of contract is dictated by the funder. (See the Glossary for definitions of each type.)

Unlike a contract, a GRANT is typically awarded for a project that is initiated by an organization, which may not have all of the details of the project determined. Grants are frequently awarded for research or experimental projects or for general support of organizations. They typically permit more latitude in shifting funds among budget categories, more flexibility in the timetable, and more freedom around procedures.

A SPONSORED PROJECT is a specific activity or program that is financed by funds which come from a source outside an organization. The term EXTERNALLY FUNDED is also used to describe this type of project.

When and How to Respond to an RFP

All proposals fall into one of two categories: unsolicited or solicited. UNSOLICITED PROPOSALS are initiated by the grantseeker, who submits a proposal after seeing information about the funder and the funder's giving program and determining there's a possible fit. Unsolicited proposals are part of a competitive process that is open to any organization that fits the funder's guidelines. SOLICITED PROPOSALS are initiated by the funder, who contacts preselected organizations and invites them to submit a proposal for a specific kind of project or constituency that the funder has already identified as a giving program priority. Whether solicited or unsolicited, whether the project addresses a need identified by the grantseeker or the grantmaker, a proposal responds to an opportunity announced by the funder in an RFP (request for proposal).

Government agencies and some private foundations use RFPs to announce opportunities for grants or contracts. RFPs are usually issued by funders who have a particular outcome they wish to achieve and hope to discover which organization is most qualified and has the best ideas to carry out the desired goals. This competitive process gives funders more control over the types of projects they fund, rather than reacting to whatever comes in. Funders use RFPs to publicize their highest priorities with precision. Most funders also believe the RFP process may lead to more successful outcomes because RFPs require organizations to do more rigorous planning before submitting a proposal. Finally, some funders feel that using RFPs decreases the possibility of charges of unfair competition from organizations that are not selected for funding.

While there is no uniform format for an RFP, most contain the following information:

- The purpose of the request and the desired outcomes
- The total amount of money to be awarded by the funder, sometimes including the maximum amount that would be awarded to any single organization
- Instructions for how and when the organization should respond
- Instructions for how the organization should demonstrate capability
- Technical details on the content of the program, including expected tasks and products, usually called the scope of work
- An explanation of legal issues or other requirements, such as compliance with guidelines about accessibility for people with disabilities, fair hiring practices, or accreditation
- Instructions for preparing a budget, which may require budget information to be reformatted to fit the funder's categories in order for the funder to be able to make a uniform comparison across all proposals
- A list of required forms and compliance statements to be submitted along with the proposal

When deciding whether to respond to an RFP, you must determine whether the topic is one your organization wants to participate in and whether it is capable of being competitive. In making this evaluation, it is helpful to consider the criteria described below and in Figure 5.1.

Relevance

Before responding, determine whether the RFP is relevant to your organization's mission. A clear match between your organization's mission and the purposes of the RFP will increase your chances of successfully being funded.

Your organization should focus on projects that are relevant to the organization's current interests. Because RFPs often require much more detail about proposed implementation plans and budgets than do other types of proposals, responding to RFPs is particularly time-consuming. Such proposals are also frequently more expensive for an organization to prepare. For example, funding sources issuing RFPs often invite organizations to attend a technical conference (sometimes called a bidders' conference) where they give more information on the proposed program and provide an opportunity for organizations to ask detailed questions. However, organizations have to bear the costs of attending these meetings. Some government agencies that issue RFPs now offer online tutorials, which are much less expensive. But generally, it is not worth the cost in time and resources to respond to an RFP unless it matches your organization's top priorities.

Eligibility

Most funders include *explicit* eligibility requirements in their RFPs, which specify the types of organizations that may submit a proposal. For example, an RFP may be limited to local government agencies or to nonprofit organizations that have 501(c)(3) status from the Internal Revenue Service. Often, there are hints about *implicit* eligibility requirements in RFPs, such as a statement that organizations have specific kinds of prior experience or be able to conduct a project within a particular geographic area. Organizations that cannot meet either the explicit or implicit eligibility criteria will not be considered.

Feasibility

Another way to determine if your organization should respond to an RFP is to evaluate whether the proposed project is feasible for your organization to accomplish. Sometimes, RFPs are issued for projects that are very difficult for any organization to implement successfully. Think about the number and scope of products or activities expected from the project; the amount of available time and funds your organization can provide; the availability of the necessary technology or knowledge within your organization; the political environment in which the project must be implemented (funding sources sometimes overlook the influence of an unfavorable political climate or local opposition to a proposed project); the degree to which cooperation or participation by other organizations or individuals will be required; the extent to which your organization already has those collaborations in place; the decision-making process for the RFP and whether it appears to favor certain organizations over others; and the kinds and amount of monitoring, reporting, and evaluation data that must be provided by the funded organization. In addition, double check the proposed funding plan for the RFP to make sure that it also is feasible. Determine if the funder is offering enough funds to cover the entire cost of the project or if some parts of the RFP need to be subsidized by your organization. If the RFP as originally written is not feasible, your organization should determine if the funding source is willing to entertain suggested modifications that will increase the project's chances of success. If a project described in an RFP seems like something your organization can successfully carry out, it is worth applying for. If not, it is a better use of your organization's time and funding strategy to find other funding opportunities.

Flexibility

Before responding to any RFP, first determine how flexible the RFP and project are. Flexibility can take two forms—the first is the flexibility available to your organization in its response to the RFP. For example, an RFP is flexible if alternative methodology or approaches can be suggested for completing the work or if your organization has a better idea for how to achieve the desired outcomes. This type of flexibility helps you determine whether your organization's interest and capability matches the funding opportunity.

The second type is the flexibility your organization will have in managing the project. Realistically, it is impossible to anticipate every event or factor that will influence a project. Funders should be aware of this by specifying, in the RFP or at the technical conference, a process that can be used to negotiate needed changes once the project is underway. If not, you should carefully consider the consequences should your proposal be funded, and make sure your organization is experienced in planning and managing that particular type of project.

Capability

Also, before responding to an RFP, your organization must determine if it has all the kinds of resources (including personnel) that will be needed to implement the project, or can get them in time to meet the project's deadlines. Your organization should decide if it has the institutional infrastructure in place to make timely decisions. Most RFPs call for much tighter implementation deadlines and much more detailed performance requirements than do other types of proposals. If your organization isn't ready to make the necessary program and resource decisions, you might want to delay responding to RFPs until your organization is fully capable.

Competitiveness

The evaluation criteria included in an RFP are indicators of how competitive the RFP process will be. These criteria usually indicate the extent to which factors such as previous experience, available support services, staff qualifications, and proposal content will be weighted in selecting organizations for an award. In particular, your organization must determine whether it has the resources (e.g., time, money) to apply.

Another issue to consider is whether your organization has the resources required by the RFP. Some organizations have various resources or services that they can provide for the project without charge, while others must consider all externally funded projects to be essentially self-supporting. Some organizations have unionized staff, which affects their per-person costs for such projects. Other organizations are located in areas where salaries are higher than elsewhere in the country. Still other organizations will find that their distance from the funder will result in much higher transportation costs than closer organizations would incur. Cost is often a major criterion when a funder evaluates competing responses to an RFP. All applicants need to think the costs through carefully before committing to a project.

Your organization needs to determine which other organizations will be competing for the award and survey the broader political environment. Politics often influence RFP selection processes. Strong competitors can usually be identified by participating in the RFP's technical conference. Only the most serious applicants tend to participate in such meetings. You should also identify any individuals whose endorsements would be particularly useful in responding to the RFP, such as key elected officials, the heads of organizations that need to cooperate to make the project successful, or community leaders who are very familiar with key decision makers of the organization issuing the RFP. Try to determine, by speaking directly with one of the funder's program officers, if the RFP was developed in response to criticism from a particular source or in response to legislative action sponsored by

FIGURE 5.1 CHECKLIST FOR PREPARING TO COMPETE FOR AN RFP

❏ Is the RFP relevant to your organization's mission?

❏ Is your organization eligible to respond to the RFP?

❏ Is the RFP compatible with your organization's interests?

❏ Is the project in the RFP feasible?

❏ Is flexibility available to your organization in responding to the RFP?
  Is there flexibility available in managing the project?

❏ Is your organization capable of implementing the RFP?

❏ Can your organization be a competitive applicant?

❏ Does your organization have the needed resources?

❏ Is there a favorable political environment around the RFP?

❏ Does another organization already have the inside track?

a particular group. Then examine the kinds of relationships your organization has with these influential groups or people and determine if they will support your organization and, if so, if your organization can work with them.

One final point to keep in mind is whether another organization might already have the inside track for a particular RFP. In theory, if a government source intends to give a grant or contract to an already-selected recipient, it is supposed to declare the project a SOLE-SOURCE OFFERING. For various reasons, this often doesn't happen. Identifying RFPs that are already "locked up" is sometimes difficult, even for organizations that have a good information pipeline. But experienced proposal writers and savvy organizations claim the content of the RFP itself may give the necessary clues. Things to look for include: evaluation criteria that can be met by only a few organizations, a very detailed scope-of-work statement that indicates the project has been tailored to the plans of a specific organization, or the level of detail on projects already underway or that have already been completed by another organization.

From the Funder's Corner
Grantseekers need to look at the type of funding they are looking for and how that matches or fails to match the type of funding that a funder provides. For instance, if an organization is simply raising money for its annual budget, there are certain foundations that may be interested in that while others will not. Likewise, if an organization is looking for a grant for equipment, capital, or another type of one-time expense, there are other more appropriate sources for that.

This breakdown leads to another step, having the organization look strategically at its operating budget. For example, by looking ahead, an organization may see certain items that may be "grantable," such as a brochure redesign, small equipment, and so forth. These items may now be paid out of operating cash. But if you can write a grant for such items, it allows you to preserve your cash for those expenses, such as salaries, that can be more difficult to fund with grants. —*Ken Ristine*

Summary
Before you begin to look for funders who can fund your proposed idea, make sure you understand what types of awards are available and which kinds are most suitable for your particular idea. Clarify whether you're submitting a proposal because you're initiating the approach or because you're responding to a request for proposals announced by the funder.

Key Terms
CAPACITY-BUILDING GRANT or TECHNICAL ASSISTANCE GRANT: An investment in an organization's ability to function more effectively, scale up, or become more self-sustaining.

CAPITAL CONTRIBUTION: Funding that helps an organization secure land, build or remodel facilities, or acquire equipment. Also called CAPITAL GRANT.

CHALLENGE GRANT or MATCHING GRANT: Money provided by a funder as an incentive for others to contribute. Challenge usually implies that the recipient must raise a specified amount of contributions from others before the grant money will be awarded, while matching usually means the grant funds will match other contributions dollar for dollar up to a particular amount.

CONTRIBUTED INCOME: Money generated by an organization by asking individuals, organizations, or small businesses to make charitable gifts.

CONTRACT: An award for a project solicited through an RFP (request for proposal). The funder will have already identified the need and the expected outcomes, selected an acceptable cost range, and estimated the time required to complete the proposal.

EARNED INCOME: Money generated by an organization through sales of products or fees for services. Examples include tuition, fees, concert tickets, conference registration, books or how-to videos, adventure travel to habitat preserved by the organization, or contracted transportation for clients with disabilities.

ENDOWMENT: Money that an organization puts into restricted, conservative investments so that the interest earned can pay for program or operating expenses.

FELLOWSHIP or **SCHOLARSHIP** or **INTERNSHIP:** Funding awarded to organizations or institutions that then offer financial support to students.

GRANT: An award of financial support, equipment, or other assistance, based on a proposal written in the format and to the guidelines required by the funder. A grant does not have to be paid back to the funder.

LOAN GUARANTEE: A form of assistance in which a grantmaker uses its good reputation to help an organization secure a loan.

OPERATING GRANT or **GENERAL PURPOSE GRANT:** A grant that supports an organization's operating costs, with no expectation that the money will be used for a specific activity.

PILOT GRANT or **DEMONSTRATION GRANT:** Specific financial support for a demonstration project or pilot project, which aims to show the effectiveness of a model or approach that could later be replicated by the grantee or others using funds from elsewhere.

PILOT PROJECT or **DEMONSTRATION PROJECT:** Project that aims to show the effectiveness of a model or approach that could be replicated by others. Pilot projects are often funded by a specific type of grant called a pilot grant or demonstration grant.

PROGRAM-RELATED INVESTMENTS: Very low-interest loans from foundations for program-specific purposes such as economic development, low-income housing, or minority enterprise encouragement.

PROJECT GRANT or **PROGRAM GRANT:** A grant that supports the costs of a particular activity, as distinct from an operating grant, which supports the whole organization. Activities with fairly limited initiative are usually called projects; activities with wider scope or longer duration are usually called programs.

REQUEST FOR PROPOSAL (RFP): The notice released by funders to invite grantseekers to submit a proposal.

SEED MONEY or **START-UP MONEY:** Funding that helps launch a new initiative or new organization.

SOLE-SOURCE OFFERING: An RFP in which the funder intends to give the grant or contract to a preselected recipient.

SOLICITED PROPOSAL: A proposal submitted in response to an invitation initiated by the grantmaker. The funder contacts preselected organizations and invites them to submit a proposal for a specific kind of project or constituency that the funder has already identified as a funding priority.

SPONSORED PROJECT or **EXTERNALLY FUNDED PROJECT:** A specific activity or program that is financed by funds from a source outside the organization.

UNSOLICITED PROPOSAL: A funding request submitted as part of a competitive process that is open to any organization that fits the funder's guidelines.

6 FINDING A SUITABLE FUNDING MATCH

This chapter details how and where to look for prospective funders and how to determine which ones will be the most suitable match for your organization and your project. The chapter begins with suggestions for how to canvass your own organization and local community for potential funders, then discusses how to search beyond your current contacts for more options and learn more about them. The second half of the chapter offers strategies to narrow your list of funders and discusses how to select the best options for a good funding match.

For your project to achieve maximum results, your organization should be supported by multiple funding sources. It takes a significant amount of time and effort to learn all you need to know about a funder before tailoring your proposal, so figuring out a targeted list early on in the process will save you time and money later on.

Know Your Own Organization First

Before you begin searching for grants, assemble the organization-level information gathered in Chapter 1 so you will understand how well a prospective funder fits with your organization's mission, geography, constituency, size, and reach. You want to find a true match rather than reimagine yourself in order to "chase money." Here is a list of what to have at your fingertips:

- Your organization's mission statement
- Your organization's strategic plan
- The demographic profile of the beneficiaries you currently reach and the ones you hope to reach
- The geography of your organization's activities, current and proposed
- The poverty rate of the communities served, where appropriate
- Details about the specific need your organization will address
- Your organization's current programs and activities
- Annual reports, financial reports, and other reports available from your organization
- Annual reports, financial reports, and other reports available from the potential funder
- A list of your organization's current funding sources
- A list of previous grant proposals that were not funded, and why they failed

- A list of your organization's funding streams, including recent grants awarded
- A list of your organization's current collaborators and partners, with a brief description of their constituencies, programs, size, and reach, in case it's more appropriate for a partner organization to apply and include you as a subcontractor
- A short list of successful past partners and collaborators and their involvement
- A current list of prospective funders

Look in the Right Places

Begin your search for funders by looking within your own organization for connections. Then expand your search to your local community and beyond.

Your Constituents

Grantseekers should first consult the people affiliated with their own organizations when searching for funding options. Board members, co-workers, volunteers, those served by the organization, members, donors, and vendors belong to service clubs and professional associations, work for businesses and government agencies, and socialize or worship with all kinds of funders. A simple request at a board meeting or in your newsletter may bring forward priceless connections.

If you work with a major institution, such as a hospital or university, there may be prospect research staff whose job it is to help you find appropriate sources. Be sure to check with development department staff.

Don't forget to ask your own people to help identify funding sources.

Prior Funders

Approach the funders who have supported your organization already and ask for suggestions, introductions, or referrals to other funders. If funders have already invested in your organization or your proposal idea, they want it to succeed and carry on.

Vendors

Companies your organization does business with want you to succeed so you can continue doing business with them. They may have their own corporate giving program. Or they could introduce you to others in their industry or companies *they* do business with.

Peer Organizations

Research other organizations and institutions that do similar work to see who has funded them recently. Your search could be as simple as looking at the list of funders in the annual reports of peer organizations. Or you could consult some of the online resources listed on the Getting Funded website, www.gettingfundedbook.com, to see who else is doing similar work and who has supported them in the past.

"We have to spread our resources across a large community with a lot of varied needs, so we can't give to the same organizations year after year. Our guidelines stipulate that we can fund an organization only once every three years. But we don't want our investment to lose momentum either. So grant recipients should ask us if we know a fellow grantmaker who may be interested in carrying on where our grant left off."

—CEO of a community foundation

Elected Officials

Contact the staff of elected officials who represent your community on the local, regional, or national level to see if they know about funding opportunities. It's in their interest to help attract money that will serve their constituents. Ask if they periodically notify organizations of RFPs or if they know of other potential sources, especially governmental agencies, that might be suitable for your organization to approach.

Online Resources

There's no need to reinvent the wheel when thousands have traveled the road before you. The Internet contains a rich array of websites that are dedicated to helping grantseekers benefit from their colleagues' experience, including websites that offer helpful suggestions for preparing proposals to private foundations, corporations, or government funders.

> When a grocery cooperative was expanding to a second store, they invited some of their largest vendors to a meeting to explore who might fund the expansion. An employee of one of the distributors who delivered truckloads of food to the co-op every week offered to approach several of the distributor's business associates for money, and those allies alone gave enough money to fund the new store.

All federal grant opportunities can be found both on Grants.gov and on the relevant U.S. government department's website. All other publicly funded grant opportunities, such as those offered by state and local government agencies, will be found on the website of the funding agency.

Most foundations have websites of their own, with the exception of very small foundations and those who do not accept unsolicited proposals. Information about corporate foundations or corporate giving programs, however, may not be included on corporate websites or on other sites that compile corporate data. Ask whoever is in charge of a company's marketing for direction.

And since grantmaking isn't the primary function of some of the other private funders mentioned in Chapter 4, there might not be any reference to their giving on the web. But countless resources do exist on the Internet and can be found through Google and other Internet search engines.

Online directories, some available free and some by subscription, have taken the place of comprehensive printed directories of grantmakers. The definitive online grant directory for the United States is the Foundation Center's *Foundation Directory Online Professional*, available by subscription at http://fconline.foundationcenter.org. Another exhaustive online directory, GrantStation, is available by subscription or for free at many public libraries. See the Resources section for a list of other helpful online resources, and check the Getting Funded website, www.gettingfundedbook.com, for extensive, up-to-date lists of resources for grant research.

Your Local Library

Libraries have bountiful information about grant sources. Many will have printed directories for use on-site as well as online databases. Look for industry-specific newsletters and specialty publications and databases. Foundations provide valuable information on their tax returns, filed as Form 990-PF, which can be searched at libraries. From 990s, you can research which organizations a funder has awarded grants to, including award amounts. In addition to actual listings of potential funders, libraries will also have background information on the government agencies, companies, foundations, or organizations you're considering, including their history, their leaders, financial and stock information, business relationships, and more. Hundreds of public libraries host Foundation Center

Collections, which are robust compilations of publications and online resources about fundraising and grantseeking. Check with your local public library, the libraries at nearby colleges or universities, and even librarians in private corporations.

Research Potential Funders Thoroughly

Once you have gathered a long list of funders, you will want to learn as much as possible about each funder before deciding who is most appropriate for your proposal. The more homework you do early in the process, the more likely you will be to find funders who are a good match for your organization and project. Below are resources that will help you target your list of potential funders.

Funders' Guidelines

Most private funders provide GUIDELINES to inform grantseekers of their goals and procedures. Few grantseekers read them closely. Savvy grantseekers pay careful attention to the information in a grantmaker's guidelines or RFP, watching for the funder's overarching motivation for awarding grants or contracts. Do not try to squeeze your square program into a funder's round hole. If a grantmaker states that it will fund only education reform efforts in local school districts, don't ask for funds for an after-school arts program. Make sure that your proposal truly helps the funder accomplish its own goals.

> No funder is giving you money just because you need it. Funders have their own goals. And if you can show how your organization's work furthers their goals, they're more likely to consider partnering with you.

For example, some groups that were applying for funding from a city's Department of Neighborhoods complained that the funder created hardships for them by requiring collaborations among the local chamber of commerce, schools, and community councils. But one of the stated goals of that department was to strengthen neighborhoods by increasing communication and cooperation among existing neighborhood groups while they worked toward a common goal.

Look for the funder's goals. You can save valuable time and money by ensuring your eligibility before approaching a prospective funder. Since one of the most prevalent complaints among funders is receiving proposals from applicants who don't fit the guidelines, set your organization apart from other grantseekers by pointing out how you do meet them.

Funders' Annual Reports

Public companies must report certain financial information to their shareholders as well as to the U.S. Securities and Exchange Commission. Annual reports, quarterly reports, or ownership filings can be read online or requested directly from companies. Annual reports for any type of funder contain useful information that can provide clues about how appropriate your proposal idea will be to the funder. Look to annual reports for information such as the following:

- What types of people make up the leadership
- What accomplishments are showcased
- What the total assets are and how the stock is doing
- How the total assets and stock relate to previous years
- How much was given away last year, to whom, and for what
- What range of grant amounts was awarded
- Whether the funder uses stories and photos or statistics and citations

- Whether the funder emphasizes products and outcomes or process and anecdotes
- Whether the funder emphasizes partnerships with others or distinctions from others

Funders' IRS Form 990-PF

Private foundations must submit a FORM 990-PF (Return of Private Foundation) annually to the IRS. This document includes a list of all grantees, details on finances, giving interests, restrictions, application procedures, and deadlines. You can read this information at Foundation Center libraries or online at GuideStar. (See the Resources at the end of this book.) By checking which organizations a foundation has funded in the past, for what projects, and for what amounts, you will clarify whether your idea is suitable for that funder. Resourceful grantseekers even reach out to prior grantees to see what they learned about the funder in their grantseeking process.

Funders' Websites

Funders' websites hold a treasure trove of information that will help you determine whether there's a potential fit with your organization. Of course you'll look for their guidelines, but look between the lines for other clues about their internal culture and views. From funders' websites, you can start to understand their goals, core values, initiatives, and current priorities. You can learn about these aspects:

> *"We count how many people walk in the door. We count how many items each checker scans in an hour. We count how many dollars are spent at each register during a shift. You'd better be putting some numbers in your proposal to our company!"*
>
> —Corporate giving officer at a membership grocery warehouse

How funders present themselves to the world:
- Do they seem folksy or formal?
- Do they lean toward text or photos?
- Do they feel exclusive or welcoming?
- Do they seem more focused on facts and statistics or stories and feelings?
- Do they seem more interested in people and processes or results?

Whether and how funders make themselves accessible to grantseekers:
- Do they make it easy or hard to connect?
- Do they prefer phone, mail, or electronic communication, such as email or text?

How funders position themselves among similar organizations:
- Do they mention being part of a larger picture, e.g., coalitions, alliances, or systemic approaches?
- Do they view themselves as cutting-edge and singular?

Who a funder's leaders are, so you can find out more about their positions on issues.

Indications of a funder's history and future goals.

Funders' Industry Publications

If you're approaching a company, association, religious group, or special interest group, you may be able to find articles about them, and about trends in their field, in industry or association newsletters, journals, and magazines, or on field-specific websites.

Conversations with Funders

You can glean more subjective information by contacting program officers at government agencies or recipients of previous grants for answers to the following questions:

- Do they agree that your project addresses an important need?
- Do they think you have thought of a good way to solve this problem?
- Do they have suggestions about what could be changed to strengthen your chances of being funded?
- Can they offer advice about how closely your project matches the program priorities and selection criteria of this particular funder?
- Do they know of any political factors you should know about before applying?
- Can they tell you how many of the grants awarded recently went to first-time applicants?
- Can they suggest which sections of the proposal are consistently the most important ones to reviewers?
- Do they have warnings about the most common mistakes made by previous applicants?
- Can they tell you what information applicants typically leave out that the funder wants to see?
- Do they know of any discretionary funds, unsolicited proposal funds, or as yet unannounced programs you might qualify for?
- Do they know of other programs that might be more appropriate for your organization to apply for?

Look for Common Ground

Proposals that closely match a funder's goals—whether those goals are implicit or explicit—are the only requests that will be considered seriously. These goals could be prompted by legislation or politics, by the personal values and interests of a foundation's originator, or by a corporation's need to fund projects that will increase its visibility and stock value. It's up to you to do enough background research to be able to articulate why the proposed funding partnership makes sense.

Funders can tell when grantseekers have not narrowed their search enough to find good matches. To convince a funder that your project is worth considering, you must explain why you believe there's a compelling connection between your goals and theirs, and why funding your proposal idea is an opportunity they won't want to miss. Proposal reviewers can also tell when they are getting a one-size-fits-all grant proposal. They feel like they're being approached by someone in a bar who's

From the Funder's Corner

Nonprofits should remember that you have to connect to funder values. Even though grant money is given away, it is given with a purpose in mind. A funder is not buying a tangible good, like materials for a manufacturing process or something his or her organization will consume. The funder is buying something for the community, whether it's increased access to health care for children or leadership development through youth groups. —*Ken Ristine*

using the same tired line to pick up anyone who might respond. Indeed, countless funders have received proposals with another funder's name inadvertently left in the text.

As you narrow your search for potential funders, look at the organization-level information you gathered about your own organization in Chapter 1 and compare it with the information you've compiled about potential funders in order to look for the following characteristics.

Shared Mission

The funder's goals clearly relate to the goals of the grantseeking organization and the proposal.

Examples: A residential real estate company whose purpose is to get families into their dream homes has a company foundation that consistently funds Habitat for Humanity projects, domestic violence shelters, runaway teen shelters, homeless shelters, and first-time homebuyer programs. A foundation that promotes international affairs funds organizations that encourage dialogue and shared experiences among people from different cultures.

Shared Constituency

The funder's members, employees, or customers have common characteristics or shared experiences with those to be served by the project.

Examples: A union whose members include chambermaids in hotels, kitchen prep workers in big restaurants, and janitors in downtown high-rises supports a program championing immigrants' legal rights, because so many of the union members are immigrants. A toy manufacturer funds a group offering support to families who have lost their homes in disasters, and another group that provides counseling to child victims of sexual assault. The foundation created by a family whose members share a genetic propensity for a degenerative disease funds an organization doing research on the disease and another group that offers direct services to people with the disease.

Shared Culture or Values

The funders share the core values of the grantseeking organization, such as how it's governed, or the ethnic makeup of the population served.

Examples: A company run by Chinese immigrants provides funds for the construction of a nursing home for Chinese elders. An alternative medicine clinic supports a group exploring nonpharmaceutical approaches to depression. A public foundation rooted in a feminist governance model funds nonhierarchical nonprofits that promote cooperation and mediation.

Shared Image

The funder and grantseeking organization share the same name or perceived status, or a company's corporate tag line could be applied to the program.

Examples: A cellular phone company whose tag line is "Imagine No Limits" supports a ski program for people with disabilities. A timber company whose tag line is "The Tree Growing Company" supports a neighborhood tree-planting campaign. A community symphony that has chosen to perform a whole season of music by American composers looks for partnerships with companies with "American" in their name.

Shared Market

Determine who is making money from your constituents. Regardless of the economic status of the people you serve or those who support you, someone is making money from them. Your constituents may be partial to a particular clothing line, model of car, or vacation destination. There may be a type of beverage they usually drink (are they wine people or beer people, soda drinkers, or bottled water folks?), or an information management system they prefer (do they seem to use one type of computer or phone more than another?). There may be certain pharmaceuticals they take due to their age or medical condition. Picture a sugar substitute company sponsoring an event for a group fighting diabetes.

Also think about companies that would *like* to be making money from your constituents. Corporations can position themselves powerfully in front of the people you associate with by giving a gift that affords them signage at an event or logo placement on your materials. Look for products or companies seeking visibility, possibly because they're new to your community, and be prepared to define the demographic profile of your constituency so the company can see the value of a partnership.

Shared Opportunity (Damage Control)

Sometimes a funder's image has suffered for political, economic, or environmental reasons. An invitation to support your work gives such a funder an opportunity to reposition itself among the community your organization serves.

Examples: A transportation provider that recently had an accident, a food purveyor responsible for an *E. coli* contamination, a toy company that had to recall dangerous toys, or a manufacturer accused of polluting or allowing an explosion may be looking for opportunities to connect with your constituents.

Finding common ground with potential funders isn't hard—it just takes a little time to learn more about them. They will appreciate that you know who they are and what they hold important. It will set you apart from the competition.

Summary

Prepare for your funding search by assembling information that will help you find the most suitable funding opportunities for your organization, your project, and

---

From the Funder's Corner

Getting past the list of usual suspects is critical because those groups—the funders everyone's heard of—get more requests than they can possibly fulfill. Here's a suggested strategy: collaboration. Talk to another grantwriter or development officer, or two, that you could partner with on this project. They don't have to be with groups that offer the same sort of services. In fact, it might be more productive if they aren't. Here's a chance for a human services group, an arts group, and an environmental group to partner, for example. Share ideas about publicly known prospects that may not fit your organization but may be a fit for another group. This approach applies to foundations and other publicly known giving entities.
—*Ken Ristine*

your constituency. Look for only genuine matches, based on shared priorities, values, constituencies, geography, and scope, and do not stretch yourself into something that you are not, as this will lead to mission creep, lower funding rates, and wasted time. You will find funding opportunities through your own networks, at the library, online, and from referrals from current funders and elected officials.

Don't use a broadcast approach in the hope that one among the many applications will find fertile ground. However, look for multiple funding sources that fit, because no funder wants to be the sole source of funding. Few foundations will fund a project alone, especially if it is a sizeable one. They simply won't believe that there are no other possible sources among industries, businesses, individuals, and public, private, and corporate foundations.

Key Terms

FORM 990 and FORM 990-PF: Internal Revenue Service form filed annually by public charities and private foundations, listing assets, receipts, expenditures and compensation of officers. Form 990 is filed by nonprofits. Form 990-PF, filed by private foundations, includes a list of all grants made during the year.

GUIDELINES: A funder's description of what it hopes to accomplish by giving money, as well as a description of who may apply and instructions and rules for how proposals must be assembled and submitted.

7 MAKING A GOOD FIRST IMPRESSION

This brief chapter shares how best to make your initial approach to a funder and how to cultivate a relationship prior to asking for support. The pragmatic advice and constructive examples herein will help you develop and maintain good relationships between your organization and the funders whose support you seek.

Grantmakers want to get to know you—so reach out to them before your proposal's due date. How you initiate and cultivate a relationship with them greatly affects their opinion of the ultimate proposal.

Here are some steps to take to foster good relationships.

Do your homework.

Find out as much as you can about the funders before contacting them. The more you know about their leaders, their history, their culture, and their process, the more receptive they will be to your advances. Thoroughly reading their guidelines demonstrates respect and professionalism, and your acknowledgment of recent developments in their world shows that you're paying attention to them, not just thinking about your own needs.

Approach funders as they wish to be approached.

If the guidelines say, "No phone calls," don't call. If the guidelines request a letter of inquiry, submit one. (If they don't ask for one, don't submit one.) Funders have their own processes, and they want them followed as requested. If you find listings that have no contact information for the funders, don't spend a lot of time sleuthing out how to reach them—these funders have purposely decided to remain unreachable because they don't want to hear from people they don't have a relationship with. People who insist on contacting funders who have sought privacy dampen their enthusiasm for the whole grantseeking community.

> *"The best way to ensure that you won't get funded is to introduce yourself to me in a proposal on deadline day."*
>
> —Head of Corporate Social Responsibility for a national bank

A corporate funder at a commercial bank was plagued by the chaos created by a merger between her bank and a former rival bank. Every day when she showed up for work, she would find a new challenge: her staff had been cut; her budget had been cut; her office had to move; their funding guidelines had to shift. Yet every day, eager grantseekers would call her asking for money or volunteers or in-kind gifts. She said, "I just wish someone would have called without their hand out, and said, 'Your life must be hell right now. Hope things settle down around there soon.'" Funders notice and appreciate it when you show them you're paying attention to their world too.

Initiate the relationship.

If your first contact with a funder is by phone or email, plan your approach ahead of time, writing out a draft of your main points or questions, in order. Show your respect for funders' time by being clear and brief—don't try to engage in a longer conversation unless they invite that. Let them know right away that you've read their guidelines, then ask some clarifying questions to see if they agree that there's a fit between your idea and their goals. Thank them for their time.

Send the information they request.

Some funders ask grantseekers to first submit a LETTER OF INQUIRY (LOI) or QUERY LETTER—a brief synopsis of your request—before sending your FULL PROPOSAL. Funders use these letters to screen out organizations that don't fit their guidelines or that have a proposal idea that won't be competitive. Craft your letter exactly as advised. If a funder doesn't give directions, refer to the suggestions in Chapter 15, "Crafting Letters of Inquiry." Then wait for a signal from the funder before taking any more steps.

A National Science Foundation program officer advised grantwriters to call federal funding staff to find out about national trends and share what they were learning while engaged in their work. He said program officers used to be in the trenches doing the work and missed having robust conversations about cutting-edge work with practitioners. He suggested grantseekers ask program officers for advice and offer suggestions for great articles or links, even highlighting the text that might interest them.

Cultivate a relationship with the funder before asking for support.

Funders want to develop relationships with the organizations they support. Here are some suggestions of steps you can take before asking for funding:

- Show potential funders you've been paying attention to what's going on in their world by congratulating them on an award or good news coverage.
- Invite potential funders to an event that showcases your organization's mission, or offer a tour of your facility.
- Email a link to a brief YouTube video that illustrates the impact of your organization's programs, possibly featuring a testimonial by someone who has benefited from your work.
- Ask potential funders for an in-kind gift of goods or services—something besides cash—that they have in abundance and can give with minimal effort.
- Find out if any of your volunteers are connected to the funder. Many nongovernmental funders want to know that their employees or members are participating in your work already.
- Mail a copy of an article from a trade journal that helps make the case for the type of work you do.

> *"Grantwriting is a contact sport."*
>
> —Grants Manager for a metropolitan school district

A trust officer in a bank managed several family foundations, each with different guidelines. Some required letters of inquiry and some did not. At least once a week, she would receive full proposals addressed to foundations that required two-page query letters, and query letters for the foundations that didn't want them. Each mistake required her to spend precious time calling or emailing the applicants, many of whom argued with her about the process. The trust officer was appreciative of organizations that took the time to follow directions carefully.

- Share the findings of recent research about your field, so funders can see that you want them to understand the context, not just know about your organization.
- Ask potential funders to participate in a focus group or ask their advice about something.

Make sure that whatever you do to invest in the relationship with potential funders is indeed adding value for them, offering them something they can't easily get on their own. Simply telling them about your organization is not really cultivation.

Follow the rules when you apply.

If funders say applications are due at a particular time, be sure to send yours in on time rather than ask for an extension, especially a last-minute one. If funders ask for your proposal to be sent in a particular way (electronically, or with five copies, no staples), do exactly as they say. Your ability and willingness to follow directions will affect how funders perceive your organization.

Give funders time and keep them informed.

Once your proposal has been turned in, let the funder take the time needed to process it. You will most likely hear directly as soon as there is an answer. However, if you have new information about your project, such as a commitment from another funder, or progress with pending legislation, be sure to let the funder know.

Summary

Grantseeking is a lot like a romance, so unless you're instructed not to, you'll want to make an effort to invest in the relationship before asking for a commitment. Funders are people too, and they want to be shown courtesy and respect—not be viewed as deep pockets, only to meet your needs. Pay attention to what each funder wants out of the relationship, and make sure the whole process is a satisfactory experience.

The Director of Philanthropy at an international technology company told the audience at a grantwriting conference that 80 percent of the proposals submitted to the company failed to meet the eligibility requirements published in the guidelines. Organizations turned in proposals that were outside the funder's geographic boundaries, fields of service, and budget sizes; eligibility requirements that were clearly articulated and widely accessible. She said, "It's hard to be generous with people who don't pay enough attention to see what we care about!"

A grantseeker who knew she would soon be approaching a bank for a grant initiated contact by asking to borrow piggy banks bearing the bank's logo for centerpieces at an event. She acknowledged the bank from the podium and in the printed program at the event, then took pictures of the piggy banks on the tables and enclosed them in a hand-written thank-you note the next day. A few months later, she called to ask if there were corporate employees who could help with a three-hour volunteer project, and once they were on-site, she gave them special attention, made sure they got to visit with beneficiaries of the organization, took photos of them in action, and sent personal thank-you notes to each one, plus their supervisor and the corporate contributions officer. When it was time to ask for money, the bank already had warm feelings about its relationship with the organization.

One corporate funder shared that her biggest pet peeve was applicants who submitted proposals that had been stapled or bound, when the guidelines specifically said, "no binding." Since she had to make multiple copies of each proposal for her board, she said taking them apart not only wasted her time, it sometimes ruined her fingernails, which didn't make a good impression.

Key Words

FULL PROPOSAL: A proposal that is detailed and from five to two hundred pages long. Most often, grantmakers provide a template and explicit instructions that they want grantseekers to follow. (See also the chapters in Part III on writing a proposal.)

LETTER OF INQUIRY (LOI) or **LETTER OF INTENT** or **LETTER OF INTEREST** or **QUERY LETTER:** A one- to three-page synopsis of the full proposal in business letter format, used as a first step to get an invitation to submit a full proposal. (See also Chapter 15.)

PART THREE
Write and Submit a Competitive Proposal

Each funder has its own priorities, and each will ask for answers to particular questions in a particular order. There is no single standard proposal outline to follow. But there are certain topics that appear regularly in funders' application forms. To create a compelling proposal that stands out among all the others, you must carefully plan and craft each of your answers to demonstrate what makes *your* project more fundable.

Part III will show you how to strengthen your case for support, tighten up your presentation, and avoid common mistakes in each of the typical elements of a proposal. A strong final document will be clear, concise, readable, compelling, and free of jargon. It will demonstrate that you have done the following:

- Identified an important need or problem that relates to your organization's mission (see Chapter 9, "Composing the Need Statement")
- Documented how your work differs from or builds upon that of others (see Chapter 10, "Writing the Project Description")
- Planned an effective and feasible approach that will result in worthwhile outcomes (see Chapter 11, "Designing an Evaluation Plan")
- Justified the requested resources and planned for future funding (see Chapter 12, "Developing the Project Budget")
- Shown that your organization and staff have the skills and experience to succeed (see Chapter 13, "Establishing Your Qualifications")

And to review, before you begin to write the proposal, you'll want to have completed the following steps:

- Gathered information about the funder or funders you will approach (see Chapter 4, "Identifying Potential Funders")
- Ascertained the relevance of your work to the funder's priorities (see Chapter 6, "Finding a Suitable Funding Match")
- Determined what type of grant to ask for and what mix of earned and contributed income will be most appropriate for your project (see Chapter 5, "Deciding How to Fund Your Project")
- Begun to find common ground and cultivate a relationship with the funder you have chosen to approach to support your project (see Chapter 7, "Making a Good First Impression")

8 PREPARING TO WRITE

This chapter outlines the necessary steps for planning your proposal-writing process. These steps include preparing a timeline, setting clear expectations about the process, building a team, and clarifying what lies ahead to prevent surprises.

Careful preparation is essential to a competitive proposal. The time you spend thinking ahead can also help you do the following:

- **Develop a useful schedule for implementing the project.** Many problems that can occur at the beginning of the grantwriting process can be avoided.
- **Provide a framework for project management up front** by establishing the roles and responsibilities within your organization. For example, if staff from another part of your organization will be essential to the success of the project, you can negotiate for their time during the proposal-writing process. Evidence of these decisions, referenced in the application, can strengthen your proposal.
- **Ensure that you have anticipated costs accurately** and requested adequate resources, including time, money, staff, and facilities.
- **Inform others about the goals and plans for the project.** This prevents surprises among staff who will be affected once you get funded.
- **Test the true degree of internal commitment to the project.** Commitment to the project among your organization's top leadership is especially important. In larger organizations, project ideas may emerge from one department or from a single researcher, yet if funded, the project may involve other departments. By the time you've obtained all of the required internal reviews and signatures, it will be clear whether your organization is enthusiastic about your project and will honor the commitments you've written into the proposal or not. You should not submit a proposal if you think your organization might not deliver on its promises.

The checklist in Figure 8.1 can help you plan to write a competitive proposal. The topics in this checklist were drawn from the answers to a survey of over one hundred private foundation and government program officers.

Most importantly, a strong proposal must engage funders in your excitement about the project and prove to them that you are capable of carrying it out.

FIGURE 8.1 CHECKLIST FOR PREPARING TO WRITE A PROPOSAL

Have you:

- ❑ met with your organization's administrator, program manager, and finance manager to discuss the project, the proposal, and the assignment of roles for completing the proposal on time?

- ❑ created a timeline for the proposal-writing process and scheduled appointments to check in through the deadline?

- ❑ verified that your organization can and will sign any compliance statements required by the funder on such things as antidiscrimination policies, subject protection, animal research, or drug-free status?

- ❑ identified who in your organization must provide these assurances of compliance and contacted those people early in the process? These documents often require action by your governing body, so allow plenty of time to secure them.

- ❑ read all of the forms and instructions provided by the funder and paid close attention to those regarding format, length of each section, required style manual, overall number of pages, required content, attachments, and any other specific directions?

- ❑ made a checklist of all the requirements to refer to often throughout the proposal-writing process?

- ❑ found out if electronic templates are available for any of the required documents, such as compliance forms, budgets, or timelines?

- ❑ developed an outline that includes the major points you want to make in each section of the proposal?

- ❑ identified all the sections that will need input from other sources and indicated who is responsible for which on your master copy of the schedule?

- ❑ let those who must submit content know as early as possible? Send each person a copy of the RFP or guidelines, highlight in color the section for which their information is needed, and clarify precisely what you need from them.

- ❑ given all contributors a deadline of at least one week before you truly need their information? Send out regular friendly reminders, with offers to answer clarifying questions or help out if necessary. Remind your collaborators that this isn't just your project—the grant will further the work of the entire organization, and may even help pay their salaries.

- ❑ found out if some sections (such as evaluation) will need to be prepared by consultants and arranged for their participation as early as possible?

- ❑ identified external entities from whom you could request letters of support, and provided suggestions for what to write, as well as an early deadline?

As you begin planning your proposal writing project, taking the following steps will help streamline the process:

- Collect information about your organization discussed in Chapter 1: gather statistics, quotes, photos, reports, previously submitted proposals, Form 990s, operating and project budgets, the most recent strategic plan, lists of board members and advisors, and other documents that will help you compose the proposal. Put them in a clearly labeled folder to save time in the future.

- Schedule uninterrupted work time in significant blocks so you can focus on writing. Build in time near the end of the process for weaving together all the pieces submitted by others to ensure that the proposal has a consistent voice and style.

- Register for ELECTRONIC SUBMISSION, if that's what the funder requires. Electronic submission, now more prevalent than paper proposals, has greatly altered the grantseeking process. To participate, you must obtain an identification and tracking number, called a DUNS NUMBER (Data Universal Number System, issued by Dun & Bradstreet), which is a prerequisite for submitting an application through Grants.gov, the official federal portal. Once you've obtained your DUNS number, you will designate an individual within your organization as the E-Business Point of Contact (E-Biz POC) with CENTRAL CONTRACTOR REGISTRATION (CCR). See www.grants.gov/applicants/organization_registration.jsp or www.bpn.gov/ccr for the detailed 5-step process. This process can take several weeks and must be done in advance, since many federal grants offer only a month from announcement to due date. You'll find more details on electronic submission in Chapter 16.

Getting letters of support, recommendation, collaboration, and cooperation can be hard, as people tend to procrastinate. Start requesting these letters well before the deadline and persist until you get them.

Focus your thoughts and stoke your enthusiasm by interviewing those who benefit from your organization's work and capturing their quotes and stories to use in proposals. Their responses may characterize your work with fresh words and phrases, which will give heart to the statistics and other data in the proposal.

Consult The Grantsmanship Center's *Program Planning & Proposal Writing* for guidance as you devise your project plan and prepare to write your proposal.

Establish a Proposal-Writing Timeline

As with everything else in grantwriting, there is no perfect or standard model for the proposal development process. You just have to do the best job you can with the time that is available.

All government funders and most private foundations and corporations have hard deadlines for their grant programs.

Typically, it takes funders six months to a year from the date a proposal is submitted to make their funding decisions. Some funders may have even longer delays. One reason for these delays is that funders must determine how much money they have available to distribute in that funding cycle before they can decide how much money they will allocate to new and CONTINUING SUPPORT.

Ideally, your proposal-writing process should begin at least a year in advance of when your project or program is expected to begin. This provides ample time

A critical step early in the process is to develop a detailed work plan that specifies the major information needed for the proposal, who will prepare it, when and in what sequence, and when the necessary internal reviews must be completed in order to meet the application deadline.

FIGURE 8.2 PROPOSAL DEVELOPMENT TIMELINE

MONTH	ACTIVITY
1	Identify the problem, need, or opportunity. Hold preliminary discussions with colleagues to assess your organization's capability to successfully pursue this idea. Decide whether to proceed.
2	Identify a project director and others who will be involved in planning and/or writing the proposal. Approach other agencies whose involvement is critical to the project's success and determine their role in preparing the proposal. Prepare a detailed work plan. Make preliminary assignments. Conduct a needs assessment. Identify prior work or related activities of other organizations. Develop a case for how your work differs from or complements others'. Discuss optional approaches to the problem. Begin to identify potential funders. Hold meetings with top administrators to get buy-in. Establish the legal eligibility of your organization. Make contact with other organizations that could serve as the fiscal agent if necessary.
3	Complete the research to identify potential funding sources and begin cultivation. Be aware of any compliance requirements and ensure that your organization can meet them. Secure any required assurances of compliance with government regulations.
4*	Reach an agreement on the final version of the need statement, project idea, and approach. Develop the first draft of the proposal and seek feedback from colleagues who have previously received funds from this source, agency administrators, partners, and collaborators. Discuss with your organization's legal counsel any issues that might arise if a grant document or contract is negotiated.
5	Modify the proposal using input received during previous months. Complete the final version and translate it into the formats required by the funders. Submit the proposal for internal reviews. Seek review and clearance as necessary from other agencies. Submit the proposal to the funder.
6–9**	Verify receipt of the proposal by the funders and find out when a decision is likely to be made. Stand by while funders conduct their initial review of the proposal and request additional information or clarification. Plan for a site visit by the funder.
10–11	Receive approval or rejection. In either case, obtain reviewers' comments. Prepare to negotiate with funders in case they want to modify the project or the budget.
12	Receive a check or authorization to expend funds. Start the project. If funding is for only one year, begin planning for re-funding efforts.

*Proposals to funders that request a letter of inquiry will require greater advance planning, as it is difficult to craft an effective letter of inquiry before the full proposal has been drafted. See also Chapter 15.

**The activities conducted by the funder during the latter half of this process are not under the control of the grantwriter. It is a good idea, however, to include these steps in your timeline so you know that you've started developing the proposal early enough, given the date on which you'd like to begin your project.

for your organization to explore related work, develop a compelling need statement, clearly think out the project's outcomes and approach, negotiate any cooperative arrangements, develop plans for project evaluation, create a detailed budget, identify and prepare requests to several funders that may co-fund the project, gather the necessary compliance or assurance statements, and complete any internal proposal review and approval processes. Not only does such advance preparation lead to a thoughtful, compelling, and competitive proposal, but it also allows you to make a positive first impression on funders who request first contact via a letter of inquiry. See Chapter 15 for information about crafting letters of inquiry.

Figure 8.2 summarizes the major activities involved in developing a funding proposal and how they are typically sequenced.

Another tool many grantwriters find useful is called a CASE STATEMENT. A case statement is an internal document that compiles all the data you've collected on the need for the work you propose to do, including who else is working on the issue, what the most recent research and experience indicates about how best to approach the situation, how you have chosen to address it, and why your organization is uniquely suited to do the work. Case statements often also detail all the opportunities for others to support your work, such as making in-kind contributions, making connections and opening doors to other funders, and making financial contributions, as well as the benefits available to donors at various levels.

Case statements are seldom shared in their entirety with external audiences. A case statement is meant to be a master source for all your fundraising messages. Once you've developed your case statement, you will have everything you need to communicate with all your stakeholders in one document, and you can pick and choose which elements to share with whom as each opportunity arises. You should be able to draft website copy, appeal letters, grant proposals, thank-you letters, annual reports, news releases, and other communiqués based on what's compiled in your case statement, tailoring each message to the appropriate audience. All your thinking and planning becomes a mother document from which everything else emanates.

> "Taking insufficient time to prepare a good proposal is the single biggest reason for proposal failure."
>
> —Program Officer at a federal funding agency.

> "We spent two years fundraising for a new child care center building. Only as we prepared to break ground did we learn that the city had changed the zoning in this area and we now had to find an extra $50,000 for required landscaping and an automatic irrigation system."
>
> —College Administrator

Identify the Components of the Proposal

There is no such thing as a standard proposal or format suitable to every funder. Although there was an effort in the 1990s among foundations and corporations to accept a common grant application developed by national or regional associations of grantmakers, few private funders seem to favor them any more. However, there is growing consensus about the major elements that should be included in a proposal.

Figure 8.3 lists the major questions that need to be answered in a funding proposal, together with sample answers from a fictional project. Answering these questions in a worksheet of your own can help you organize your thoughts as you begin to prepare your proposal.

FIGURE 8.3 MAJOR QUESTIONS TO ANSWER IN A GRANT PROPOSAL

PROPOSAL COMPONENT	UNDERLYING QUESTION	SAMPLE RATIONALE
Need	Why do this?	An increasing number of youth are dropping out of high school in X community at rates well above the state's average. Research shows that high school dropouts have low self-esteem and a limited sense of future opportunity. They are often unemployed or in low-wage jobs; are more likely to engage in crime, become poor parents, and perpetuate a cycle of poverty; and are more likely to experience physical and mental health problems.
Goal	What do we want to do?	To reduce the high school dropout rate in X community by X percent by X date.
Importance	To what end?	So more young people can be self-sufficient, be prepared for college and/or higher paying employment, become better citizens and parents, and be physically and mentally healthier.
Project Description	How will we do it?	Combine existing neighborhood services for tutoring, recreation, counseling, health education, and parent training into a new center and assign mentors to troubled youth.
Evaluation	How will we know what has changed as the result of our efforts?	School attendance records, test scores, and the degree of change on self-esteem inventories will be used to measure progress toward the project's outcomes. Records will also be kept on the number of mentors matched with teens, and the number of parents who complete training. Over several years, an increased graduation rate among those served by the center is expected.
Qualifications	Why choose us?	Our agency has prior experience managing after-school programs and working with teens. It has previously collaborated with all of the other agencies whose services would be combined in the new center and has a large number of volunteers who could serve as mentors.
Budget	How much will it cost?	As most of the services are already budgeted by other agencies, and the new mentoring program will be managed by existing staff, operating the new center will cost $100,000 per year and $10,000 annually for evaluation.

Proposals to Government Funders

Proposals to government agencies, while longer and more complex than proposals to private sources, come with very clear expectations.

Public agencies are demanding about their forms being completed precisely as directed. Almost all government agencies now require applications to be submitted electronically, which has led to increased standardization in proposal formatting. If required documentation is not included in the electronic submission or major questions are not answered, the computer program used to screen applications will eliminate the proposal in the first round before a human reviewer ever sees it. Read more about electronic submission in Chapter 16.

Figure 8.4 lists the components commonly found in applications to government agencies. The information normally contained in each section is listed in Figure 8.7 at the end of this chapter.

> Private foundations and corporations typically want less information and shorter proposals than do government agencies. Private funders often have small staffs and do not want as much information as government funders, who must collect specific information to comply with regulations.

FIGURE 8.4 MAJOR COMPONENTS OF PROPOSALS TO GOVERNMENT FUNDERS

- Cover Sheet or Title Page
- Signed Assurances
- Executive Summary, called Abstract in research proposals
- Statement of Purpose
- Statement of Need
- Project Description, called Procedures in research proposals
- Sustainability Plan
- Evaluation
- Qualifications
- Budget
- Attachments

Include only those components and attachments listed in the RFP or your whole proposal may be disqualified.

Proposals to Foundations and Corporations

Foundations and corporate funders vary widely in the type and amount of information they want. The more established and formal the funder, the more complicated the application process and the more rigorous the expectations of your proposal. The major components of proposals to foundations and corporations are listed in Figure 8.5. They are similar but not identical to the components of proposals to government funders. More detail about each element can be found in Figure 8.8 at the end of this chapter.

It is common courtesy to include a cover letter with your proposal to private funders. Consider your cover letter the "face" on your proposal, an opportunity to connect with the reader, be gracious and warm, and fill in any compelling information that you weren't able to include in the answers to the funder's questions. Think about inserting a quote, from someone who benefits from your organization's services or someone the funder knows, mentioning your organization's ability to make an impact. The best cover letters are brief and pack an emotional punch.

FIGURE 8.5 MAJOR COMPONENTS OF PROPOSALS TO FOUNDATIONS AND CORPORATIONS

- Cover Letter
- Executive Summary
- Problem or Need or Opportunity Statement
- Project Description
- Organization Background
- Evaluation
- Qualifications
- Budget
- Sustainability Plan
- Attachments

Include only those components and attachments listed in the guidelines or your whole proposal may be disqualified.

Assemble Your Proposal-Writing Team

Sometimes, writing a proposal with a committee is the only way to be competitive. The information needed to complete the proposal is seldom known by only one individual, so you'll often need the cooperation, input, and wisdom of multiple parties to cover all essential points. A foundation program officer who had been a university faculty member previously and had routinely prepared proposals using committees provided the following suggestions.

> Give everyone an internal deadline that's at least one week (two weeks for federal grants) before proposals are really due, or people's procrastination will lead to sloppy, last-minute work.

Hold an initial meeting with a few colleagues to brainstorm the project idea and do a preliminary assessment of your organization's capability. If you will be submitting your proposal in response to an RFP, use the criteria provided in Chapter 5 (in the section "When and How to Respond to an RFP" and in Figure 5.1) to guide your conversation. Make a checklist of all of the information you will need to complete the application. Then use Figure 8.6 to help you plan ahead to complete your proposal on time.

From the Funder's Corner

When you present your proposal to a program officer, she must represent that proposal to the next level of decision makers. Often that is in a meeting where she is asked, "What is this proposal about?" Your success depends on the program officer being able to provide a succinct and compelling summary: a sound bite. So ask yourself, How well do you answer that question in your proposals? Do you provide one or two sentences that clearly state what the proposal is all about? Or are you relying on the program officer to find the right words? —*Ken Ristine*

FIGURE 8.6 CHECKLIST FOR COMPLETING A PROPOSAL

Have you:

❏ verified that the project aligns with your agency's mission and priorities and held preliminary discussions with top administrators to get buy-in?

❏ selected who will be "lead" for proposal development? This person should lay out the work plan for completing the proposal, make assignments and oversee completion, secure compliance documents, determine what internal reviews are necessary, and serve as the project's spokesperson. Ideally, this individual will also be the project director.

❏ assigned one person to check professional literature and informational sources on related work, and to create a preliminary statement of how your project is different from or complementary to others?

❏ scheduled as many brainstorming and progress report meetings as needed and as time permits? Use email to monitor and report progress. Much of your time will be spent encouraging other members of the team to complete their assignments on time. You should either meet with or communicate with your team every week or the momentum will evaporate.

❏ identified at the same time one person to do research on potential funders? This person should find out if letters of inquiry are needed, secure all necessary forms, verify deadlines, and arrange preliminary contact with potential funding sources. The lead proposal developer should gather all of the components and translate them into the various formats required by the different funding sources. If time is really tight and proposals to several different sources are needed simultaneously, the task of filling out the different forms and preparing the various narratives can be shared among the committee using ironclad internal deadlines.

❏ arranged a final "mock-up" meeting that lays out the proposal in outline form? Use the questions in Figure 8.3 to be sure that there is an internal logic to the flow of ideas. Different individuals can then quickly write various parts of the proposal knowing that their work will be consistent with others. At this point, have someone who is experienced in preparing budgets create the financial plan for the project. It should specify what will be sought from this funder, what is already in hand or will be sought from other donors, and what will be contributed by your organization. The lead proposal developer should begin discussing any financial commitments needed from the organization with key administrators as soon as possible. Make certain key administrators are comfortable with the indirect costs (overhead) allowed by the funder. If that rate is less than normal, discuss with them the types of expenditures and amounts to include in the budget as direct expenses.

❏ secured early approval from your organization's internal legal staff if the proposal is for a project that will require a written contract with the funder or has any unusual legal issues? Do not wait until you hear from the funder before discussing your plans with your internal lawyers. Otherwise, you may not be able to start your project when planned.

❏ asked a colleague to do a thorough and objective critique of the final draft? Have new readers assess the proposal's persuasiveness and internal logic. Have someone with good editing skills look for grammar, consistent style, flow, and readability.

❏ made certain that someone who is very careful about details gives each proposal a final review before it is submitted to your top administrator for signature? This review should verify that all of the required information is included and that the proposal package is complete. Determine how many copies of the proposal need original signatures. After you've secured the signatures and the copies of the proposal are returned to you, do one final review to ensure all are complete. Pieces of a proposal sometimes get lost or mislaid during the internal review and signature processes. It is up to you to ensure that the full package is sent to the funding source.

Summary

Strong proposals are the result of careful planning. Before you even begin to start writing, it's important to gather those team members who will be involved in the process and create a list of tasks that need to be accomplished, with clear expectations for who is responsible for what by when. By creating a timeline, worksheets with assignments, and checklists, you will avoid surprises along the way.

Key Terms

CASE STATEMENT: An internal document that collects and distills all the data you've collected on your proposed project so that everything you need to communicate with supporters—from volunteers and collaborators to government agencies, private grantmaking organizations, the media, and individual donors—is available in one document.

CENTRAL CONTRACTOR REGISTRATION (CCR): All grantseekers who wish to submit a proposal to the federal government must first register with CCR in order to use the online portal Grants.gov. Go online to www.bpn.gov/ccr for details.

CONTINUING SUPPORT or CONTINUATION AWARD: A grant or contract that renews support of a previously funded project. Most continuation awards must be reviewed and reapproved; they may or may not require a complete proposal at each approval period, depending on the funder.

DUNS NUMBER: An organizational identification number necessary to apply for federal grants. Federal funders use the nine-digit DUNS (Data Universal Number System) numbers to track applicants. Grantseekers can obtain a DUNS number for free through Dun & Bradstreet or Central Contractor Registration.

ELECTRONIC SUBMISSION: Turning in an application for funding online, usually through a formal process on the funder's website.

Cover Sheet or Title Page

Project title; name and contact information of the project director; name and address of the applicant organization; name of the government program and agency to which the proposal is being submitted; inclusive dates of the project; total project budget and amount requested in the proposal; signatures of persons authorizing submission. (See also Chapter 14.)

Signed Assurances

Description of any required assurance or compliance statements. (See also Chapter 14.)

Executive Summary or Abstract (in research proposals)

Self-contained, ready-for-publication synopsis of the project: need, purpose, significance, outcomes, objectives, procedures and methods of evaluation, and dissemination. Emphasize the end products and benefits of your project. Normally 200–250 words long. (See also Chapter 14.)

Statement of Purpose

Specific, detailed description of expected goals, objectives, and outcomes to be attained through this project.

Statement of Need

Well-documented description of the problem to be addressed and why it is important. Establish significance, timeliness, potential for replication, and contribution to other work. Use credible sources for all statistics. (See also Chapters 2 and 9.)

Project Description or Procedures (in research proposals)

Plan of action for achieving project outcomes, and rationale for choosing this approach as the most effective. Discuss how your project is different from or complementary to others. Emphasize collaborations and other ways that you will leverage the request. Explain how you will share results with others to demonstrate far-reaching benefits from the funder's investment. (See also Chapters 3 and 10.)

Sustainability Plan

Plan for how the project's activities will be supported after this grant ends. Some agencies ask for this in the project description or in the budget section; others want it to be a separate component. Be specific about your plans for future funding, including other grantmakers, individual donors, and earned income. (See also Chapters 5 and 12.)

Evaluation

Plan for measuring the change that occurs as a result of the project. Describe the questions to be asked, the methods to be used to gather and analyze data, and the plans for using and reporting information. A logic model for outcome-based evaluation is often required and always a good way to be more competitive. (See Chapter 11 for further discussion of evaluation. See Chapters 3 and 10 for discussion of logic models.)

Qualifications

Overview of the organization's mission, history, programs, and relevant experience; explain why your organization is ideally suited to undertake this work. Describe specific project staff, their qualifications, their duties, and the percentage of their time dedicated to the project. Most government sources want résumés of major project staff, and many require a specific format. Also list any consultants, their roles, and their qualifications. Name any cooperating organizations and describe any memorandums of understanding between the organizations. (See also Chapter 13.)

Budget

Detailed description of project costs for each year of operation, displayed by major line items, usually in prescribed, detailed budget forms. Itemize what is being provided by your organization, what is being requested, and what will be contributed by other sources. Use footnotes or a budget narrative to explain and justify how you arrived at various costs. Include a plan for future funding that shows income from a variety of sources. (See also Chapter 12.)

Attachments

Attachments include but are not limited to the tax determination letter from the IRS (your organization's 501(c)(3) letter or other IRS designation letter), a list of board members (or whatever body governs your work) including names and affiliations, the organization's most recent audited financial report, and letters of support or agreements to participate from any collaborators whose involvement is essential to the project's success. It may be useful to include a letter of support from your congressional delegation or, if applying to the state, from key legislators: ask the program officer if this would be appropriate. Be very careful to follow the funder's guidelines about what can be included as an attachment. Funders do not want brochures, newsletters, or other collateral material, but copies of news articles germane to your request may be of interest. (See also Chapter 14.)

Include only attachments listed in the RFP or your whole proposal may be disqualified.

Cover Letter

Acknowledgment of the funder's goals and guidelines; name and goals of the project and why it fits with the funder's goals; total project budget and amount requested from this source; amount secured for the project from other sources (if any); the names of others being approached to co-fund the project; name and signature of the person authorized to approve submission of the proposal on behalf of your organization, such as the president, dean, department chair, or principal investigator at a university, or the executive director or board chair of a nonprofit organization; and contact information.

Executive Summary

One- to two-paragraph summary of the problem, need, or opportunity; project plan; outcomes; and reason these are relevant to this funder. Include a sentence with the specific request, such as, "We respectfully request $124,000 for three years to fund an after-school program for 85 at-risk teens." Include a short description of your organization and make a compelling case for why funding this project should be a priority. This section determines whether the reviewer will read the rest of the proposal. (See also Chapter 14.)

Problem, Need, or Opportunity Statement

Description of the problems, needs, or opportunities to be addressed; the target population; and the geographic scope. Show how the proposed work is relevant to the funder's guidelines. Answer the "So what?" question (i.e., why this project, why now, how will it benefit society, what difference will it make). This section summarizes your organization's mission, history, major programs and services, and how these relate to the project. (See also Chapters 2 and 9.)

Project Description

Description of the strategy and methods to be used and justification for why these will be the most effective. Include a timeline with major milestones and show how the project differs from or complements similar efforts by others. Collaboration and other kinds of leverage will strengthen this section. This section details the goals, objectives, activities, and outcomes that will result from your project and why these matter. This section also explains how you will share results and recognize project funders. (See also Chapters 3 and 10.)

Organization Background

Description of the organization's mission, history, programs, and relevant experience (i.e., what its track record is with projects similar to the one proposed). Indicate whether others in the community or field have recognized or funded your organization's work. This section provides funders with clues that signal whether your organization is sufficiently well positioned to accomplish the proposed project.

Evaluation

Plan for measuring the change that occurs as a result of the project. Evaluation measures and results must cross-match to your goals, objectives, activities, and outcomes. Indicate whether an outside consultant will conduct the evaluation, how you will use the results, and what reports the funder will receive and when. (See also Chapter 11.)

Qualifications

Description of why your organization is best suited to do this project. Describe the organizational structure for the project; provide a sentence or two on the duties of each of the project staff; provide names and summarize the backgrounds of those who will fill key staff and consultant positions; and list any partners or cooperating agencies (include letters indicating their support for the project and willingness to participate). Include an attachment showing your board members' names and affiliations. Detailed job descriptions for key project staff may also be included as attachments, particularly for larger projects. (See also Chapter 13.)

Budget

Detailed budget for the project that shows what is being requested from the funder and what will be contributed by your organization. If the project is to last more than one year, show planned expenditures and income for each 12-month period. Provide the names of other funders, the amounts received, and pending requests, and describe what parts of the project those funds will cover. Make sure funders understand that they are not the project's only supporter. (See also Chapter 12.)

Sustainability Plan

Description of how the project will be supported once the requested funding ends. Be specific: name any secured funding or fees-for-service that will commence; indicate if your project is a short-term project. Do not say, "We'll raise additional monies to support this." The most convincing strategy is to show that your organization will absorb an increasing percentage of the project budget over time. (See also Chapters 5 and 12.)

Attachments

Attachments include but are not limited to the organization's 50l(c)(3) letter or other IRS designation letter; the names of the organization's board of directors (or other leaders) and their affiliations; the organization's latest audited financial statement, current budget and major sources of revenue, and latest annual report; and up to three letters of support or commitment, as well as recent media reports or press releases. (See also Chapter 14.)

---

9 COMPOSING THE NEED STATEMENT

This chapter discusses the importance of the need statement and provides information and ideas to help you write it. The need statement shapes every other aspect of the proposal, so it must be as well-crafted and compelling as possible. To develop a persuasive statement of need, you'll want to understand what the funder is looking for, compile the information that supports your case, and then write an effective statement.

Understand the Importance of the Statement of Need

Ask a room full of grantseekers to pretend they are grant*makers* and draft a sample grant application form, and they will usually generate a list of questions very similar to those posed by funders. But one question grantseekers often fail to include is, What's the problem? When you're immersed in your work, the problem seems obvious, and it's easy to forget that someone else might not understand the issues the same way you do. That's why funders ask grantseekers to state clearly what problem or need in the community or the world the proposed project will address. The section of the proposal where you will answer this question may be called the STATEMENT OF NEED, NEED STATEMENT, PROBLEM STATEMENT, or OPPORTUNITY STATEMENT.

The need statement identifies the problem and how it came to be, and clarifies the connections among the problem, its causes, and your proposed solution. The need statement establishes the rationale for the proposed activity. It also ties a need in the community to a need for the funder's involvement. This section of the proposal demonstrates the following:

- That you have a thorough understanding of the problem your project intends to explore, address, or resolve
- That this problem is important, not only to the people to be served by the project but to the wider society
- That a critical analysis of field shows that there is a significant gap that this project could fill
- That the need is timely, and the reasons it should be addressed now
- The ways your work relates to that of similar organizations in your community or your field

- The innovative nature of the effort, at least locally, and if it duplicates previous efforts, why additional resources should be allocated to the problem
- The need for replication or application by others, and reasons to believe your project could help resolve other similar or related problems
- The beginning of your rationale for the methods, approach, and plan of action that will be fully discussed in the sections of the proposal that follow
- The reasons you care about the problem, including the relationship of the problem and its proposed solution to the interests and capabilities of your organization
- The ways the need you intend to resolve dovetails with the funder's goals

Many foundations' application forms ask, Why are you asking us to fund this project? This question can be interpreted three ways:

- Why are *you* asking us to fund this project? That is, why is your organization concerned about the issue, and why is your organization the most appropriate organization to deal with it?
- Why are you asking *us* to fund this project? That is, how did you determine that our foundation was the most appropriate funding source to approach to help solve this problem?
- Why are you asking us to fund *this* project? That is, of all the things your organization does, and of all the things our foundation is asked to fund, what makes this the effort most worthy of support?

These are all important questions, and the funder probably wants to know the answers to all three. Carefully assessing the need for the proposed work (see more about need assessments in Chapter 2) should give you the information you need to respond to all three questions concisely within the allotted space. Keep these questions in mind as you collect the information to build your case and write the statement, and then assess your argument to make sure you have a compelling response to these questions in your statement of need.

It's easy to digress as you're composing the answer to a question. You get going on a train of thought, and the train picks up steam, and at the end of the allotted space, you may not have actually answered the question. One grantwriter kept her writing focused and on topic by typing the funder's question at both the beginning and the end of each section of her proposal draft. As she finished her answer, she would rediscover the question and check to make sure she'd answered it accurately.

Build Your Case

As you develop your need statement, you'll want to evaluate the proposed project from many different angles. Considering each of the factors described below will help you build the case for your proposed project.

Community Significance

Even if you have already shown that the project relates to the funder's general interests, you can strengthen your proposal by demonstrating that the specific problem or need you are addressing is of special importance to the broader community. This is a competitive landscape, and grantseekers who can position their issue as critical and timely—without diminishing the important work of others—will look especially appealing. Answer the question, Why is this problem you describe more urgent or important than others under consideration by the funder?

Relevance to the Grantmaker

Emphasize how well the need relates to the funder's goals.

To emphasize why this specific need is of unique or direct importance to the particular funder, consider whether your solving this need will do the following:

- **Help the funder respond to a legislative mandate.** For example, say the state legislature has mandated that counties whose schools have test scores below a certain level must implement strategies to improve these scores. If the funder is an educational service district or a school district foundation, your project could help them meet their own goals.
- **Help the funder protect an investment they've already made in a community.** For example, imagine that a funder has made significant contributions toward rebuilding a decaying downtown core. If your organization's project will extend the effort by helping emerging businesses attract more customers and manage their businesses more efficiently, you increase the likelihood that the funder's intent will be realized.
- **Help the funder use their gift to leverage support from others.** For example, if the funder is interested in supporting your project but has limitations—perhaps they can make only one grant to you every three years, or don't have as much to give this year—you could suggest they offer a challenge grant to encourage other funders and donors to give, or award a grant knowing other funders will follow their lead. Or you could ask for a loan guarantee, which gets funding for your project without the funder having to provide it directly.

Funders will respond positively to your interest in meeting their needs while you meet a need in the community or the world.

Research and Analysis

Funders want you to demonstrate that you have critically analyzed the appropriate literature, and that your analysis has played a role in shaping your project. It will not be enough to simply include a bibliography. You are establishing your professional competence by how you interpret the information you cite and relate it to your organization's work. Funders are impressed by proposals that demonstrate that you compared the relative merits of various methods for solving the problem and arrived at your approach only after careful analysis of possible solutions.

Demonstrate that you understand what ideas have already been funded. Reviewers for the U.S. Department of Defense have said that in fully one-third of the proposals they receive, it is clear that the writers never bothered to find out what had already been done to address the problem. Make sure that any statistics you cite are current, accurate, and from credible sources.

If the problem you propose to address was brought to light through a needs assessment conducted by you or others, be sure to mention this. If the results of the assessment are lengthy, include an executive summary and offer to send the entire report from the needs assessment separately.

Context

Acknowledge the existence of other groups and show both how you are distinct from and how you are cooperating with your colleagues. Prove that the problem or opportunity is big enough or complex enough to require the efforts of several groups to solve it. (For more on why collaboration with other organizations is a strength, not a sign of weakness, see Chapter 1.)

If numerous organizations or institutions are dealing with the same issue, make sure your need statement explains how your work will complement but not duplicate the efforts of others. To position your organization in the context of others addressing the need, mention the following in your need statement:

- **Geographic scope:** Describe the scope of the region you hope to serve. How does geography affect the scope of the problem? Is it worse in certain places because of climate, transportation, lack of water, or limited access to resources? Are there other groups in the same geographic scope working on the issue?
- **Participant profile:** Describe the age, ethnicity, gender, sexual preference, ability, or relationship to the issue of the people served. If some groups are affected more deeply than others by the problem, why is that so? Explain why your organization is especially concerned about a particular subgroup, if that's the case.
- **Methodology:** Differentiate how your chosen methodology relates to other organizations' ways of addressing the need. Will you specialize in a narrow band of the problem, hoping for deep impact, or offer a full spectrum of services to cover many aspects of the problem? How does your methodology complement or build on that of other organizations?
- **Experience:** Note how your organization's experience has shaped your understanding of the need.
- **Time frame:** Help the funder understand the urgency of the need. Will your proposed work fill an immediate need or build toward a long-term solution?

Project Feasibility

A need statement that is sufficiently focused assures reviewers that given the time and resources requested in the proposal, there is real hope for a solution. Limiting the scope of the project to a manageable level demonstrates experience and thoughtful project development. A proposed solution that is obviously too complex or too expensive for the requested resources may strike funders as a sign of inexperience and is likely to cast doubt on the feasibility of the proposal.

Corroborating Data

Statistics alone do not prove a need. On the other hand, it's difficult to corroborate need without them. And some funders' guidelines require statistics from specific sources. In your need statement, include sufficient statistical data to substantiate your case, and demonstrate that you can interpret the data, not just regurgitate numbers.

A grantwriter who was working with a Boys & Girls Club asked the Executive Director if it was okay to say in the grant that if kids came to the club, they wouldn't join gangs. The ED laughed at the suggestion, saying, "There are so many factors affecting these kids, we couldn't possibly promise that." "What *can* we promise?" asked the grantwriter. The ED replied, "Well, if we can keep that little boy, who has violent tendencies, from decking anyone for the two hours he's here each day, we call that success. And if that little girl, who's usually unpleasant and unkempt, can walk in here after school and have someone welcome her and engage her in positive activities, we call that success." The grantwriter asked, "So what do I put in the grant?" The ED suggested, "Say these kids will have a safe, nurturing environment where they can engage in stimulating activities." Your need statement should reflect a situation you can reasonably expect to affect.

When you write your need statement, weave hard facts and statistics into your narrative and include charts, tables, and graphs to tell your story. In addition to statistics from other sources, also gather data from your own organization's experiences. For example, if you operate a shelter and you're having to turn away people due to a shortage of beds, capturing those numbers will strengthen your case. A strong statement of need will use both HARD DATA (statistics) and SOFT DATA (anecdotes or quotes) to paint a vivid picture for the funder.

Statistics should be gathered from sources with a high level of veracity and standards. Citing facts from Wikipedia, for instance, is inappropriate. Statistics that are more than a few years old do little to make your case.

The Resources section at the end of this book provides a list of online resources that may be useful for corroborating the need for your work. The Getting Funded website, www.gettingfundedbook.com, offers regularly updated links to these resources and others.

Write the Argument

Now that you have compiled information that supports your case, you're ready to write the statement of need. Use the model below, which demonstrates the five components of a strong need statement, as an example to follow for your own statement. Then assess your draft statement against the tools that follow: a list of characteristics of a strong need statement, the worksheet in Figure 9.1, and the list of common pitfalls funders see in grantseekers' need statements.

Model of a Strong Need Statement

A strong statement of need answers all of the following five questions.

1. What is the need?

Example: The *problem* is a 10 percent increase in homelessness among students in Canyon County over the past five years. In the two high schools in the community of Dexter, homelessness affects 10 percent of the students each year (for a total of 200 students), while the incidence of homelessness is 2 percent in the state, and an unknown percentage nationally.

2. What are the causes of the problem?

Example: The *causes* of the increase in student homelessness are undocumented but are assumed to be related to high unemployment and unprecedented mortgage foreclosures in this area. The primary cause of this problem appears to be the closing of the ABC Company, the major employer in the area.

3. What are the costs of the problem?

Example: Compounding the significant impact of homelessness on each affected individual, the problem *costs the county* an additional $3,500 per student per year in prevention efforts, direct services, and remediation. Others affected by this problem include the nonprofit agencies that serve homeless families, and the school district, which loses per-student funding for each homeless student who drops out. The consequences of not addressing the problem include a higher dropout rate and potential for increased crime.

4. What are some promising strategies?

Example: Several *promising strategies* have been developed to address student homelessness. [Include strategies for each specific population to be targeted.] At the local level, the following agencies provide these services: the state Department of Labor, the local community college, and the following nonprofit agencies...

For the last decade, those engaged in this field have believed that [title or term for strategy] strategy reflected best practices, but research by [researcher name and date] has revealed that the [title or term for new strategy] strategy results in more positive results.

Based on current research in the field, consideration of the barriers indicated below, and our own organization's experience, the most promising approach for this community may be [phrase that describes proposed strategic approach].

5. What are the major barriers?

Example: Barriers to addressing the problem of student homelessness in this community include severe cuts in school district funding, the decrease in grant and contract funding of nonprofits serving the homeless population, and the elimination of some bus routes serving this area. *Additional barriers* that keep homeless students from gaining access to community services include low levels of literacy, lack of transportation, inadequate clothing, and hunger.

Characteristics of a Strong Need Statement

The statement of need is a pivotal element in any proposal. It sets the stage for the rest of the document, as your response to every other question hinges on how you define the problem. Your description of scope of work, methodology, evaluation, and even the budget must reflect—indeed parallel—your statement of the problem.

Make it easy for funders to see the relationship between your need statement, your proposed solution, and your promised outcomes. Use parallel visual structure, such as bullets, numbered items, or subheads; parallel word choice; and parallel depictions of scope or scale in each section, so funders can see the thread that connects your argument throughout the entire document, holding it all together. (On writing outcomes and the evaluation plan, see Chapters 10 and 11. On writing the budget and budget narrative, see Chapter 12.)

These are characteristics of a strong need statement:

- It is concise.
- It clearly describes who or what is affected by the situation.
- It includes statistics that are current and accurate.
- It uses ratios and percentages as well as raw numbers.
- It uses charts, diagrams, and quotes to make the need come alive to the reader.
- It documents need in the community or among clients, students, arts patrons and audiences, or other stakeholders.
- It describes the scope of the problem in relation to the same population profile in a different community or geographic area.
- It focuses on need within an identified target group.
- It provides realistic cost estimates.
- It makes a case for the need for cooperation with other organizations and agencies, the community, and the beneficiaries.
- It illustrates a need for replication in other areas.
- It explains how the need fits with the funder's mandate, mission, and current priorities.
- It correlates clearly with the project description and anticipated outcomes.

See Chapter 2 for discussion of how to describe the need for projects that are not about a problem.

When complete, your fully filled out statement of need will tell a compelling story of need and include pictures, quotes, and data to illuminate and reinforce the story you are telling.

The worksheet in Figure 9.1 can help you assess your draft statement of need. The most compelling need statements include answers to all of the questions in this worksheet. After you have answered these questions, reflect on your developing statement of need and evaluate how well it aligns with the funder's aims.

Review Your Statement of Need

When you have finished writing your statement of need, make time for either you or another person on your team to read it one more time, checking it against the common mistakes described below.

Funders are investors. Describe the need in a way that clearly aligns with their priorities. You are creating the change they want to see.

Common Pitfalls to Avoid

Funders read many proposals each year, so when you review your draft, make sure you've avoided these common pitfalls that will detract from the strength of your argument:

- **Don't paint a picture so bleak that the problem appears insurmountable.** To avoid this pitfall, make sure that the scope of the problem you describe relates to the scale of the solution you propose. For example, if you describe a problem that is truly monumental in scope, such as global warming or AIDS, narrow the discussion of need to a more manageable scope. For example, discuss the situation in your community and whether an investment in local efforts could improve things in a particular town, with a particular targeted population. Give readers hope without misleading them.
- **Don't present the problem as simply the absence of the project you propose to provide.** Funders object to circular reasoning such as this: "There is no place for senior citizens to gather in our community. Therefore, we need money to create a senior center." Funders know, and expect proposals to acknowledge, that there are many ways to address senior citizens' needs. To

FIGURE 9.1 WORKSHEET FOR ADDRESSING IMPORTANT QUESTIONS IN THE STATEMENT OF NEED

- What is the problem?
- How does the problem create a need?
- Who is affected by the problem?
- What is the impact on those who are affected?
- What are the implications of the problem to the community?
- Why does this situation exist? What are its root causes?
- What has been your organization's prior experience with this problem?
- What does external research reveal?
- Who else is working on the same issues?
- What barriers have they encountered?
- What other challenges do you anticipate?
- What responses have been considered?
- What models or research have been explored elsewhere?
- What is the experience of your organization or others with those approaches?

avoid this pitfall, you might start with a wider perspective on the need: "Seniors in this community are experiencing declining physical and mental health due to poor nutrition and a sense of isolation. Both issues could be addressed by creating a senior center that offers healthy, inexpensive meals, physical activities, and social interaction."

- **Don't attribute the need to your organization.**
  Funders read too many proposals that use the words "we need" instead of "the community needs" or "the people we serve need." Eliminate the words "we need" from your vocabulary. Remember, your organization's role is not to have needs—it's to meet needs. To avoid this pitfall, make sure your description of the need refers to the needs of those your organization serves.

Chapters 2 and 3 discuss need and designing projects based on need in more depth.

> Make sure that your program plan, evaluation, and budget emanate from the need.
> Make sure that the problem or need described is in scale with your organizational capacity.

From the Funder's Corner

The real lesson is that grantmakers, like anyone, enjoy a good story. And they really respond to a good story that intertwines facts, mission, and passion. —*Ken Ristine*

Summary

The statement of need is the basis for every other element of your proposal, as it justifies the need for investment in your project. A well-crafted statement of need draws a clear picture of exactly what the situation is and why it merits attention. It also explains why the need is particularly timely now, what the implications are if it isn't dealt with, and how it relates to your work as an organization. Most importantly, the statement of need makes a sound case for why the need your project will answer should rise above other urgent needs the funder is being asked to support.

Key Terms

HARD DATA: Information that is concrete and objective. Examples include test scores, the number of animals who were adopted, or the number of "bed nights" in a shelter. Data must be properly cited, up to date, and from a verifiable and well-regarded source.

PRINCIPAL INVESTIGATOR (PI): The person in charge of, and responsible for, an experiment or research project.

SOFT DATA: Information that is subjective and less than concrete. Examples include anecdotes or quotes; responses from participants in surveys, interviews, or focus groups; observations made by a professional; or changed perceptions, attitudes, or behaviors reported by the target audience.

STATEMENT OF NEED or NEED STATEMENT or PROBLEM STATEMENT or OPPORTUNITY STATEMENT: The section of the proposal that answers the question, What is the problem (or opportunity) that warrants attention? This is the section that identifies the problem, who else agrees it's a problem, and what data lead you to believe that.

10 WRITING THE PROJECT DESCRIPTION

This chapter describes the heart of the proposal: the project description is where you help the funder understand what your organization would do with the requested funds and what difference you think your organization's work will make. In addition to explaining each element of the project description, this chapter will also cover how to handle common problems that with this section of a proposal.

Different funders use different terms to refer to the project description and the elements included in it. Research proposals, which are usually submitted to federal funders, call this the methods section, and the methods seek to solve a problem. In proposals that are submitted to foundations and corporations, this section may be called the project description, program plan, approach, or plan of action, and the project is intended to address a need or opportunity.

A project can be anything from direct client services to an architectural element in a capital campaign to a one-time effort such as a conference or performance or delivery of a truckload of bicycles to a township in Africa. A program is a more general characterization of an organization's work. Each program may have several projects. For example, a school may have a literacy program that comprises several projects with different aims, all of which help to achieve the overall program goal. Projects could include one for students with dyslexia, one for English language learners, and one focused on purchasing books.

Study the Composition of a Project Description

The project description helps the funder understand what your organization plans to do if your proposal gets funding. It should demonstrate that you have considered many options for addressing the stated need (see Chapter 9, on writing the need statement) and have devised a logical, step-by-step approach to achieve your goals, thereby solving the problem or maximizing the opportunity.

A strong, comprehensive project description will include several elements:

- **An introduction or overview:** Your general approach, rationale, and course of action
- **The goals:** What your organization hopes to achieve by doing the project
- **The objectives and activities:** Specifics about how you will reach your goal
- **The participants:** Who or what the project will serve or benefit

- **The work plan:** What will happen when and who will do it
- **The management plan:** How the project will be administered or managed

OUTCOMES, OUTPUTS, and LOGIC MODELS may also appear in the project description or in the evaluation section of your proposal. (See more about outcomes and logic models in Chapter 3 and Chapter 11.)

Length and Format

Private and public funders want the same types of information to be included in this section of your proposal, but private funders typically expect much less detail.

Some funders limit project descriptions to just a few paragraphs, for instance, while other funders allow descriptions as long as twenty pages. Both types of funders understand that the information necessary to describe a research project will differ greatly from that needed to describe a training, service, demonstration, or development project.

> Good proposal storytelling uses quotes, client profiles, and other real-life examples woven through the technical data to give life to the proposal or "business plan" that you are presenting to a funder.

The requested format for project descriptions will also vary greatly, but since it's such a critical section of any proposal, consider presenting your information in several ways, such as in narrative text, a logic model diagram, a work plan, and a timeline. Make it as clear as possible. You're trying to portray a great deal of information concisely.

Figure 10.1 is from the project description in a proposal to a foundation for a CAPITAL GRANT. After an opening section that explained the nature of the organization's services and the reason a new facility was needed for the organization to better serve its clients, the grantwriter included this chart.

Anticipate Challenges

Attempts to predict where obstacles might occur will help you build into the project sufficient time or resources to correct difficulties that arise. When you flag

FIGURE 10.1 SAMPLE CHART USED TO PRESENT INFORMATION CONCISELY

PROBLEM: Old facility	SOLUTION: New facility
Old building	Newer building
Not near highway	Central to county, near freeway access
Poor general visibility	Good corner visibility
Inadequate parking	40-car parking lot
Outdated mechanical and electrical system	New or improved systems as part of the remodel
No inside van loading or parking	Space for eight vans and for van loading
Small, poorly divided office space	Office division based on program requirements
Lack of good meeting space for trainings and volunteers	Small and large group space for classes and volunteers

potential problems and acknowledge the potential need for corrective action, you signal to the funder that you have thought through the process painstakingly. Failure to prepare for adjustments may leave your organization vulnerable, as the funding you receive may stipulate that you engage in or produce particular activities that become no longer appropriate or workable.

To avoid having to repeatedly seek approval from the funder for project modifications, suggest in your project description one or more of the following possibilities:

- **Field tests** for all unproven methods, materials, and activities, to provide for necessary revision or refinement
- **Sequential phases** of activities, such that periodic assessment might inform modifications in the remaining steps
- **Scheduled checkpoints**, for the project staff to evaluate data and make decisions about any necessary modifications
- **Periodic consultations** with the funder to discuss necessary changes

You can avoid unnecessary project delays by identifying check-in times and indicating that consultations with the funder will generally be limited to these times.

Write the Necessary Components

The project description will likely be the longest portion of a proposal, will include many separate kinds of information, and will involve technical and sometimes complex material. This section describes each element of a compelling project description.

Introduction

When you write a proposal, you're essentially telling a story, and like any good author, you will want to pay attention to both the flow of the narrative and the construction of the plot. Unlike the storyteller, however, the proposal writer does not want to leave the reader guessing about what will come next or making things up to fill in gaps. Begin your project description with an introductory section to set the stage. Make it easy for the reviewer to see how your description will be structured.

A good introduction or overview will perform the following tasks:

- Introduce the approach to be used in the project, with a brief justification
- Illustrate how the proposed work correlates both to the need and to your organization's mission
- Clarify what outcomes your organization hopes to achieve
- Call attention to the aspects of the project that make it particularly distinctive, e.g., special populations or innovative activities, materials, equipment, or technology

Approach

The project description includes a description of the overall approach or strategy your organization has chosen to carry out the work, the specific activities in which your organization will engage, and your justification for choosing this particular path. As mentioned in Chapter 3, the description of your proposed strategy should cover its relevance to the community, to your organization's mission and goals, and to the funder. You want to show how the proposed project will build on past efforts and your organization's prior experience and capability. This section of the project

FIGURE 10.2 ELEMENTS OF A PROJECT LOGIC MODEL

	GOALS	PARTICIPANTS	ACTIVITIES	INPUTS	OBJECTIVES	OUTPUTS	OUTCOMES	IMPACT
DESCRIPTION	The ultimate result(s) expected, possibly beyond this grant	Who will implement; who will benefit	The methods used to carry out the specific project	What your agency brings to the project	Actions taken to reach the goal	The number and duration of units of service or products of activities	Short-, medium-, or long-term changes anticipated	In general, what will be different 10 years from now.
SAMPLE PROJECT	Reduce intergenerational poverty by increasing high school graduation rates in Valley County	3 university research fellows; 39 students from Valley View Elementary	Direct service delivery, research, events	Staff, money, clients	Each student will read with support for 2 hours, 3 times a week from the ABC reader	Yearly student progress reports; attendance records	Increased attendance; documented increase in student enthusiasm about going to school and learning	Increased high school graduation rates

description should confirm that your choice of methods and activities was based on research, best practices, and conversations with others in your field.

The section on approach (sometimes called strategy) should do the following:

- Discuss why your approach is significant or innovative, and why you're confident that it's feasible
- Describe the scope of the project
- Discuss why your chosen approach is particularly timely (if appropriate)
- Name any partners who will cooperate or collaborate with you and describe the value they will add
- List the roles of any consultants or advisory bodies, including how they will be selected
- Describe how unexpected events or results will be handled (one paradox of project development is the need to plan for the unanticipated)
- Assure the funder that your plan includes opportunities to monitor progress and adjust course, and that you will seek the funder's approval for such adjustment

Goals, Objectives, and Activities

Grantmakers favor proposals that demonstrate both a plan and a rationale for what will change as a result of your work. Well-crafted project descriptions include a section on GOALS, OBJECTIVES, and ACTIVITIES. These items signal the overall intent of the project, the tangible results to be achieved, and the benefits to those served and the larger community. They also make an explicit connection between the stated need and the results you hope to achieve.

While all parts of a proposal are important, this section of the project description is among the most critical. The goals, objectives, and activities are the fundamental building blocks for the project design. Make sure they are clear and compelling, match the grantmaker's interests, are appropriate to the scale of the project, and are informed by the need statement.

A GOAL STATEMENT is a broad description of the intended results of the project. It helps the funder gain an overall orientation to the longer-term purposes of the project, but does not address the specifics of what will be accomplished or what your organization will be held accountable to produce. Limit the number of goals to what your organization can realistically accomplish.

In the following examples, a nonprofit community development agency is applying to a private foundation for funds to secure safe housing for homeless alcoholics. The project description section of their proposal might have a goal statement like the following:

- *Example of a goal statement*: To reduce the cost of first response in Jefferson County by building permanent housing for chronic inebriates.

An OBJECTIVE STATEMENT describes a specific and measurable result of the project. Each *individual objective* states specifically, in measurable terms, one thing the project will accomplish.

Each objective should be SMART:

S   Specific
M   Measurable
A   Achievable
R   Realistic
T   Time-bound

Use the SMART RULE to guide you when you write objectives. Then incorporate the information into your objective statement. For example, an objective statement for the goal above could be this:

- *Example of an objective statement:* Finance and construct fifty units of subsidized housing in the downtown core over the next three years.

An ACTIVITIES STATEMENT describes the specific tasks and timelines that you will use to reach your goal. They include the who, what, where, when, and how aspects of your project. Activities tell funders exactly what they will be supporting in terms of your day-to-day work.

An activities statement for the example above could be this:

- *Example of an activities statement:* In year one, we will work with lenders, architects, and city planners to plan the facility. In year two, we will work with contractors to build the facility. And in year three, we will create the policies and procedures to manage the building and hire medical, social work, and security staff who will be on duty twenty-four hours a day.

Figure 10.2 shows how goals, objectives, and activities fit into a program logic model. Figures 10.3 and 10.4 present more elaborate versions of logic models. Go to the Resources section or to the Getting Funded website, www.gettingfundedbook.com, for more about goals, objectives, and logic models.

FIGURE 10.3 SAMPLE LOGIC MODEL

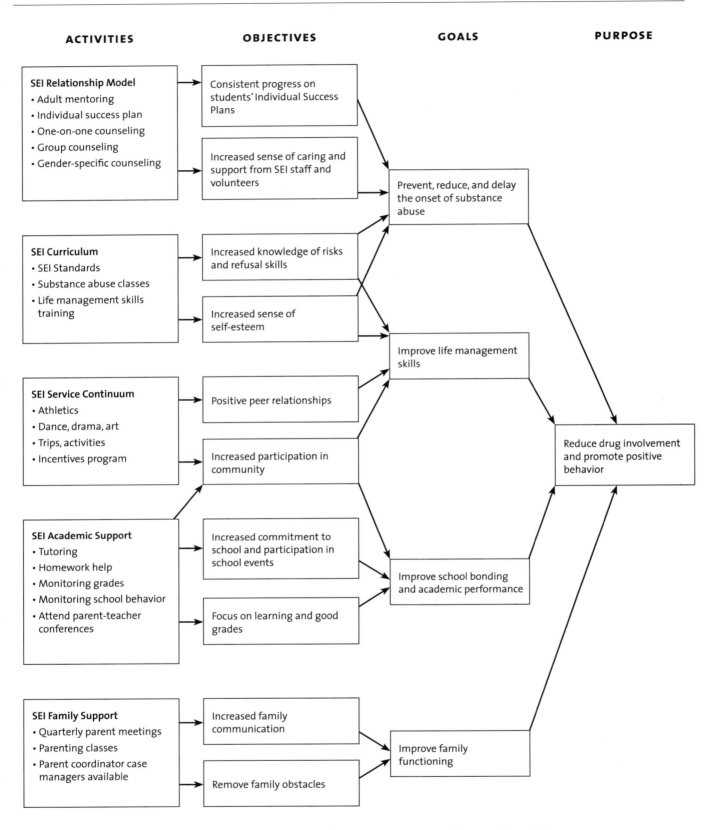

From *Grantwriting Beyond the Basics, Book 1: Proven Strategies Professionals Use to Make Their Proposals Work,* by Michael Wells.

FIGURE 10.4 SAMPLE COMPLEX LOGIC MODEL

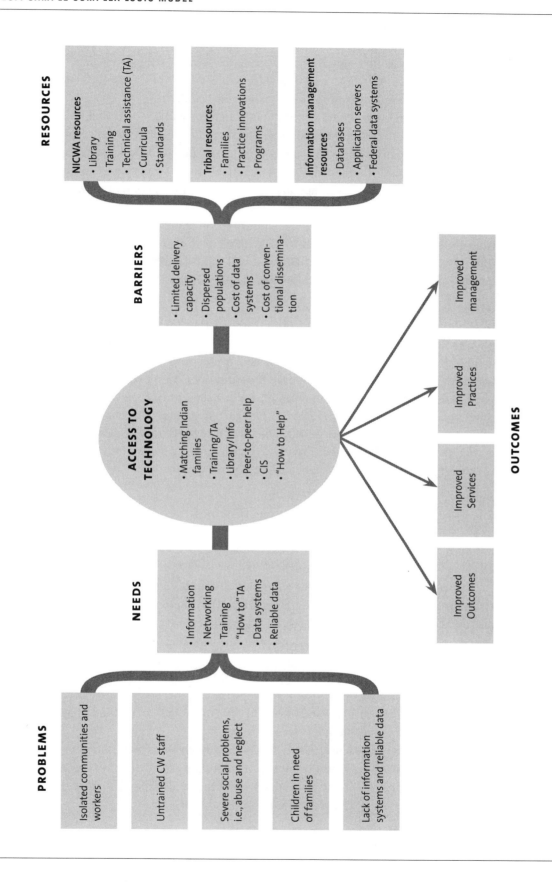

From *Grantwriting Beyond the Basics, Book 1: Proven Strategies Professionals Use to Make Their Proposals Work*, by Michael Wells.

Participants

In the section of the project description that describes participants, include a demographic profile of those who will be affected by your project or program, whether as clients, audience members, students, residents, or fish. You should convey why and how this particular population was deemed worthy of attention. Again, as with the goals, you'll want to tie this section of the project description to your need statement. (See Chapter 9 for composing the need statement.)

In this section, describe how participants were or will be identified, recruited, screened, and managed, and how they will be served or affected by the project. Say how long participants will be affiliated with your organization, to what degree they will be involved, and whether they will be charged for participating or not. If there are potential issues related to language, ability, or cultural competency, indicate what you will do to accommodate those issues.

The participants section can include information about groups that will benefit from the project but will not be direct participants. By writing a paragraph about those who might benefit tangentially, you will indicate to the funder that the requested support will be leveraged for even greater results.

Work Plans and Project Timelines

In a subsection of the project description, indicate the dates by which major accomplishments and products will be completed, and show the funder how the activities will be spread throughout the project period. Many proposals include the specific activities and their planned sequence in the subsection on approach. Even so, it is a good idea to summarize plans and timelines in a separate subsection clearly identified by a label such as "Work Plan" or "Project Timeline." Use charts, graphs, or other types of diagrams to present timelines for key activities. Unless the project is very short or has only a few activities, visual elements will be important aids to reviewers who may otherwise become lost in the narrative.

Suggestions for Developing a Work Plan.
There are many ways to present plans and timelines. Read the funder's guidelines or the RFP carefully to determine what is required and how best to present your material. Some common tools that can be adapted to your needs include Gantt charts, PERT charts, and logic models.

A GANTT CHART is a type of bar chart that illustrates a project schedule. Gantt charts are most useful for depicting dates in relation to activities. Some Gantt charts also show the relationships between activities. Gantt charts can be used to show current schedule status using percent-complete shadings and a vertical "Today" line.

A PERT CHART is a project management tool used to schedule, organize, and coordinate tasks within a project. PERT stands for Program Evaluation Review Technique. PERT charts are most useful for showing the intended interrelationships among events. The Critical Path Method (CPM) is a similar methodology developed for project management.

A LOGIC MODEL can be a useful tool for creating work plans too.

See Figures 10.5 and 10.6 for examples of Gantt and PERT charts in use. See the Getting Funded website, www.gettingfundedbook.com, for links to further resources about Gantt charts, PERT charts, and logic models.

Suggestions for Developing a Project Timeline.
To create a project timeline, first write each step in the process in chronological order, then summarize it in a timeline chart or narrative and insert it into your project description.

FIGURE 10.5 SAMPLE GANTT CHART

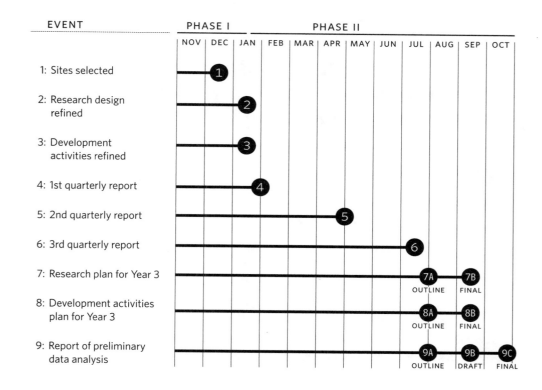

Consider including the following information:

- The amount of time necessary to negotiate the contract with the funder
- The order in which each activity must be accomplished
- The amount of time necessary to carry out each specific project activity
- The amount of time that will elapse between receiving notification of funding and beginning the project
- The amount of time it will take your organization to set up internal processes for managing the grant funds
- The amount of anticipated project downtime due to holidays, vacations, sick leave, or delays related to managing collaborative work with other organizations

It's better to be realistic than optimistic when it comes to your project timeline. Funders recognize that promising too much work in too little time is a sign of lack of experience with project design. For example, it's unrealistic to suggest that new staff will be hired as soon as the grant is awarded, because it generally takes a month or two to post and fill a new position. Have an experienced colleague review your timelines to ensure that they are realistic.

If after consideration you feel that the projected timeline will exceed the anticipated period of funding, consider modifying your activities. If that seems impossible, you may want to go back and scale down the entire project. Limiting the promised outcomes can help.

See Figures 10.7 and 10.8 for examples of simple and more complex project timelines.

FIGURE 10.6 SAMPLE PERT CHART

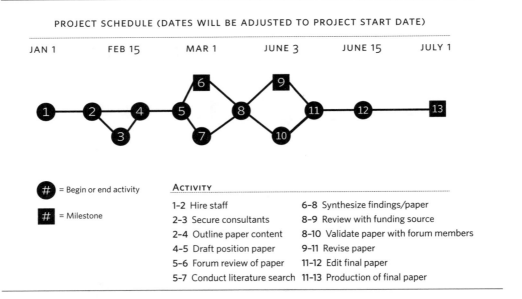

PROJECT SCHEDULE (DATES WILL BE ADJUSTED TO PROJECT START DATE)

| JAN 1 | FEB 15 | MAR 1 | JUNE 3 | JUNE 15 | JULY 1 |

= Begin or end activity

= Milestone

ACTIVITY

1–2 Hire staff
2–3 Secure consultants
2–4 Outline paper content
4–5 Draft position paper
5–6 Forum review of paper
5–7 Conduct literature search

6–8 Synthesize findings/paper
8–9 Review with funding source
8–10 Validate paper with forum members
9–11 Revise paper
11–12 Edit final paper
11–13 Production of final paper

Deliverables

Deliverables are tangible products created during the course of a funded project. Examples of deliverables include manuals, curricula, videos, reports, teaching tools or methods, service delivery models, mobile displays, scripts, and research papers.

> Promise only what you can produce.

Not every project produces deliverables, but if you intend to develop one, include a description of the deliverable near the end of the project description. Check with your organization's legal advisors to determine who will own the copyrights or patents, and include this information in your proposal. If the proceeds from sales of such products will help sustain your work beyond the period of funding being requested, your project will be even more appealing.

Replication

Some projects have the potential to serve as demonstration projects. If a proposed idea works well in one community, it may solve similar problems in other contexts. Research and exploration with other experts in your field can help you determine whether your project has potential for REPLICATION. If you see potential replicability, include this information in your project description along with your rationale and quotes from experts who endorse this potential. You should include responses to the following questions:

What elements of your plan can be copied? If your sexual assault program depends on the cooperation of police, the county health department, the local child protection agency, and school counselors, it's safe to assume that all but the most remote communities will likely have similar entities, making replication of your cooperative model possible.

What products will you create that could be used by others? Perhaps your project will result in print and digital materials useful in prevention education, or a health-promotion curriculum, or a design for a crisis intervention phone system that others could copy or purchase.

FIGURE 10.7 SAMPLE PROJECT TIMELINE

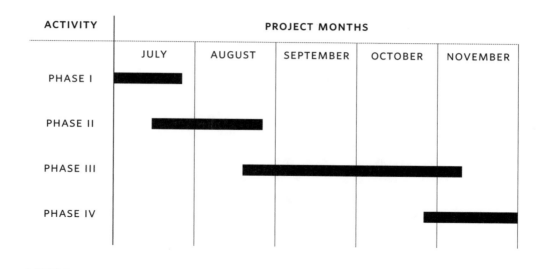

Who else do you think could benefit from your experience? Perhaps you belong to a regional or national network or association whose members could learn from your project. Government agencies you work with or other organizations working in your field may want to adopt, adapt, or participate in elements of your plan.

Replication, made possible by the dissemination of reports, methods, and lessons learned, is very important to funders. It demonstrates a ripple effect of learning and positive change in society from their investment in your work. This makes funding your work an attractive return on investment.

Dissemination

Funders also want to know that the lessons you learn might be shared with others and have the potential to affect the standard practices in your field. Determine to whom you will disseminate results or findings from your project, and list these groups in your project description. Here are some possibilities:

- Project participants
- Your board, staff, advisors, and key volunteers
- Donors, including individuals and both public and private funders
- Collaborating organizations and agencies
- Local umbrella groups such as United Way, arts councils, church councils, or environmental councils
- Professional associations, networks, or clearinghouses in your field
- Academics in your field
- Regulators in your field
- Policy makers and advocates, e.g., elected officials, lobbyists, and coalition members
- Subscribers to particular trade publications, blogs, or electronic newsletters
- The broader community

FIGURE 10.8 SAMPLE COMPLEX PROJECT TIMELINE

	Year One								Year Two											
	May	Jun	July	Aug	Sep	Oct	Nov	Dec	Jan	Feb	Mar	Apr	May	Jun	July	Aug	Sep	Oct	Nov	Dec
Task 1: Consultations (landowners & agencies)	X	X	X	X	X	X	X	X	X	X	X	X	X	X	X	X	X	X	X	X
Task 2: Contracts, Permits, & Plans	X	X	X	X	X	X	X	X	X	X	X									
Task 3: Revetment Installations				X	X	X	X	X							X	X	X			
Task 4: Riparian Plantings						X	X						X	X				X	X	
Task 5: Education	X	X	X	X	X	X	X	X	X	X	X	X	X	X	X	X	X	X	X	X
Task 6: Volunteer Recruitment	X	X	X	X	X	X	X	X	X	X	X	X	X	X	X	X	X	X	X	X
Task 7: Reports						X						X						X		X
Task 8: Monitoring	X	X	X	X	X	X	X	X	X	X	X	X	X	X	X	X	X	X	X	X
Task 9: Project Evaluation					X						X								X	

Mechanisms for sharing the information might include the following:

- Your organization's or department's electronic or print newsletter
- Your organization's annual report
- Your organization's website, blog, Twitter account, or RSS news feed
- A written or electronic letter to colleagues in related professional associations
- Letters to funders, participants, and partners or collaborators
- Gatherings, e.g., luncheons, focus groups, salons, and forums, in which you share findings with supporters
- Articles in industry magazines, trade publications, or scholarly journals
- News releases to local, regional, or national media
- Webinars, teleconferences, or videos shared electronically
- Presentations at conferences
- Funders' newsletters, websites, or annual reports

Administration

In the project description, you also have the opportunity to explain how your project will be administered. Begin by describing the key staff positions necessary to carry out the project and what their roles will be. Common positions include the executive director, program manager, and finance chief. Unless the funder has requested a separate section of the proposal called "Personnel" or "Qualifications" (see also Chapter 13), mention your leaders' qualifications here. Most funders will specify whether they want résumés or curricula vitae to be included. The information on key staff, whether presented in the project description or a separate section, serves four purposes:

- To explain clearly who will be responsible for the project and its various activities
- To clarify the hierarchy or chain of command among staff
- To verify that your organization has competent people in charge of the project
- To justify the salary- and benefit-related budget requests

Also report what other project staff will be necessary and how they will be selected. If project staff will be funded by more than one source, detail how their time and tasks will be delineated and how the split was determined. Identify the chain of command and describe how project staff will relate to other units of your organization.

Sustainability

End your project description with a section that describes how you intend to carry on your work after this particular grant has ended. Funders are investing in your project or program, and they want to be assured that it will continue without their support.

Depending on what's appropriate for your organization, you might include some of these options for sustaining your work:

- Inviting other funders to follow this funder's lead
- Convincing a legislative body to include your project in its budget appropriations
- Attracting contributions from individual donors

- Absorbing project costs into the organization's annual operating budget
- Generating earned income from deliverables produced while the project was funded by this grant

These and other ideas for future funding are discussed in Chapter 12, "Developing the Project Budget."

Even if your project is a one-time effort, such as purchasing equipment, constructing a building, or hosting a performance or conference, funders will want to see how you intend to maintain their investment. Describe how your organization will maintain or replace capital items, or keep the influence of the performance or conference alive in the community after the event is over.

Acknowledgments
Whether it's directly requested or not, always include in your proposal, in the project description section or elsewhere, how you plan to acknowledge the funder. You'll find a list of ideas in Chapter 17, "Investing in Ongoing Relationships."

Explore Variations for Specific Project Types
Particular information will be needed in your project description if you are seeking an operating grant, capacity-building grant, or capital grant.

Operating Grants
OPERATING COSTS, also known as OVERHEAD COSTS, INDIRECT COSTS, or ADMINISTRATIVE COSTS, are those costs that are not a direct part of a project. They might support staff salaries, recurring phone bills, building maintenance, or other administrative costs. An OPERATING GRANT funds these costs.

Operating grants can be more difficult to find due to the history of grantmaking itself. When private foundations were becoming more common in the 1960s, partly due to their appeal as tax havens, foundations viewed their role as supporters of innovation through special projects, and perceived rent, utilities, insurance, janitorial services, and other such indirect costs to be the responsibility of the organization. Many private funders still feel that funding general operations makes organizations dependent on foundation support, and therefore isn't sustainable. But doing the work of projects is difficult if there aren't enough resources to nurture the host organization. Since the beginning of the twenty-first century, foundations and corporations have become more willing to support general operating costs, and have acknowledged that a continual focus on innovative projects may get in the way of the important work grantseeking organizations are doing on an ongoing basis.

Operating grants are intended to support the organization as a whole, so orient your project description toward a general view of your organization rather than specific detail about a project or program. The components of the project description remain the same, as you tell a story, describe a problem, name activities designed to reach a goal, and identify measurable outcomes, all with an external focus on the need

> "I may choose to fund you in subsequent years. I just don't want you to rely on that."
>
> —Executive Director of a private foundation

> "Operating grants are for healthy organizations, not for solving debt problems or saving you from a crisis."
>
> —Executive Director of a public foundation

your organization will meet. The project description for operating grant proposals should cover the same elements as in a service delivery proposal, including replication and dissemination.

For example, successful operating requests describe how the requested funding will position your organization for growth in an important new direction, or add ballast during rough economic times. Another of many good reasons for operating support is that your organization is engaged in innovative work or inquiry and should be supported as it tries to yield more results.

When you are searching for funding opportunities, make sure you know each funder's attitude about operating costs. Some will fund these costs as part of a program or project request, but many disallow support of operating costs altogether. Government grants usually allow operating expenses as part of a project request, whereas private funders often do not.

From the Funder's Corner

If your organization runs a campaign for general support, you should consider offering a message of change as it relates to what your organization has learned over the past year and how it will apply those lessons next year. Ask yourself, what has changed for us in the past year? What changes will continue to affect us, and what does that mean for how we deliver services? For example, perhaps because of an economic downturn you are seeing people coming to your organization for the first time. In addition to being new to your organization, they are traveling a greater distance. Your organization originally selected its site because historically there was a concentration of need. But now that more people need your help, you also find that they are more geographically dispersed. Whatever those changes are, they can be the kernels for telling compelling stories about what your organization is doing for its community today. —*Ken Ristine*

Capacity-Building Grants

CAPACITY-BUILDING GRANTS, like operating grants, help organizations strengthen their ability to meet needs. Capacity-building grants cover aspects such as creating strategic plans, installing new accounting software, and offering staff or board training. They are used to help organizations address increased client demand or growth in territory or services, or to increase an organization's skills, infrastructure, and reach. Capacity-building grants are generally awarded to healthy organizations, not to bail an organization out of debt or to solve poor planning or leadership.

Sometimes programs and projects can grow so much that they endanger the organization. Capacity-building support may be in order to keep internal operations in proportion to external demand. Capacity building can help an organization reach a new constituency, measure breakthrough results, or overcome barriers to cultural competency. Proposals for capacity-building grants are more likely to succeed with funders who already know your organization and already believe in your organization's cause and constituency.

Project descriptions for capacity-building grants follow the same format as for any other type of proposal. Include a need or problem (identified after a thorough assessment), a proposed strategy, clearly named participants, and measurable outcomes. Remember to maintain an external focus that shows how building your organization's capacity will help you better serve your community. Be prepared to suggest a potential increase in results, such as greater numbers served or more land preserved.

Capital Grants

Capital grants cover the costs of buying durable goods or building or repairing buildings. The goal of project descriptions in capital requests is to show how the building or equipment requested is a means to an end.

Example: The Birchwood Community Hospital is the only hospital in a 500-square-mile area that includes two tribal reservations. Only 5 percent of the Birchwood region's women have had a mammogram, and the incidence of breast cancer is 300 percent higher than the national average. Acquisition of a mobile mammography van will make mammograms accessible in the area's rural communities, where limited transportation, a culture of fear of talking about cancer, and reluctance to leave livestock deter nonurgent trips to the hospital. The mobile nature of the van will assist with coordination among tribal and nontribal outreach workers as they seek to change the culture of cancer awareness in the region.

In this example you can see why the equipment is needed, but more importantly, what difference it will make. It will help change a culture, offer access, diagnose disease, and promote treatment.

Example: The 220-seat Johnson Auditorium in rural Lincoln will provide a venue for a literary series, for the high school theater and community orchestra, for city hall meetings open to the public, and for an emergency shelter. The community will participate in the building design, the township of Lincoln will donate the land, and the Friends of Johnson Auditorium will spearhead fundraising and management once the building is constructed.

In this situation, the theater represents artistic expression; disaster preparedness and community conversations, learning, and pride. The description demonstrates an external focus, with the auditorium a means to solve community isolation and division.

If you are requesting capital support for a new building, include these project design elements:

- Major benchmarks, e.g., groundbreaking, completing construction, opening for business, with planned dates
- Costs to complete each activity
- Cost per client contact
- Cost per square foot
- Cost of included equipment

These are some additional concepts to keep in mind:

- Funders will compare your budget with the cost of similar projects, so explain any issues that may increase the cost of your building. Costs may be higher due to the special nature of a facility or its location.
- Renovating a building may cost more than constructing a new one, but may also save a special building.
- Cheaper isn't always better, but more expensive isn't always better either.

- Funders often ask for pro forma operating budgets, i.e., budget projections that extend for many years into the operation of new facilities. Consider how much maintenance and repairs in the new building will cost you, or save you.
- New facilities are generally built on the promise that more people or animals will be served. Consider how your organization will support the costs of providing a higher level of service.

Avoid Common Pitfalls

Funders say they see certain common weaknesses in many grantseekers' project descriptions. You can make your proposal stand out by making sure none of these mistakes appear in yours.

Overpromising

The scale of your project design is particularly important. One of the most common problems in proposals is overpromising. It's difficult to strike the proper balance between promising to achieve important results and committing to project outcomes that really can be achieved given the time, staff, and budget included in your proposal. However, achieving this balance is critical to preparing an effective and feasible proposal. Being honest and reasonable about the scope of your project increases your chances of getting funded.

Internal Focus

Another common problem seen in project descriptions is a focus on problems and benefits internal to the organization rather than external, in the world. You and others in your organization live with organizational needs every day. However, funders are looking for proposals that have an external focus. They're not in the business of supporting organizations, but rather solving problems and improving life in communities.

Example: An organization serving abused children is told after an inspection that it will have to bring its facilities up to code or risk losing accreditation. The organization submits a funding proposal that focuses on its need for accreditation, rather than on its young clients' need to be served in a safe environment.

Even in the case of operating support, and capacity-building and capital grants, the focus must still be on external benefits.

Example: A case worker at a social service agency has an old, slow computer.

- **Internal focus:** The case worker needs a new computer because working on the old one is frustrating.
- **External focus:** A new, fast computer will allow the case worker to perform twice as many new client intakes per week, eliminate the waiting list, and result in one hundred more people getting services each week.

Weak Plan of Action

Sometimes, grantseekers haven't thought through all the steps necessary to implement their proposed project.

Example: An application to a private foundation says that the goal of the project is to open a new food bank. The rest of the proposal is devoted to justifying why hunger is a social problem and why more food banks are needed. It provides no clues about why this specific food bank is necessary, where the food bank will be located, how the facility will be retrofitted, what population it will try to serve, how the food will be obtained and stored, how the availability of the food will be publicized, or how many staff and volunteers will be needed to operate the food bank.

Mismatched Scope

Another common occurrence is for a proposal to describe substantial numbers of people or acres affected by the problem, yet in the project description indicate that only a fraction of that number will be served.

Example: The project description of a health clinic says it will provide health care to thousands of low-income residents, but the project outcomes promise treatment for only a tiny segment of that population and for only one specific malady.

Unsubstantiated or Unproven Claims

Proposals that suggest methods or activities or strategies that haven't been proven effective are likely to raise red flags. Make sure your project description includes the following:

- Evidence of other studies or projects that have used similar procedures, with examples suggesting that the methods will likely achieve the intended results
- Strategies that have been separated into distinct and manageable activities that can be matched to measurable outcomes
- A plan of action with activities arranged in a sequence of logical and complementary phases
- Evidence that your organization is aware of any potential problems with the suggested activities and has some plan in mind for handling these problems

Faulty Alignment

The most prevalent weakness in project descriptions is faulty alignment. If you don't pay close attention, it's easy to end up describing need in one way, anticipated outcomes in another way, and evaluation methods in yet another way.

> Make sure the budget and the program description tell the same story, mutually reinforcing each other.

The most common mistake is that the priorities articulated in the project description aren't reflected in the budget.

Example: The stated purpose of a grant proposal is to launch a new type of reading program, but over half of the budget is dedicated to buying new computers and software. The funder may well decide that the real purpose of the request is to upgrade the school's equipment, and thus reject the proposal.

Sometimes grantseekers articulate a clear need, but don't make an explicit connection in the project description between that statement of need and the project being proposed.

Example: A large national group applies to a corporation to underwrite a conference targeting the lack of communication among scientists involved in acid rain research. The proposal devotes several pages to justifying why acid rain is a significant issue. But it provides no justification as to why communication among scientists might be the most important aspect of this problem to address, or why a conference could be expected to make any lasting change.

Sometimes grantseekers articulate a compelling need, but the project description doesn't provide enough information to prove that the plan will be sufficient to meet that need.

Example: A nonprofit organization mentions the high incidence of drug use among teens, and suggests that a teen drop-in center would help. The project description fails to list the activities the center would provide to prevent drug use, and fails to acknowledge that the problem is complex and might require multiple types of programs to be successfully resolved.

Sometimes the stated project objective is contradicted in the details of the project description.

Example: A university proposes a program to encourage public school personnel to become self-sufficient at conducting classroom evaluations. Yet the suggested methods call for producing courses, materials, and models that will always require the involvement of university faculty as trainers or consultants. One part of the proposal offers to create independence, but another part of the proposal simply calls for a new form of long-term dependency.

Often the need is described as a gap in services, while the project description mentions only the acquisition of something—a piece of equipment, a building, or a staff position—without explaining how having that item or person will affect the need.

Example: A rural hospital describes the need in terms of patients not being served in the emergency room. But the proposal is to purchase trauma response equipment for the emergency room, and the project description fails to spell out how purchasing equipment will affect the gap in service. Later, the outcomes and evaluation sections of the proposal promise only the completion of purchase and related construction.

Strive to align your project description with every other element of your proposal. If your statement of need has three main points, repeat those same three points in your project description, in the same order, using the same terms, and referring to the same scope and scale. Then employ the same parallel construction in your evaluation plan. And finally, ensure that all budget items clearly relate to what you've put forth in the project description.

Recognize the Risks

Failure to craft a sound project description can have negative consequences for your organization, even if the project gets funded. If a funded project has been poorly defined, project staff may flounder through the initial several months of the funded period arguing points that should have been settled at the time the proposal was developed. Other negative consequences are also possible:

- The budget or timeline for the project may turn out to be unrealistic.
- Important partners may become frustrated at the confusion and withdraw from future collaborations.
- The project may become embroiled in a political fight in which staff and clients or constituents disagree about what the funds were intended to achieve.
- The delay in clarifying project outcomes may lead to time running out and/or the money being spent with little to show for it.

Summary

The project description, sometimes referred to as methods, program plan, approach, or plan of action, paints a picture for funders of a sound idea that your organization knows how to implement. The project description is often the longest section of a proposal, as it includes many components: what you intend to do and how, why you chose this strategy, who will be served and in what way, what you hope to achieve, how you plan to sustain the work after the grant, and how you intend to share what you've learned with others. A compelling project description focuses on the need you hope to meet and the difference you hope to make among external audiences. Regardless of whether your proposal is for research activities, program funding, capacity building, or capital items, your goals, objectives, and outcomes should mirror the other sections of your proposal, especially your statement of need, your evaluation plan, and your budget. Using a logic model may help you craft clearer project outcomes and a tighter, more compelling project description.

Key Terms

ACTIVITY: A specific step that will be taken so that an organization's methods or tactics work.

ACTIVITIES STATEMENT: A statement of the specific tasks and timelines that will be used to reach the project's goals.

CAPACITY-BUILDING GRANT: An investment in an organization's ability to function more effectively, scale up, or become more self-sustaining.

CAPITAL GRANT: Funding that helps an organization secure land, build or remodel facilities, or acquire equipment.

DISSEMINATION: The process of sharing the lessons learned and the knowledge and results gained by doing a project.

GANTT CHART: A type of bar chart that illustrates a project schedule.

GOAL: One of the overarching targets you hope to achieve through the proposed work.

GOAL STATEMENT: A broad description of the intended results of your project.

LOGIC MODEL: A graphic representation of a project that shows the relationships between what you propose to do and the results you will achieve.

METHOD or TACTIC: The way that an organization implements a project and/or evaluates the results of a project, including the steps taken to achieve project outcomes.

OBJECTIVE: A specific, measurable indication that you are making progress toward your goal. There are at least four types of objectives: behavioral, performance, product, and process.

OBJECTIVE STATEMENT: A specific statement that describes a specific and measurable result that your project will accomplish.

OPERATING COSTS or INDIRECT COSTS or OVERHEAD or ADMINISTRATIVE COSTS: The costs of administering the organization as a whole, so that the organization is in a position to implement the project.

OPERATING GRANT: A grant that supports an organization's operating costs.

OUTCOME: A specific, measurable change in decision making, knowledge, attitude, or behavior resulting from your project's outputs.

OUTCOME STATEMENT: A narrative description of the project's outcomes.

OUTPUT: A quantifiable item or unit of service resulting from the activities you propose.

PERT CHART: A project management tool used to schedule, organize, and coordinate tasks within a project.

REPLICATION: An event in which another organization uses your project as a model to do their own, similar project.

SMART RULE: A list of recommended characteristics for goals: Specific, Measurable, Achievable, Realistic, and Time-bound.

SUSTAINABILITY: A project's ability to continue after the grant funds end.

11 DESIGNING AN EVALUATION PLAN

This chapter explains why evaluation is so important to funders and how to determine what you will evaluate. The chapter also provides step-by-step guidance to help you craft a well-thought-out evaluation plan, and answers to frequently asked questions about evaluation. The evaluation section of your proposal demonstrates that you have built into your project the means to track and measure the change that results from your work. Grantmakers want assurance that the funds they provide are making a difference.

Examine the Reasons for Evaluation

Evaluation helps you measure success. It explains what you will consider success by defining what difference you hope to make and how you will know whether that change happened. *There is no single best way to do evaluation.* There are many models and techniques that are viewed as legitimate by most funding sources.

The *W.K. Kellogg Foundation Evaluation Handbook* (which can be downloaded without charge from the website www.wkkf.org) defines evaluation as the "consistent, ongoing collection and analysis of information for use in decision making." Or, to put it another way, evaluation is a systematic way of providing responses to the key questions that you and others want to ask about your funded project.

Evaluation verifies the results of the work and informs continuous improvement by doing these things:

- Asking the right questions
- Collecting information
- Conducting measurement
- Analyzing the information
- Reporting results

Evaluation helps everyone involved in your project remember the key reason for engaging in this work, and stay focused on the project's goals and outcomes. For this reason, most funders now require some type of evaluation component in the projects they fund. But there are at least five other reasons why doing evaluation, whether required or not, is in your own best interests:

- Evaluation can help you determine if the various parts of your project are working as envisioned, and if not, can allow you time to take corrective action before all of your grant funds are gone.

- Evaluation can provide meaningful opportunities for reflection and discussion within your organization and with others.
- Evaluation can prove whether your approach is effective or not, and thus offers credibility when you attempt to disseminate and replicate your ideas.
- Evaluation can help generate information about your project's results, and thus supports future requests for funding.
- Evaluation can serve to educate the funders and the field.

Distinguish Among Types of Evaluation

While the specifics requested by each funder may differ, there are four common types of evaluation.

> State how findings will be used for ongoing programmatic and organizational improvement.

BENCHMARK EVALUATION: Before you begin your work, you must document the current situation so that measurements taken during and after project implementation can be compared to the starting point. This is called your benchmark assessment. Subsequent measurements are called benchmark evaluations.

FORMATIVE EVALUATION: The second type is called formative because it produces information that is helpful to you *as the project takes form*. It judges the effectiveness of the project while it is being implemented. Formative evaluation focuses on the *process*. These are examples of formative evaluation:

- Testing the arrangement of lessons in a textbook before its publication
- Tracking changes in teenagers' attitudes over the course of a drug prevention class
- Collecting continuous feedback from participants in a program in order to revise the program as needed

SUMMATIVE EVALUATION: The third type is called summative because it measures and reports what was achieved *at the project's end*. It judges the effectiveness of the project after it has been implemented. Summative evaluation focuses on the *product*. These are examples of summative evaluation:

- Determining students' subject comprehension level after using a particular textbook in a training course
- Assessing teenagers' attitudes about drug use at the end of the class
- Collecting data on the impact of a program after a year of operation in a community

IMPACT or OUTCOME EVALUATION: A fourth type of evaluation, which is also summative, is called impact or outcome evaluation, because it evaluates *what has changed* among individuals, groups, the community, or the knowledge base as a result of the project. It provides data to assess the larger consequences of what you have achieved.

These are examples of impact or outcome evaluation:

- Measuring the degree to which users of the textbook had increased proficiency in the subject matter
- Quantifying whether teenagers reported a decrease in acceptance of drug use among their peers
- Determining whether participants in the program were behaving differently six months later as a result of the program

There are two types of data used in project evaluation: quantitative and qualitative.

QUANTITATIVE INFORMATION is concrete, objective, and countable. It is often referred to as hard data. Examples include test scores, the number of animals who were adopted, and the number of acres preserved. This information usually reflects your outputs.

QUALITATIVE INFORMATION is less concrete and more subjective, stemming from observations, impressions, and feelings. It is often referred to as soft data. Examples include responses from participants in surveys, interviews, or focus groups; observations made by a professional; or perception, attitude, or behavior changes reported by participants.

A word of caution: Some grantmakers will ask for *outcomes* (changes in behavior, skill, knowledge, or attitudes), when what they really want is *outputs* (results that can be counted or that you can see and touch). For example, if the instructions ask you to specify the *number* of participants who will be able to do something as a result of your project, the funder likely wants *outputs*. On the other hand, if the request is about *how well* the participants will perform, the funder is more interested in *outcomes*. Be sure to answer the question the funder is asking.

Develop an Evaluation Plan

There are four steps to designing an evaluation plan: deciding why you're conducting an evaluation, deciding what and how to evaluate, then how to analyze your findings, and finally, how to plan and implement the process.

Step 1. Purpose: Decide what to evaluate.

- Determine the main purpose of the evaluation by referring to the needs assessment and promised outcomes.
- Decide from whom evaluation data will be collected, e.g., the school counselors, the parents, or the teens.
- Identify what questions to measure.

Step 2. Data: Decide what information you need and how to collect it.

- Identify the specific information needed and how to pose the questions to get it.
- Clarify from which specific populations or sources the information will be gathered.
- Select data collection methods.
- Capture initial baseline information and set targets for change.
- Determine what clearances and permissions will be needed.
- Establish a timeline for data collection.

Students at an elementary school were asked to turn off their televisions for an entire month as part of a grant-funded project. The benchmark evaluation measured how much time they spent watching television before the project started. The formative evaluation measured how many students participated for how many days throughout the month; the summative evaluation measured whether students' behavior on the playground and in the lunchroom had changed by the end of the month; and the impact evaluation measured whether families reported spending less time watching TV and more time reading, being outdoors, or being engaged in cooperative activities. Evaluating a project's success can be done using all four types of evaluation: benchmark, formative, summative, and impact.

An organization engaged in downtown revitalization efforts might measure quantitative results in terms of how many downtown buildings got new facades, awnings, or planters, while measuring qualitative results in terms of whether citizens felt more inclined to spend time downtown. Other information that could be tracked later in the process might be whether downtown businesses counted more customers in their stores (quantitative) and how residents felt about shopping downtown (qualitative).

Step 3. Analysis: Decide how to analyze and report the information.

- Select methods for analysis, synthesis, and reporting.
- Determine what information will prove that the project has affected the stated need.
- Decide what reports to produce for which audiences and decision makers.
- Choose which reports to provide to the funder and when.
- Establish a timeline for data analysis and reporting.

Step 4. Roles, Responsibilities, and Resources: Determine what resources you need for the evaluation.

- Determine who will play what roles in designing and performing the evaluation.
- Identify an outside evaluator if necessary.
- Identify how much evaluation activities will cost and include this in appropriate places in the proposal's budget.

The sections that follow discuss these four steps to designing an evaluation plan in more detail.

Step 1: Decide what to evaluate.

First, clarify the purpose of your evaluation by referring to your stated need for the project and your promised outcomes. If the need is clearly defined and your goals, objectives, and outcomes are realistic in scope, it should be apparent what needs to be measured. And sometimes preparing for evaluation helps grantseekers rethink what they can promise as goals and outcomes.

As you determine what to evaluate, you will need to understand your starting position. If you're trying to reduce logging of old-growth trees, you need to know how many are currently being cut down so you can tell if the rate of logging has changed. Pre-project research or testing is often necessary to get a clear picture of the current situation. You will also need to determine what is a reasonable amount of change. Don't suggest more aggressive rates of change than are reasonable.

It's critical to decide who you will ask to respond to data collection surveys. Answers to your evaluation questions may vary widely, depending on whom you ask. Trained professionals may view a situation differently than volunteers do, and people whose jobs rely on the grant income might see results that elude an outside evaluator.

Returning to your logic model (see Chapter 3) can help you plan how to evaluate your project. Each column of a logic model holds things that can be measured, and it might be a helpful exercise to see what you would measure in each category. But you will definitely want to plan to evaluate your outcomes, objectives, and goals, for your own sake and for the

Design your evaluation to match your organization's capacity, budget, and skill set. Be sure to include evaluation costs in your project budget.

The organization that studied what would happen when elementary students turned off their televisions sent one funding proposal to a grantmaker that promoted literacy efforts and sent another proposal to a grantmaker that was intent on decreasing violence and the use of forceful language in schools. Both grantmakers supported the project. The project was conducted according to its project description, but what was measured at the end differed for each grantmaker. One evaluation focused on whether the students read more (for the literacy funder) and another evaluation focused on whether the students' behavior changed on the playground (for the anti-violence funder).

A counselor was assigned to work with a troubled family in which no one got along and communication was difficult. At the end of the assignment, an evaluator asked the family members how it had gone. They responded, "We all hate that woman, and we all agree she wasn't worth the time." When the same evaluator asked the counselor how it had gone, she replied, "It was a classic textbook success. My goal was to get disparate members in the family to coalesce against a common enemy—me!"

sake of your funders. Remember to align what you evaluate with the priorities of each funder of your project.

Step 2: Decide what information you need and how to collect it.

The second step in designing an evaluation plan is to identify the specific information needed to answer the evaluation questions of the different audiences. Consider these two examples:

Example 1: The goal of the project is to reduce the number of teenage pregnancies in a community. The evaluation plan is to collect data on teenage pregnancy rates at the start, middle, and end of the project. That data is already available from the county health department, so there is little additional cost to the project.

Example 2: While the goal of the project is the same, the evaluation is designed to determine which activities are the most effective at reducing teenage pregnancy, and thus must specify what questions to ask about each activity. This evaluation design will require a multifaceted and more expensive approach to collecting data, such as individual participant interviews.

How questions are asked has great bearing on the results of your evaluation. Take time to ensure that the questions don't steer respondents in a particular direction. And make sure you're asking questions that will elicit responses you can use.

> Request funders' report forms prior to submitting your proposal, and use the report questions to design your evaluation activities

As you choose your evaluation activities, consider the amount of time and money that each one will require. Also consider the suitability of each among those from whom you will collect data, including how often you'll be able to contact those individuals, and when those contacts are likely to occur. For example, if your organization has no way to stay in contact with individuals who have successfully completed a program, do not design an evaluation that requires you to collect post-program data from participants.

Jane Reisman and Judith Clegg in *Outcomes for Success!* provide a useful summary of major types of evaluation designs and their relative costs.[1] Further information is available in the Resources section of this book under "Evaluation and Outcomes," and online at the Getting Funded website, www.gettingfundedbook.com.

Here are just a few examples of data collection options:

- Ask participants to keep a journal.
- Ask participants to fill out a questionnaire or online survey.
- Interview participants.
- Give participants a test to see what they've learned.
- Conduct a focus group with participants.
- Ask colleagues whether they've noticed changes.
- Have a professional, e.g., a social worker or educator, observe and codify behavior.
- Collect data from existing sources, e.g., government agencies.
- Take measurements before and after the project, e.g., water, soil, or air quality, or water or energy usage rates.

> Managers of a program designed to help expose students of color to math, science, and engineering thought that they should be measuring whether students chose careers in those fields after participating in the program. But with careful guidance from an evaluation consultant, the program managers realized that what they should be measuring is whether the students believed that they *could* have a career in those fields. Ultimately what they measured was an increase in students' sense of self-determination.

1. Jane Reisman and Judith Clegg, *Outcomes for Success!* Seattle, WA: The Evaluation Forum, 2000, p. 41.

A summary of several types of evaluation designs together with the level of resources required is provided in Figure 11.1.

You will need to decide whether to create your own data collection instruments or use existing ones. You'll find many available resources on the Internet. Some federal agency websites include inventories of the data collection instruments used in projects they've previously funded. One example is the Juvenile Justice Evaluation Center Online at the Department of Justice, at www.jrsa.org. Many universities have excellent online resources with links to other websites covering evaluation, assessment, measurement, research methods, and reporting. Go to the Getting Funded website, www.gettingfundedbook.com, for more information.

Clarify from which populations or sources you will gather information. If you plan to glean information from people who have been served by your project, make sure you have a way to reach those people directly. In some cases, participant records may be confidential, or staff responsible for the records may not be willing to share them.

FIGURE 11.1 TYPES OF EVALUATION DESIGN

EVALUATION DESIGN	INDICATOR	RESOURCE NEEDS
Participant feedback surveys	Participants' reports of satisfaction with services they received (e.g., quality, access, friendliness, results).	Low
Post-program measurement	Use of evaluation tools to describe outcomes (e.g., behavior, attitudes, experiences, knowledge) following completion of the program.	Low
Pre- and post-program measurement	Use of evaluation tools to describe expected outcomes (e.g., behavior, attitudes, experiences, knowledge) prior to a program and following completion of the program.	Moderate
Pre- and post-program measurement with a comparison group	Same as pre- and post-program measurement approach, but with the added component of collecting similar scores for a comparison group.	High
Post-program measurement and benchmarks	Same as post-program measurement approach, except similar scores are also collected from partner organizations or other targets selected for benchmark comparisons.	High
Pre- and post-program measurement and long-term, post-program measurement	Same as pre- and post-program measurement approach, with additional scores obtained again at a later point in time (e.g., six months, one year, two years).	High

Determine whether you will collect evaluation data from cooperating agencies or partner organizations. This is an increasingly important decision because so many funders are interested in funding collaborative projects. For example, one grantseeking organization asked representatives from other area organizations that served the same population to help corroborate the need for and validate the design of a proposed program. A year after the program began, the other organizations were invited to discuss what changes they had seen. Their insights helped alter future projects and methods.

> If you'll be collecting information from people who speak another language or have hearing loss, you'll want to factor in the time, cost, and advanced planning required for interpretation.

Find out whether you can get the clearances and permissions needed to collect the information you need. Grantmakers get very nervous if they receive a proposal, especially one involving human or animal subjects, that fails to provide evidence that the grantseeking organization is aware of, and fully in compliance with, federal, state, and local regulations. These requirements may be specified in the grant announcement, be embedded in state law, or be part of your organization's established procedures. Increasingly, funders also want information on how you will ensure adequate representation of minorities and women in the population you serve or study. Federal agencies are particularly sensitive on this subject and expect it to be addressed explicitly in all research or experimental projects. The time needed to carry out the procedures required to protect human or animal subjects or to gain permission to study minor children or other vulnerable populations must be built into the evaluation timeline for any research project.

Funders of research projects may ask for more detail on instrumentation, data collection, and analysis. Depending on the length and complexity of your description of these topics, you might address them in a single subsection of the evaluation plan, or in separate ones. Be sure to include an appropriate level of detail on issues such as the following:

- Variables to be addressed or specific information to be obtained
- Specific instruments to be used to collect the necessary data
- Description of the background and content of any evaluation measures that may not be well-known to proposal reviewers
- Psychometric data or any other relevant evidence to justify suitability, technical soundness, and comprehensiveness of the evaluation measures
- Sources from which specific information will be obtained
- Rationale for data collection activities, including how they are consistent with your objectives
- Data collection schedules, data retrieval methods, and data preparation and storage plans
- Data analysis information, including data analysis models, units of analysis, and justification of these choices
- Plans for ensuring that the data is complete, recorded accurately, and transcribed correctly for analysis, including procedures for obtaining a high response rate from study participants and for editing and preparing data for analysis
- Data reporting plans, including audiences, types of reports, and reporting schedule
- Data use and application

In your evaluation plan, identify any audience that must review and approve your data collection instruments or procedures. Identify the amount of time estimated for this review, which can be surprisingly long. Also describe how modifications to your data collection plan will be made, if necessary. Remember that all federally funded projects that involve the administration of surveys to large groups of people must have clearance before the project begins. Details should be sought from the appropriate federal agency.

Step 3: Decide how to analyze and report the information.

First create a timeline for your entire evaluation process, beginning with the end product and working back to the beginning. Allow some flexibility, as elements of your plan are bound to shift during the process.

Most funders do not require much specificity on analysis techniques in a proposal, unless it is for a research project or highly experimental program. Regardless, you'll be better off if you know at the outset what activities you will engage in to analyze the data you collect. Funders will expect you to articulate how you will know whether you have affected the stated need, how much, and for how long.

Your evaluation plan should list the reports you will generate and their audiences, along with the planned distribution dates. Also indicate what kinds of decisions your reports will influence. Sorting all this out can be more complicated than it first appears. Will you share evaluation data with program participants, cooperating agencies, other organizations working in your field? When will you provide evaluation data—periodically or only once at the end of the grant period? Funders are especially interested in knowing what evaluation reports they will receive. Some funders specify their own reporting requirements in their guidelines. Others leave it to you to propose an evaluation plan and reporting schedule.

Figure 11.2 shows one way to plan for evaluation reports. Some proposals might include this type of table either in the project description or as an attachment. Other proposals might use pertinent information from the plan in the overall description of procedures and timeline.

> Evaluation reports are a subset of overall grant reports, which have their own timelines and requirements.

Step 4: Determine what resources you need for the evaluation.

Your plan for carrying out your project evaluation process will need to take into account the resources required, including both financial costs and staff time and expertise.

Normally, funders expect evaluation to cost 5 to 10 percent of the total project budget. But there are also legitimate reasons for an evaluation budget to be much higher. Costs that typically need to be considered include salary and benefits for evaluation staff and consultants; travel costs; purchase of questionnaires or data collection tools, office supplies, and relevant equipment or software; and printing costs. Unless the funder requires you to display the evaluation budget separately, you can include the evaluation costs in your overall project budget (see Chapter 12).

Your team will need to decide whether to have the evaluation activities performed by internal staff, by consultants, or by a mix of the two. The *W.K. Kellogg Foundation Evaluation Handbook* (see Resources) has an extensive and useful discussion of how to make this decision, how to select a consultant, and how to develop the evaluation budget. Major considerations are staff qualifications and experience and the complexity of the evaluation design.

FIGURE 11.2 SAMPLE PLAN FOR DATA COLLECTION, ANALYSIS, AND REPORTING

Outcome	Evaluation Design	Person Responsible	Instrument	Schedule	Analysis	Reports
By the end of the school year, the 4th-graders in this program will have increased their reading scores by an average of 25%.	pre-test / post-test	Title I reading teacher	Woodcock Reading Mastery Test	Sept. 15–18, May 12–16	Calculate post-test scores to see if growth was significant compared to the test's national norms.	June 15 to state department of education

Figure 11.3 provides an example of how evaluation responsibilities can be divided among project evaluators, whether they are internal staff or external consultants. This type of table could be a useful component in your proposal, particularly if the costs of your evaluation may exceed 10 percent of the total project budget or if extensive use of consultants will be required.

Frequently Asked Questions about Evaluation

The rest of this chapter addresses some questions about evaluation asked by many grantseekers.

Do all proposals require an evaluation component?

Requests for evaluation plans depend on the funder. For most government funders and larger foundations, your ability to show results is weighted heavily in the review process and may be the deciding factor in requests for renewal of funding. Some types of projects, such as facility construction, equipment purchase, or even general operating support, require an evaluation report showing that the money was spent as indicated in the budget or contract. Funders frequently expect evaluation details even in proposals for small amounts ($25,000 or less). However, some very large foundations explicitly state that you should not include an evaluation plan and budget in the original proposal, as the funder will negotiate an evaluation plan and the funds to implement it soon after announcing the award.

Are all evaluations complicated and expensive?

Evaluations need not be complicated nor expensive. Most funders simply want to know if you succeeded, and if not, what you learned from the experience. Since most funders are interested in particular causes, the lessons you learn, good or bad, can help them understand the field better. Just make sure you try to discover whether you were successful or not.

For example, a social worker who led a group of Native American fathers through a nine-week parenting class expressed to the class her concern about how to report on the program's success to the funder. A shy father in the back row quietly said,

TASK	EVALUATOR RESPONSIBILITIES	PROJECT STAFF RESPONSIBILITIES
Coordination	Designate a person to be a primary evaluator for this program.	Designate a person to coordinate the evaluation responsibilities for this program.
Evaluation Plan	1. Prepare a general evaluation plan in cooperation with the project staff. 2. Finalize and approve the project's revised evaluation plan.	1. Review the general evaluation plan, revise as necessary to fit the project, and return the revised plan to the external evaluator.
Evaluation Instruments	1. Prepare a draft copy of all instruments to be used. 2. Provide the project with a sample set of standardized instruments to be used together with cost information and an order form. 3. Review any project-developed instruments if requested by the staff.	1. Prepare copies of all evaluation instruments. 2. Develop any local monitoring or evaluation instruments. 3. Have each proposed evaluation instrument reviewed and get approvals for using them.
Data Collection	1. Provide the project with a schedule and plan for data collection. 2. Provide written directions for administering nonstandardized evaluation instruments. 3. Prepare common codes and coding directions for all answer sheets and data collection forms.	1. Schedule and administer all evaluation instruments identified in the evaluation plan. 2. Collect and code data specified in the plan. 3. Code responses to all instruments as needed. 4. Get code sheets to the external evaluator for processing.
Data Analysis	1. Verify the correct scoring and/or coding of all instruments. 2. Codify and analyze data.	1. Determine whether there is any special data analysis the staff would like to have run that has not already been included in the evaluation plan.
Reporting	1. Prepare a draft copy of the evaluation report and give it to the evaluation coordinator for review. 2. Prepare a final copy of the evaluation report. 3. Prepare a camera-ready copy of an evaluation report abstract.	1. Identify the information needs of the people in the project if any have changed since the evaluation plan was prepared. 2. Review the draft evaluation report for any factual errors or misrepresentations. 3. Print the required number of evaluation reports and abstracts.

"With all due respect, ma'am, you could ask us." He was right. It would have been enough. But it's best to figure out at the front end how you plan to evaluate your project.

How do you handle evaluation of prevention programs?

Admittedly, designers of projects whose success is judged by what *didn't* happen may face a special challenge. So, how will you know it didn't happen? And how will you know it didn't happen because of your efforts? There is usually some type of indicator (such as dropout rate) and data source (such as school attendance reports) that you can use to measure progress and monitor your degree of success, even if it isn't required by the grantmaker. Selecting the indicator and citing your data source is a very simple and commonly used approach to evaluation. You may also want to learn which of your prevention activities worked the best. As the Native American father said, you can ask your participants.

How do you evaluate the effectiveness of the arts?

All fields can be evaluated. Regardless of what the money is for, funders expect you to be able to articulate something that will change as a result of their support and then let them know whether that change occurred. For example, here are some ideas about how arts organizations could evaluate their work:

> Indicate in your proposal how your short-term outcomes will inform your long-term activities and outcomes.

If you're bringing a specific artist to the community to deepen people's understanding and appreciation of a particular music genre, you could interview a certain percentage of audience members before and after the concert to see if their level of understanding or appreciation changed. If you seek funding for an artist in residence in a school, you could say the project aims to encourage movement among sedentary children, or to expose them to the art of another culture, or to trigger a conversation about an issue they're studying or that's relevant to their community. Progress toward any of these goals would be fairly simple to measure.

How can you prove results if your grant is for operating costs?

Even proposals for operating costs must detail what will be different at the end of the grant period. Some organizations choose an element of the operating budget that is difficult to get funding for—such as fundraising expenses, marketing and communications, or insurance payments—applying the grant money to that activity. At the end of the grant period, the organization can share what happened as a result of having that line item on the operating budget covered by the grant. Examples might be reducing the cost per dollar raised, reaching 1,000 new stakeholders with electronic marketing efforts, or managing technology cost-effectively. If you choose to apply the grant to your organization's entire operating budget, you can still quantify how many people benefited from the organization's work during the year or the number of endangered species that were protected. You can also measure how an operating grant helped fill a budget shortfall or improve organizational capacity by synching up the donor database with the accounting software.

Some organizations choose to use funding for operating costs in a highly strategic way and then track progress as results. An example would be exploring the feasibility of a highly risky project, such as permanent housing for chronic drug abusers. The organization would codify the conversations about approaches and costs and share that information as if it were program outcomes. Sharing the lessons learned and being honest about any failures would build trust with the funder who supported the proposal.

Some organizations use their operating grants to build readiness for unknown and unpredicted challenges. For example, when steep cuts in health care funding are promised by the legislature, it can take months for organizations to learn how much will be cut and from which departments. When closures of public health facilities are also promised, health care nonprofits know they will probably see greatly increased demand for services at the same time that funding from their government contracts will be cut. An operating grant can give an organization flexibility, as administrators can use the funds where they are needed most as the situation unfolds.

How rigorous an evaluation do grantmakers want?

There was a time that one could confidently predict that government agencies would require much more extensive evaluations than private foundations or corporations would. That is no longer true. Grantmakers are investors. They want to know whether their investment has resulted in the goals and outcomes they want to support. Here are some examples of evaluation requirements drawn from a variety of public and private funding sources.

> Often, as the amount of the award increases, so does the expectation of rigor in the evaluation. With larger grants, you will see an expectation of a higher standard of evidence of change demonstrated by your evaluation.

Example 1: Please describe any evaluation efforts that you will undertake to determine that your objectives and outcomes are being achieved. Briefly describe the indicators that will be used to monitor progress. How will you use the information you gather to make your organization more effective? What are the challenges and obstacles you face in evaluating the effectiveness of your work? If you do not currently undertake formal evaluations, how do you measure success?

Example 2: The proposed project must demonstrate an evaluation component that will present clear educational outcomes to be discussed in the final project report.

Example 3: A good evaluation plan appropriate to the scale of the project will provide information as the project is developing and will determine how effectively the project has achieved its goals. The effects of formative evaluation should be described. Also include how you intend to evaluate the final project and how you will determine whether this project met your scientific and pedagogical expectations. Discuss how you plan to collect and analyze data on the project's impact.

Example 4: Describe objectives, how project results will be measured, and who will be responsible for providing financial and quarterly information.

Summary

Funders expect much more rigorous measurement of the results of funded organizations and projects than they did in years past. The most important element of assessing effectiveness is pinpointing what to evaluate, a decision that needs to be based on precisely what you promised as outcomes. Sound plans begin with a baseline measurement of original conditions and promise a desired outcome in relation to that baseline. Effective evaluation design showcases the information you deem important enough to capture and why, how you plan to collect and analyze it, and how you intend to report your findings. Remember to include in your project budget the resources needed to complete your evaluation and reporting plans.

Whether a funder requires evaluation or not, you'll want to conduct a careful analysis of your work to make sure you're being effective. If you don't know where you are going, any road will seem to take you there. If you haven't planned for evaluation, you may never know if you've achieved success.

Key Terms

BENCHMARK EVALUATION: A type of evaluation that compares measurements taken after a project is underway with benchmark assessments, which are measurements taken before the work began, or at intervals during it.

FORMATIVE EVALUATION: A type of evaluation that measures progress against goals as a project takes form. It judges the effectiveness of the project while it is being implemented. Formative evaluation focuses on the success of the process, as distinct from the end product.

IMPACT EVALUATION or OUTCOME EVALUATION: A type of summative evaluation that looks at what has changed among individuals, groups, the community, or the knowledge base as a result of a project.

QUALITATIVE INFORMATION or SOFT DATA: Information that is subjective and less than concrete. Examples include anecdotes or quotes; responses from participants in surveys, interviews, or focus groups; observations made by a professional; or changed perceptions, attitudes, or behaviors reported by the target audience.

QUANTITATIVE INFORMATION or HARD DATA: Information that is concrete and objective. Examples include test scores, the number of animals who were adopted, or the number of "bed nights" in a shelter. Data must be properly cited, up to date, and from a verifiable and well-regarded source.

SUMMATIVE EVALUATION: A type of evaluation that measures and reports what was achieved by the end of your project. Summative evaluation focuses on the product. It judges the effectiveness of the project after it has been implemented.

12 DEVELOPING THE PROJECT BUDGET

This chapter explains what a project budget consists of, clarifies what funders are looking for in both your project budget and your organization's operating budget, and discusses how to create budgets that paint a vivid picture of your project's goals and plans and your organization's financial diligence.

A budget is a numerical representation of your plans, indicating the costs incurred in carrying them out and how you plan to cover those costs. The budget narrative helps an outsider interpret the numbers and understand how you arrived at them. The BUDGETS and BUDGET NARRATIVE (allowed in many funders' applications) together demonstrate to funders that your organization has thought through the financial aspects of the project. This chapter offers a four-step process for creating any type of project budget. The budget preparation worksheets included in the chapter can help you tell your story in numbers. The budget narrative is the place to explain in text your organization's rationale for particular financial decisions, and is a very important piece of the proposal.

Understand the Role of the Budget

Budgeting is simply the process of translating the proposed project into fiscal terms. The budget components of a proposal should be developed in conjunction with the project description and according to the funder's guidelines. The budget and budget narrative, which is the explanation and justification for the budget in words, need to tell the story of the project so clearly that the reviewers will understand the project even if they do not read the rest of the proposal. The budget LINE ITEMS, which are the specific expenses and income, need to relate to and support the project's goals, objectives, and activities.

The budget preparation process is an important opportunity to evaluate the practicality of the proposed project. Funders place great importance on well-prepared and accurate budgets when they are deciding if organizations have the necessary experience and managerial capability to complete projects successfully. Mistakes made in the budget can result in your proposal being rejected due to poor budget development. If you receive funding despite mistakes in the budget, then your organization may end up professionally and legally committed to a project that cannot be completed due to inadequate resources.

Prepare your budget carefully, with an understanding of its relationship to the proposed plan of action, so that your organization will be prepared to successfully answer funders' mental questions and engage in final financial negotiations. More than one person should be involved in framing the budget. Include in the process everyone who will be involved in making the project happen, as well as grant managers and finance staff. As you discuss the need for particular elements of the proposal, consider devising two budgets—one that represents your ideal budget and one with only the bare essentials.

> *"We loved the project, but the budget request was for items that were not discussed in the proposal, and the activities discussed in the proposal were not supported by line items in the budget."*
>
> —Trustee of a private foundation

You may discover while preparing the budget that the total projected costs for the project exceed your ideas for funding. This is an opportunity for you to redesign the project. Consider reducing the project's scope or using less costly methods. Funders pay attention to whether the proposal you submit includes plans for adequate financial resources to conduct the proposed scope of work. When a project is funded based on an unrealistic budget estimate, the organization must later approach the funder to request permission for substantive changes to the project—which may compromise its ability to reach its goals—or to ask for additional funds.

As much care should be given to the budget as to the development of the rest of the proposal. *Seasoned reviewers will often turn to the budget first, before reading the proposal, because they can tell so much about your organization and your proposal simply by reading the story told by the numbers.* Some funders separate out the budget section of a proposal to be reviewed by financial experts, and then send the rest of the proposal to be reviewed by project experts. The budget must be able to stand alone and give a complete picture of the project without relying on the other parts of the proposal to support it.

Figure 12.1 is a standard project budget worksheet that includes the most common elements. See a sample project budget filled out on the Getting Funded website.

Learn the Ground Rules

Before you can create a budget for your project, you must learn the ground rules that apply to your own organization and to the funder you intend to approach. Talk to your finance staff or treasurer to find out about your organization's internal ground rules. Then make sure you understand the funder's expectations.

Internal Ground Rules: The Grantseeker

If you work for a well-established organization with a history of grantseeking and extensive infrastructure, there will likely be staff who specialize in the financial aspects of grant-funded projects. If you work for a smaller or less experienced organization, ask your finance department staff or board treasurer if there are any guidelines you must follow. Find out your organization's policies about indirect costs, defined later in this chapter, and other budgeting considerations. Check to see if your organization already has budget worksheets with itemized expense categories and an internal grant budget review process.

Your organization may also have decided what types of contracts it is willing or not willing to sign. FIXED-PRICE, COST-REIMBURSEMENT, COST-PLUS-FIXED-FEE, and COST-SHARING contracts may not all be appropriate for every organization. For example, your organization may not be in a position to sign a contract that requires it

FIGURE 12.1 WORKSHEET FOR CREATING A PROJECT BUDGET

Project Budget $_____

PROJECT REVENUE

Public

Federal	$_____
State	$_____
Municipal	$_____
SUBTOTAL	$_____

Private

Foundations	$_____
Corporations	$_____
Organizations	$_____
Federated Campaigns (e.g., United Way)	$_____
Individuals	$_____
Earned Income	$_____
Interest Income	$_____
SUBTOTAL	$_____
TOTAL INCOME	$_____

PROJECT EXPENSES

Salaries	$_____
Benefits and Taxes	$_____
SUBTOTAL	$_____
Facilities	$_____
Equipment	$_____
Supplies	$_____
Travel and Per Diem	$_____
Contract Services	$_____
Communications	$_____
Program-Related Expenses	$_____
SUBTOTAL	$_____
TOTAL EXPENSES	$_____

Note: Total Income and Total Expenses should match.

to pay all the project expenses up front and get reimbursed only every few months or once a year. And some grant contracts require the grantee to pay for organizational expenses (such as getting an audit or having a handicap accessible facility) that cannot be included in your project budget.

External Ground Rules: The Funder

Each funder has guidelines about what it will and will not fund. This information can be found both in funders' guidelines and in RFPs. (Chapter 5 discusses RFPs in more detail.) Below is a list of basic information you will want to know before you finalize the budget for a particular funder.

Allowable costs: Most public funders allow a budget to include indirect costs (defined on page 146), but private funders generally do not. In addition, many private funders do not allow items they assume to be the normal responsibility of the organization, such as information technology or accounting services, to be included in a project budget as direct costs.

Percentage of project costs: Some funders will consider requests for the entire cost of a project, while other funders expect part of the funds for any project to come from another source. Some have fixed rules about providing only a certain percentage of a project's total budget (often 10 to 50 percent). This rule ensures that there is shared ownership and a funder isn't the only one invested in your project's success.

Matching funds: Some funders, both public and private, may ask for matching funds, in which the award is contingent on your organization raising the same amount from other sources or contributing it from the organization's resources. Matching funds can sometimes be provided through in-kind contributions, which are noncash contributions such as goods, services, equipment, or space that would otherwise need to be purchased.

Changes: Funders may permit changes to the budget once it is approved. Grant-makers will often allow an organization to transfer up to 10 percent of one budget category (such as supplies and materials) to another category (such as travel) without prior approval.

Contingencies: While most funders expect to see a "miscellaneous" line item that will cover small, unanticipated expenses, they may not welcome items labeled "contingency"—a reserve for unexpected costs. They want you to budget carefully enough to avoid any surprises. Some funders expect you to include a little leeway in your projections; and some assume that costs will always end up higher than you predicted. Check to see what each funder prefers before you finalize your budget.

Estimated costs: If you are responding to an RFP, you may be able to determine an acceptable budget range by noting the amount of staff time estimated by the funder. An RFP issued by the National Science Foundation (NSF), for example, specified that the project would take an estimated "one person-year of effort." NSF used a general rule of thumb that this would cost about $80,000, a figure which became the average budget target for the proposals submitted in response to the RFP.

Reviewers: Find out who will be reviewing the budget for the funder, and whether the budget will accompany the proposal or be considered separately. Many federal agencies have contract reviewers who see only the budget, without the corresponding proposal. This may necessitate more detail in the budget to show how totals were calculated.

Timing: Some funders specify an amount of time within which all grant monies must be spent. Before you submit, make sure your organization will be able to spend the money within the time period required by the funder. One government agency was unable to award a grant to a nonprofit because the money had to be used by the end of the fiscal year, but permitting and construction time frames prevented the organization from spending it by then.

Private funding sources and government agencies require different amounts of detail in budget proposals. However, it's a good idea to prepare a detailed budget for all projects, even if you do not submit all the details in writing to the potential funder. Not only can you expect to use the information during subsequent discussions, but you will need the detail for project management.

The process of preparing budgets becomes easier as you and your organization become more familiar with fiscal terms, learn what kind of information is needed, and begin to develop your own "rules of thumb" about how much certain kinds of activities are likely to cost. However, each new proposal presents new challenges. The resource needs of each project are as unique as the proposed strategies, methods, and outcomes.

Amount to Request

Funders sometimes award less money than requested. However, it's not a good idea to augment your budget to compensate for this possibility. Even inexperienced reviewers can detect "padded" budgets, and funders respect those grantseekers who keep the numbers as realistic as possible. Many a funder has awarded *more* than requested to organizations that asked for a modest amount and didn't appear greedy.

Estimating whether the total budget amount is "realistic" can still be a challenge. This is why doing your homework is particularly important. Good research can uncover the total dollar amount available to a funder in this particular funding cycle, the minimum and maximum range of prior awards in your field, and information about whether the funder has supported the types of things you've included in your budget.

Consider asking for no more than the funder's *average* grant amount on your initial approach. While you may have seen records of very large grant amounts awarded by the funder, the recipients of those likely spent years building a relationship with and earning the trust of the grantmaker. When guidelines announce a maximum award amount, nearly every proposal requests the whole amount. Asking for a lower amount puts you at a psychological advantage. And asking for an unusual amount (such as $18,750 instead of $20,000) makes your request look more authentic and less capricious.

If you are approaching a particular funder for only a percentage of the total project cost, make sure that the items you request reflect the values and priorities of the funder. For example, an arts commission does not want to see a performer's time listed as an in-kind contribution—it is a core value of the commission to pay artists what they're worth. Some grantmakers will reject an entire proposal if the requested amount includes line items their guidelines strictly prohibit. Savvy proposal developers will not simply ask for $10,000 of a $50,000 project cost, they will choose an item in the budget that relates to the funder's guidelines and request funding for that discrete item. Be sure to determine which parts of the project budget are most appropriate to ask funders for and

A government review panel actually awarded one grantseeking organization more than they asked for because it was so obvious that they weren't being greedy, and would put the extra to good use. At the same time, they gave smaller amounts to organizations who had seemingly padded their budgets just to get them up to the maximum amount to be granted.

which are most appropriately supported by the organization or other sources. For instance, dollars raised from individuals can be used for administrative expenses, while program expenses can be raised from grants.

You may want to include a fallback position in your budget, knowing grantmakers will often fund a proposal for less than the requested amount. Don't assume that if you suggest a lower amount, they will automatically choose that number. For example, if you've asked for $20,000, but could eliminate one element of the budget that costs $2,500 and still make the project work, let the funder know. That way they're less likely to trim the award by $5,000, an amount that doesn't relate to any particular budget items.

A private foundation director became frustrated after routinely receiving proposals that didn't specify precisely what the requested amount would pay for. The foundation's guidelines listed several things they would not pay for, and she wanted assurance that their grant money would not be spent on those items.

Follow Four Steps to Develop a Project Budget

The ease with which a budget is prepared depends on the complexity of your proposed project, the procedures of your organization, and the instructions from the potential funding source. However, you will find that budgeting is essentially a four-step process, which the rest of this chapter covers in detail:

- Step 1: Identify the total costs of the project.
- Step 2: Identify potential revenue for the project.
- Step 3: Organize items by category, by time frame, and by anticipated source.
- Step 4: Transfer data into the format requested by the funder.

A grantwriter with a civic organization was confused about how to write the program description for a grant until she started with the budget. Once she asked the question "What do we want to pay for?" the plan became clear.

Budget Development Step 1: Identify Total Project Costs

The total cost of a project is calculated by adding together direct costs and indirect costs. Be sure to include all "hidden" costs, such as staff planning time, supplies, insurance, security, and bookkeeping.

As you begin building your project budget, start by filling out a worksheet such as the ones illustrated in this chapter. These worksheets help you do the following:

- Structure the budget planning process such that no probable expense is overlooked
- Record how each item was calculated so you are prepared to discuss how budget cuts proposed during negotiations might affect the project

The director of a children's arts organization was writing a grant proposal for a joint project with the children's theater next door. As she framed the project budget, she neglected to account for how much time it would take out of her already busy schedule to communicate and collaborate with the theater's director. Once that was brought to her attention, she realized that the value of her staff time alone nearly doubled the amount she needed to request. It hadn't occurred to her that while she was working on the project, she would be unable to work on any other efforts, including fundraising.

- Make sure that each budget request is sufficiently justified in the proposal narrative
- Capture the number and value of projected volunteer hours; base the value on the national United Way's annual calculations of the value of volunteer time, which are posted on the United Way website and are generally accepted by the grantmaking community
- Identify approvals that will be needed, including compliance with building codes, government regulations, and organization requirements
- Provide an expenditure plan that can be used during the actual project operation, which will be particularly valuable if the proposal writer or budget developer will not be involved in project management once funds are received

Major Budget Categories

The two main budget categories for expenses are direct costs and indirect costs. DIRECT COSTS are expenses specifically attributable to the project or program. INDIRECT COSTS, also called OVERHEAD, relate to the infrastructure that is necessary to support the organization as a whole (such as facilities, personnel, materials, and services) but is difficult to prorate separately for each grant proposal.

A project budget also must reflect the revenue your project will receive—whether from other funding sources, earned income, or in-kind donations (see Budget Development Step 2). And always remember: Make sure your revenue and expense columns add up to the same total.

Direct Costs

The direct cost categories that are normally listed in a project budget include the following, which are defined below:

- Program personnel
- Contract services
- Travel and per diem expenses
- Facilities
- Equipment
- Supplies and materials
- Program-related expenses
- Communications

Personnel: Salaries (monthly or yearly pay) and wages (hourly pay) should be computed for all staff associated with the project. The budget should also indicate the amount of time each individual will allocate to the project (shown as percentage of total salary or as number of staff days) and if the amount will be paid by this funder, the organization, or other funders to whom you are applying.

Salary and wage rates in the project budget should be comparable to your organization's usual rates. Funders generally don't allow grant funds to be used to augment people's normal pay. However, your project budget should anticipate potential salary increases due to promotions, as well as the cost of inflation. This is especially important in multiyear budgets. If you will estimate project salaries or wages based on prevailing pay in your area rather than just in your organization, contact your United Way affiliate, a nearby university, the local school district, or your city or county government for information. For international grant proposals, be sure to use the prevailing salaries of the country or locality where the project will occur.

Remember that managing the proposed project will require the time and expertise of individuals not directly involved in the project. For example, a nonprofit that is launching a new program should include in the budget a percentage of the executive director's time, an estimate of time that will be spent by those who will supervise program staff, and percentages of time that will be spent by the organization's financial services staff, technology staff, data entry staff, and so forth. When you include this information, you show funders that your organization realizes these elements are part of the cost of implementing the program. Even if your budget does not request funding for these people, the costs should be reflected in the budget and marked as in-kind support or as costs absorbed by the organization.

In addition to including the salaries and wages of all regular project staff, the personnel category may also include funds for consultants and/or advisory board members. Consultants are usually hired as private contractors at a daily, hourly, or project rate (which may be set by the funder). If your proposal requests money for travel and per diem expenses for advisory board members or consultants, be sure to explain why these people are essential to the success of the project.

Employee benefits differ with each organization. Budget items in this category might include retirement, social security, fringe benefits, unemployment taxes, and other payroll taxes. Usually these are computed by applying a certain fixed percentage against the salaries and wages of project staff. Ask your organization's business or finance staff to provide advice about the percentage to use and which types of positions to exempt. Check the funder's guidelines or RFP to determine whether or not you can include employee benefits in the budget. (See the Getting Funded website, www.gettingfunded-book.com, for more about accounting principles for grant proposals.)

> Sometimes, volunteer-led organizations are proud that their budgets don't include the cost of staff. But funders appreciate a project budget that reflects what it would cost the organization if it had to pay for staff work that is currently being done by volunteers, so they can grasp the true cost of doing business. To accurately represent the cost of volunteer hours, enter what it would cost to pay volunteers as if they were staff, and then indicate that the staff time is being contributed in kind.

Contract services: Contract services for a project will vary considerably from organization to organization. Services purchased on contract might include legal or financial help (such as bookkeeping or auditing); data management; computerized materials searches; statistical services; editing, photographic, or design services; printing and publishing services; and any other consultants or subcontractors.

Travel and per diem expenses: Costs associated with the travel and transportation of individuals connected with the project are generally presented in their own category. Some funders require that travel costs for project staff, consultants, and advisors be estimated separately. Funders may also require you to separate estimates of in-state costs from costs associated with regional, national, or international travel. Include in this category all per diem expenses (costs that are incurred on a daily basis, such as food, lodging, or parking), as well as the funds for air or ground transportation. Most funders allow costs for travel to a national professional meeting to be included in the proposal—especially if you plan to report on the progress or results of the project at that meeting. Figures 12.2 and 12.3 demonstrate one way to present these costs in a budget.

Facilities: The costs of buying, renting, and maintaining office space and other facilities necessary for a project may be assigned directly to the proposed project budget or reported as provided by the organization, either as indirect costs or as costs the organization offers to absorb. Note that if your organization plans any

FIGURE 12.2 SAMPLE TABLE USED TO PRESENT CONSULTANT FEES AND TRAVEL COSTS

NAME AND ADDRESS	SERVICE TO BE PERFORMED	CONSULTANT FEE			PER DIEM			TRAVEL	
		DAYS	RATE	TOTAL	DAYS	RATE	TOTAL	FROM/TO	TOTAL

FIGURE 12.3 SAMPLE TABLE USED TO PRESENT STAFF TRAVEL COSTS

NAME	DESTINATION	PURPOSE OF TRIP	TRAVEL		PER DIEM		
			NUMBER OF TRIPS	TRANSPORTA-TION COST	DAYS	RATE	TOTAL

renovation during the project, listing facilities costs as indirect costs may cause problems. Funds for indirect costs are usually released by the funder at the same rate that salaries and wages are paid out. For a twelve-month project, for example, only one-twelfth of the indirect costs are paid each month. Unless your organization can provide money from its own budget or other sources such as a bank loan up front, the renovation may need to be delayed several months to collect sufficient monies via indirect costs. You may want to consider including a direct cost line item for renovation or construction in your project budget.

Check all funder policies governing facilities. Some federal agencies pay a flat amount for rental space regardless of whether space is available at this rate in your area. Also, you can generally include in your project budget any costs connected with the use of facilities for field-based research, training, gatherings, and similar activities. If space for such activities is to be provided free of charge by your organization or collaborating agencies, you can estimate the cost of equivalent rent and include that in your budget as an in-kind match.

Equipment: Equipment includes items such as office desks, chairs, file systems, computer hardware and software, laboratory equipment, audiovisual equipment, and research equipment. List all equipment necessary for the project and indicate whether it will be leased, purchased, or donated to

If you are asking for funds for facility improvements or fixed assets (such as lights and sound equipment in a theater or a room outfitted with a one-way mirror for research or focus groups), be sure to let the funder know whether you own the property, as some funders are reluctant to invest in capital improvements for property the applicant organization does not own.

the project by your own organization or an external source. Carefully check the funder's policies on purchase versus rental of equipment as well as on who will claim ownership of purchased equipment at the end of the project. Be sure to include the cost of service contracts for the equipment.

Supplies and materials: Supplies and materials include all consumable office supplies, as well as costs connected with photocopying or purchasing other project materials.

Program-related expenses: This is a catch-all category for items necessary to the project that aren't really supplies or equipment. For example, an arts production may require costumes or music scores; an environmental education program may need topographic maps and specimens of flora and fauna; a children's counseling program may use dollhouses and stuffed animals. Make sure that the project description section (see Chapter 10) discusses how such items will be used.

Communications: Communications costs could include telephone costs (such as purchase and installation of equipment and phones, monthly and long distance service, and teleconferencing), videoconferencing, satellite hookups, cable access, Internet access, and so on. However, costs listed in the project budget must be essential to the project: A rural health delivery service and an urban after-school program will need different levels of communications services, for example.

Indirect Costs

Examples of indirect costs include an organization's central administration, legal services, financial services, and fundraising. Depreciation of buildings and equipment can also be counted as an indirect cost.

Most government agencies allocate a fixed amount to reimburse an organization for the project's access to such organizational resources. The amount is usually based on a fixed percent of the project's total budget. Normally, this percentage is negotiated annually between the organization and the government funder and remains the same for all projects funded by that agency.

Foundations and other nongovernment funders seldom pay indirect costs. When they do, they usually limit indirect costs to 15 percent of the project budget. When developing your budget for proposals to these types of funders, you'll want to identify items normally covered in indirect costs, such as rent, utilities, insurance, licenses, and permits, and translate them into direct costs.

Any major renovation of facilities, particularly for office space, should be justified by providing a comparison to the cost of renting such space. Funders are well aware that grants have been used on occasion to finance improvements that were not relevant to project activities. Some funders may insist that renovation be paid for out of the project's indirect costs. Others may require that the indirect cost rate be reduced to balance the direct cost request. This solution allows the renovation to be completed and paid for at the outset of the grant period.

Overhead and fees: As noted earlier, most funders recognize that there are a variety of services your organization provides that are difficult to cost out on a project-by-project basis. The term *cost out* refers to prorating how much of a line item is attributable to the project. The availability of such things as a modern laboratory, top-of-the-line computer equipment, specialized databases, and effective organizational leadership are important to the success of any project. Yet because these facilities and staff exist to serve the entire organization, it is almost impossible to determine a specific percentage of use that benefits a single program or project.

To reimburse organizations for these generally available items, federal sources have adopted the policy of paying an indirect cost—a flat amount determined as a percentage of all or part of the project budget. Regulations governing these policies change periodically, so make sure that your business office or finance staff can provide the latest version, available through Grants.gov. Usually this percentage is negotiated each year by the grantseeking organization's administrators and is simply applied to all proposals from that organization. In some cases, however, a funder may require a different indirect cost rate, may pay no indirect costs at all, or may require you to reduce the indirect cost rate as a method of cost-sharing.

You should always consult with your administrative, business, or finance staff to determine both the amount to include for indirect costs and the implications of that amount on other aspects of the budget.

In addition to overhead costs, some organizations request a fee to cover research and development activities that the organization conducts independent of any specific projects. Funders differ on whether they will honor this request. Finally, you will need to determine how to handle indirect costs or fees for any subcontractors involved in the project. Many funders will not cover requests for a second organization's overhead and will insist that this be paid out of the amount due the primary applicant.

Inflation rates: To protect yourself, make sure any multiyear budget includes calculations for yearly inflation rates. This is best done by using an estimated formula in an Excel spreadsheet. Figure 12.7 offers an example of a multiyear budget.

Per-participant cost: Many funders like to see the per-participant cost of a project and how it was calculated. This information is usually placed as a footnote to the budget and is also included in the budget narrative. If the per-participant cost is particularly high, be sure to include an explanation and rationale.

Participant costs can be calculated in two ways:

- Divide the total costs of the project by the number of participants to be served.
- Divide the amount requested from the funder by the number of participants to be served.

Project information, when presented in the format of budgeted revenues and expenses, is a vital part of almost every grant proposal. The budget justification worksheets that follow in Figures 12.4 through 12.8 offer examples of different ways budget information might be presented.

Figure 12.4 presents budgeted expenses by cost centers—by where in the organization the funds are to be spent. This example shows funds spent by just two administrative cost centers: an advisory board and the project director. Other cost centers—organizational functions or departments that have expenses but do not generate revenue—could include research and development, marketing, or customer service. The entire budget would require many pages. Advantages of this model are that it groups together all planned expenditures for each cost center and makes certain no needs are overlooked. However, this model does not account for use of money over time, and it does not organize expenditures by the categories required on most proposal budget forms.

Figure 12.5 is an example of a budget justification by activity. This example shows the costs associated with two of the activities involved in implementing a project. Again, the budget for the entire proposal would require many pages. This model has the advantage of tying specific costs to specific activities, and it allows

FIGURE 12.4 SAMPLE BUDGET JUSTIFICATION WORKSHEET BY COST CENTER

COST CENTER/ ITEM	AMOUNT	REQUESTED FROM FUNDING SOURCES	LOCAL	EXPLANATION	BUDGET NARRATIVE
ADMINISTRATION					
Advisory Board					
Salary	$3,000	-0-	$3,000	5 members x $50 each for 12 meetings	page 21, 22
Supplies	$100	$100	-0-	$20 each	page 22
Telephone					
(rental)	-0-	-0-	-0-		
(long distance)	$600	$600	-0-	$10 each for 12 months	
Travel					
(in state)	$1,800	$1,800	-0-	$30/day x 5 members x 12 meetings	page 23
(out-of-state)	$1,200	$1,200	-0-	$600 for 2 members to attend national meeting	
SUBTOTAL	$6,700	$3,700	$3,000		
PROJECT DIRECTOR					
Salary	$24,000	$24,000	-0-	$2,000 x 12 months	page 15, 17, 20
Benefits	$2,400	$2,400	-0-	Institutional rate is 10% of salary	page 20
Supplies	$480	$480	-0-	Agency requires $40/ person per month	page 17, 25
Postage	$240	$240	-0-	Agency requires $20/ person per month	page 17
Telephone					
(rental)	$240	$240	-0-	1 device x $20 x 12 months	page 17
(long-distance)	$1,200	$1,200	-0-	$100/month x 12	page 15, 25, 30
SUBTOTAL	$28,560	$28,560	-0-		

FIGURE 12.5 SAMPLE BUDGET JUSTIFICATION WORKSHEET BY ACTIVITY

ACTIVITY	DATES	ITEM	AMOUNT	EXPLANATION	BUDGET NARRATIVE
Start-up	1/1–2/15	Salaries & wages	$5,000	Director–$3,000 (45 days) Assistant–$2,000 (45 days)	Pages 13–17
		Benefits	$1,000	Calculated at 20%	
		Supplies/materials	$300	$150 each	
		Travel/transportation	$600	$200 in-state, $400 other	
		Postage/shipping	$100	$50 each	
		Rent/comm./utilities	$200	$100 each	
		Other services	$500	Consultants (5 x $100)	
Literature search	2/15–4/1	Salaries & wages	$3,000	2 Research Associates x $1,500 each	Page 20
		Benefits	$600	Calculated at 20%	
		Supplies/materials	$1,000	Acquire library	
		Travel/transportation	-0-		
		Postage/shipping	$100	$50 each	
		Rent/comm./utilities	$200	$100 each	
		Other services	$600	Computer searches (6 x $100)	

	BUDGET BY TIME PERIOD				TOTAL BUDGET
Start Date:					
End Date:					TOTAL BUDGET
DIRECT COSTS					
Personnel Costs					
Salaries					
Benefits					
Consultant claims					
Other personnel					
Travel & Transportation					
Staff travel					
Consultants' travel					
Other travel					
Postage & Shipping					
Rent, comm. & utilities					
Facility rental					
Equipment rental					
Telephone					
Utilities					
Printing & Duplication					
Printing					
Duplication					
Other Services					
Data processing					
Subcontracts					
Conference expenses					
Other services					
Supplies & Materials					
Office supplies					
Printed materials					
Other supplies					
TOTAL DIRECT COSTS					
Indirect cost @ ___%					
TOTAL COSTS					
Fee @ ___%					
TOTAL COSTS AND FEES					

for estimation of expenditures over time. However, it also has the disadvantage of not organizing the expenditures in the way requested in most proposal budget forms. For example, all salaries and wages for all activities would need to be totaled in order to figure out the type of information usually requested in the final proposal.

Figure 12.6 is a blank sample of a budget justification worksheet by time period and category. An advantage of this model is that it can collect costs by the categories frequently found in proposal budget forms. It also allows cost estimates by major time period, which is usually requested by federal agencies. However, it does not show how the sums included in each category were computed, nor are the costs tied to specific activities. The form could be made more useful if it included a reference to the location in the narrative where justification can be found. The form could also be more useful if it were completed separately for major cost centers (such as administration, training, materials, development, and evaluation).

> The grantseeking organization should contribute all the support it possibly can. If not through dollars, then through facilities, materials, labor, volunteers, or whatever else is relevant to the project. It should be clear to funders that the organization is participating fully.

Budget Development Step 2: Identify Potential Revenue

Your project budget needs to include projections for revenue as well as expenses. While few projects will have income from all these types of sources, the revenue section of your proposed budget could include the following:

Public funders: Federal, state, county, borough, and municipal agencies are examples of public funders. See Chapter 4 for information about public funders.

Private funders: Private funders include foundations, corporations, and organizations (see Chapter 4). Revenue from corporations should be itemized by type (such as event sponsorship, employer matching of employee gifts, in-kind contributions, and corporate cash contributions). Corporate foundation gifts can be listed under either category.

Individuals: Itemize revenue from individual donors by the methods your organization will use to solicit the gifts (such as mail, phone, workplace campaigns, web-based efforts, events, and personal solicitations). Your list of expected revenue from individual donations will carry more weight with funders if you name the types of individuals you intend to approach (such as family members of those served; former board, staff, volunteers, clients, or students; or members of organizations with similar missions).

Earned income: Earned income should be itemized by the ways the income was generated, such as the sale of products associated with the grant (reports, manuals, curricula, or videos) or fees for project-related services (client fees or conference or workshop registrations).

Contracts: Government funders contract with organizations to provide services they don't choose to offer themselves, such as counseling for ex-offenders or home weatherization for the elderly.

Interest income: Reports of interest income should indicate the source (such as, prior endowment gifts, reserves, or a legal settlement).

Other Support

Funders want to know who else is supporting your project for a number of reasons:

- They want to see that your organization has made a commitment of some kind, whether in cash or in kind.
- They want to know that others deem your work important, especially other grantmakers whom they view as obvious sponsors of such work.
- They want to make sure that the other collaborators in the work are entities with whom they want to be associated.
- They want to know whether your support is predominantly from government, foundation, or corporate funders.
- They want to see the level to which other funders have committed to partner in the work.
- They want to see whether they are being asked early or late in your grantseeking process.

Make sure your budget clearly indicates which sources have committed, which have been approached, and which you intend to approach. But don't ever indicate that a funder has made a commitment without having something in writing. Funders check with one another, and if they discover you haven't been truthful, your proposal will be automatically rejected and the interaction will jeopardize your prospects for future funding.

Gifts In Kind

Some of the items you need to conduct your work may be goods or services you won't have to pay for. Perhaps you already have access to them within your organization, or perhaps they are being contributed as goods or services rather than as cash. These are **IN-KIND CONTRIBUTIONS**, or **GIFTS IN KIND**. Include these in your budget. It's in your best interest to highlight how much support you have garnered from in-kind contributions, as this means you can do the work for less than the same work might cost another applicant.

Examples of in-kind contributions might include a survey company donating time to document the boundaries of the property an environmental organization is trying to preserve, or a corporation that has a print shop in its headquarters donating all the printed materials for a nonprofit organization's workshop or conference. Donated office space or event space, food or beverages, and technology hardware and software are other examples of in-kind contributions, as are the services of a graphic designer, architect, shipper, planner, trainer, or evaluator.

If entire line items on the budget are being contributed, put the in-kind items in bold or italics. If only part of a category or line item is being funded through in-kind contributions, create two budget columns: one listing total program costs for each

If you've already garnered support from one commercial bank or phone company, other similar companies may not want to fund the same project, as the company could be using its donation to your organization for marketing reasons, and being side-by-side with one of its competitors doesn't help. If a major polluter has already committed to fund you, a funder known as an environmental leader may not want to be affiliated with the project—or vice versa.

If one of your committed funders has offered $5,000 when it usually offers $50,000 grants, it may be a signal to other funders that your project didn't receive the full endorsement of your committed funder.

The corporate contributions manager at a bank once received a letter from a grantseeker that stated that a rival bank had offered to give $5,000 to their organization if this bank agreed to do the same. Thinking this sounded fishy, the contributions manager phoned his colleague at the other bank, only to discover that she had gotten the same letter that day, about his bank. Both managers agreed they would never fund that organization again.

item, and the other indicating how much of the costs will be contributed in-kind.

Some funders enjoy being bellwethers at the front end of a project and some like to make the culminating gift.

Valuing in-kind contributions is tricky. The best measure is the fair market value of the goods or services if you had to pay for them outright. If someone gives you a used item, value it as if you were buying it used, not new. The rule of thumb about valuing people's contributed time and services is this: If people are contributing skill in their field, such as lawyers contributing legal services, you record the value as the hourly rate times the number of hours. If the same people help you spread wood chips, then lawyers or no, calculate the value of their time at a standard rate per hour for that type of work.

Budget Development Step 3: Organize Budget Items

After you have established the project's total costs and the expected revenue from all sources, the next step is to organize the line items, which are the specific costs and income streams.

By Category

When arranging the line items in your budget, divide them into the broadest categories possible. This will give you more flexibility, as some funders will not allow you to move more than 10 percent of the total budget amount from one category to another, such as from training to travel.

By Time

If you seek funding for more than one year, funders will want to see how much you plan to spend each year of the project. They may match their payment schedule to your plan, or they may reimburse costs only as you incur them.

In your budget documents, display expenses on a year-by-year basis. If you propose to launch a new initiative, your costs may vary greatly from the first year (preparation) to the second year (launch) to the third year (maintenance). For example, before a church can house a new child care center in its basement, it will need to construct a fence, an outdoor play area, a stroller-accessible ramp, and sinks in each room. Some expenses will be incurred to open the center that may not recur for many years, such as developing curriculum, determining policies, hiring staff, marketing to families, setting up systems, and purchasing books and toys and furniture. But the second year the center is open, expenses may look more routine: staff salaries and benefits, supplies, snack food, communications with families, and replacement or repair of used items.

By Source

It's important for funders to know how much of the total project cost you anticipate funding yourself, how much you are asking for in your proposal, and how much you are seeking from other sources. This can be accomplished by creating four columns: total costs, your organization's contribution, your request of this funder, and funding from other sources. Funders will want to know who else is participating in the project, so whether you include a budget narrative (see "Write the Budget Narrative" later in this chapter) or just a footnote on the budget page itself, indicate who has already committed and for how much, as well as who you intend to approach and for how much.

Figure 12.7 is an example of a multiyear budget, in this case for a project that will run over three years. This model has the advantage of collecting costs by the types of categories frequently found in proposal budget forms. Because this model allows for cost estimates over several time periods, it can give more detailed explanations of how expenses change over time, such as inflation. A disadvantage of this type of budget presentation is that costs are not tied to specific activities, nor does it show how sums in each category were computed (though these could be explained in footnotes or other supporting documents).

Budget Development Step 4: Translate Your Data into Their Format

Budget formats may also vary depending on what each funder wants to know. As you develop your budget, collect all the information suggested by the worksheets in this chapter. Then, when deadlines approach, you will have the numbers you need to present in the requested arrangement. If you are submitting a budget online, be sure to make it into a PDF (Portable Document Format) file to keep your formatting intact during transmission.

Some funders will require you to transfer your budget into their own framework for easier comparison among all applicants. Your organization's budget may include items another organization does not, and vice versa, so funders will often dictate budget categories and insist that you squeeze your line items into their categories.

Identify and Obtain Required Documents

In addition to your proposed project budget, many funders will also ask for a copy of your organization's annual operating budget and its most recent audited financial statement. These funders are looking for clues about your organization's health and accountability. If you think some items in your financial documents may raise questions, put an asterisk next to them and include an explanatory note at the bottom of the page or in the budget narrative.

Operating Budget

Many funders' guidelines require both an operating budget and a project budget.

Your OPERATING BUDGET (also referred to as organizational budget) details how much money you think your organization will need to raise and spend in one fiscal year to do all of its work. It includes *all* your organization's expenses, everything from staff to maintenance to insurance to printing, and all your projected revenue, including grants, contracts, earned income, and contributed income. Your PROJECT BUDGET covers the anticipated income and expenses for the proposed project alone. The project budget is a subset of your operating budget.

Funders look to an organization's operating budget for hints of financial health or weakness. While funders understand that all budgets are just estimates, they ask for the organizational as well as the project budget because both offer signals about your organization's likelihood of succeeding if funded. Here are some of the things funders might look for in your operating budget:

- Diversified funding streams, which indicate that the organization is not dependent on any one source
- Decent salaries and benefits for staff, which tend to indicate low staff turnover
- Money being spent on the priorities stated in the organization's mission and goals
- Income equal to or greater than expenses
- Financial reserves, which indicate stability in the face of unanticipated shortfalls

FIGURE 12.7 SAMPLE MULTIYEAR BUDGET

EXPENSES	Year One				Year Two				Year Three			
	A	B	C	D	A	B	C	D	A	B	C	D
Personnel												
Salaries/Wages	$150,000	$30,000		$180,000	$157,500	$31,500		$189,000	$165,375	$33,075		$198,450
Benefits	$60,000	$12,000		$72,000	$63,000	$12,600		$75,600	$66,150	$13,230		$79,380
SUBTOTAL	$210,000	$42,000	-0-	$252,000	$220,500	$44,100	-0-	$264,600	$231,525	$46,305	-0-	$277,830
Other Expenses												
Consultant & Professional Fees		$15,000		$15,000		$5,000		$5,000				-0-
Travel	$5,000	$5,000		$10,000	$5,250	$2,000		$7,250	$5,512			$5,512
Equipment	$5,000	$5,000		$10,000	$5,250	$2,000		$7,250	$5,512			$5,512
Supplies	$2,000			$2,000	$2,100			$2,100	$2,205			$2,205
Training	$5,000	$3,000		$8,000	$5,250	$2,000		$7,250	$5,512	$1,000		$6,512
Print/Copies		$2,000		$2,000		$1,000		$1,000		$1,000		$1,000
Phone	$3,500			$3,500	$3,675			$3,675	$3,859			$3,859
Postage	$2,500	$500		$3,000	$2,625	$500		$3,125	$2,756	$500		$3,256
Rent/Utilities	$30,000			$30,000	$31,500			$31,500	$33,075			$33,075
Program-Specific Property Acquisition		$20,000	$20,000	$40,000								
In-kind Expenses	$13,000			$13,000	$13,650			$13,650	$14,333			$14,333
Other Expenses	$12,000			$12,000	$12,600			$12,600	$13,230			$13,230
SUBTOTAL	$78,000	$50,500	$20,000	$148,500	$81,900	$12,500	-0-	$94,400	$85,994	$2,500	-0-	$88,494
TOTAL PROJECT EXPENSES	$288,000	$92,500	$20,000	$400,500	$302,400	$56,600	-0-	$359,000	$317,519	$48,805	-0-	$366,324

A = Applicant Organization   B = Requested from this funder   C = Requested from other funders   D = Total

FIGURE 12.8 SAMPLE PROJECT BUDGET DRAWN FROM AN ORGANIZATIONAL BUDGET

ORGANIZATIONAL BUDGET				PROJECT BUDGET	
PERSONNEL	SALARY	BENEFITS	SUBTOTAL		NOTES
CEO	90,000	22,500	112,500		
CFO	60,000	15,000	75,000		
Development Director	60,000	15,000	75,000		
Program Director	55,000	13,750	68,750	34,375	50% of full-time salary
Program Director	55,000	13,750	68,750		
Program Director	55,000	13,750	68,750		
Education Director	45,000	11,250	56,250	14,063	25% of full-time salary
Support staff (3)	80,000	20,000	100,000	16,000	16% of support staff salaries
			625,000	**64,438**	
OPERATING					
Supplies			30,000	3,093	
Communications			14,000	1,443	project operating costs*
Staff parking			4,000	412	
			48,000	**4,948**	
BUILDING					
Rent	4,500 per mo.		54,000	5,567	project building costs**
Maintenance	450 per mo.		5,400	557	
			59,400	**6,124**	
MARKETING/COMMUNICATION					
Promotional materials			25,000	5,000	Cost of 1 publication
Printing			15,000	3,000	(out of 5)
Postage			35,000	7,000	
Website maintenance			4,000	800	
			79,000	**15,800**	
FUNDRAISING					
Printing			15,000		
Direct event costs			20,000	20,000	100% of event proceeds
Postage/Mailing			3,500		benefit project
			38,500	**20,000**	
TOTAL EXPENSES			**849,900**	**111,310**	

* Project operating costs = (organizational operating costs) multiplied by ((project personnel costs) divided by (organizational personnel costs))

** Project building costs = (organizational building costs) multiplied by ((project personnel costs) divided by (organizational personnel costs))

When reviewers compare your project budget to your organization's operating budget, they want to see what percentage of the organization's annual budget is attributed to this project. They want to see whether you have dedicated a portion of the lead staff person's time to oversight of this project, and what portion of other administrative staff, office space, and consumable supplies costs you have allocated to this project. They are looking to see if your organization has allocated any of its ongoing resources to the project or if you're asking for all project costs to be covered by outside sources. And they want to see if they're the only ones being asked to fund the project, or if you're projecting support from multiple sources.

Figure 12.8 shows how a project budget can be "carved out" of an organizational budget. An advantage of this type of presentation is that it gives a reviewer perspective on how the project fits into the organization as a whole. This example presents some details in the notes about how costs were derived. A disadvantage of this model is that it does not show the use of money over time, nor does it tie project costs to specific activities.

The checklist in Figure 12.9 can help you review your organization's operating budget the way a funder would and prepare for any questions that might arise.

Diverse Revenue Streams

❑ Is there a healthy balance of types of income?

Fundraising

❑ Is the cost of fundraising included as a line item in the organization's operating budget? Funders know it costs money to raise money, even if it's being done by volunteers.

Human Resources

❑ Does the organization take good care of its people, which affects turnover and effectiveness?

❑ Do the salaries and benefits reflect the rest of the community or field?

❑ Is professional development (e.g., training, conferences) part of the budget?

❑ Does the organization pay for memberships in professional associations or subscriptions to professional journals for staff?

❑ Does the organization spend enough money on retreats, celebrations, and appreciation for board, staff, and volunteers?

Liquidity

❑ How much of the fund balance is cash or easily converted to cash?

❑ How much is restricted funds or restricted assets?

Reserves

❑ Has the organization prepared for unanticipated events by raising and holding part of a year's budget in reserve?

❑ Is the organization poised to survive the financial effects of a natural disaster, accident, economic downturn, sudden loss of government funding, or unexpected capital repairs?

❑ Is the organization in a position to seize an opportunity (e.g., to buy its building, absorb another organization, or respond to an emerging new constituency) if the opportunity presents itself?

Deficits

❑ If the current year's budget predicts a deficit, what were the circumstances that led to it, and does the organization have a plan for overcoming it in the following year?

Sustainability

❑ Are the growth patterns healthy and sustainable, or are there huge influxes of new staff or programming?

From the Funder's Corner

What are some tools that will help you demonstrate to a funder that you've got your act together? First, have an up-to-date cash flow budget. There are several models around to use. Basically, you need to show how your expenses flow, month-by-month over the next few years, and how you estimate resources will come in.

Second, how does this budget, both resources and expenditures, relate to your focus on the key activities that promote your mission? As funders and fund seekers do the funding dance sometimes the core activities that support mission get lost.
—Ken Ristine

Audited Financial Statement

Funders often require an organization's most recent AUDITED FINANCIAL STATEMENT. This document is the result of an external professional review of the organization's finances and financial health. It often discloses information not clear from the budget, thereby answering questions about why and how the organization has made decisions. If your organization hasn't had an official audit and the cost of one will be prohibitive, ask the funder if you may substitute a less expensive and less exhaustive process, such as a COMPILATION or a REVIEW, conducted by an external financial professional.

Write the Budget Narrative

While reviewers can tell a lot about your organization and your project by looking at your budgets, a little explanation can also help avoid misinterpretation. So some funders will request a budget narrative to accompany your figures and columns. In fact, it's a good idea to prepare a BUDGET NARRATIVE for internal use whether or not it's required by the funder you approach.

A budget narrative helps anyone reading your numeric budgets understand, in words, what the numbers mean, how you arrived at them, and any implications that arise. Here are some of the ways a budget narrative might help funders understand your budget:

- **How you calculated the costs of an item.** The budget item will show a total sum, but the narrative can explain that a lump sum represents a unit cost of *X* multiplied by *Y* items needed, or that a consultant you plan to hire for 10 hours charges $200 per hour, or that your per diem rate of *X* dollars per day is dictated by your parent organization.
- **How you determined the price for a particular item.** Perhaps you got three bids for a piece of equipment, and the amount listed in the budget is the average of those three bids.
- **How you got into a particular situation.** If your budget reflects a shortfall one year, your budget narrative can explain what changed that year to cause the shortfall, whether it was a disaster, a stock market crash, a change in fundraising staff, or just bad planning.
- **How you intend to rectify a negative situation.** If your budget shows a negative balance for the prior year, your budget narrative can explain how you plan to recover that amount in the coming year's budget and how you intend to avoid similar situations in the future.
- **Why one line item might increase dramatically from one year to the next.** Perhaps your projected budget for two years from now indicates a leap in a particular type of support. Explain in the budget narrative your reasons for thinking that will happen. That way the funder can see that you are hiring staff to focus on revenue from corporations or foundations, or expect to start earning income from newly instituted fees for service. This is your chance to prove that the projected increase in income is not just wishful thinking.
- **How you justify deviations from one year to the next.** Your budget can only show the expected numbers for each year. If you're an arts organization that puts on a blockbuster every other year, you know from experience that the revenue from the well-known performance will subsidize a riskier offering the next year, and you can explain that in the budget narrative. Alternatively, you can explain that expenses, and your need for funding, are higher in the years

you take a show on tour, because facility fees are higher when you rent than when you produce a show in your own space.

To get ready to write your budget narrative, note all the places in your budget where someone unfamiliar with your project might have a question about the meaning of the numbers or how you calculated them. Then use your budget justification worksheets (see Figures 12.4–12.8) and your own understanding of the budgeting process to craft a descriptive narrative account that eliminates confusion or concerns.

Answer Budget-Related Questions

Many funders' grant applications ask these two budget-related questions:

- What will you do if we are unable to grant the entire amount you request?
- How will you continue the work after the money we award runs out?

The Question of a Reduced Award

Be prepared to answer this often-posed question: "What will you do if we are unable to grant the entire amount requested?" There are several good answers to this question, and only your organization can determine which is best for you.

- **Reduce the scope of the project.** Perhaps you can interview or serve fewer people. Perhaps the project's geographic range could be reduced, or the length of time could be shortened. Maybe you don't really need the extra support staff or that fancy computer component. Be clear about what constitutes a suitable fallback position, or decision makers won't know what would be a helpful amount to offer if they can't award the full request. For example, if they can't give you $50,000, they might still be able to fund you if they knew you could make the project work with $47,000.
- **Segment or sequence the project.** Identify which components could be done later, and offer to do the work in stages.
- **Look for other funders.** Seeking additional funders shows a grantmaker that you fully intend to carry out your project whether they fund it or not, and that you will continue to search for support until you get what you need. This strategy does not make your request of *this* funder look dispensable. Rather, it makes you look both determined and confident that someone will find your work valuable.
- **Scrap the project.** Stating that you will cancel the project without full funding signals that the amount you suggest is indeed exactly what it will take to implement the proposal, and that the project must remain intact, exactly as described, or it isn't worth doing.

The Question of Future Funding

Most funders' applications ask a specific question about how your organization intends to sustain the funded program or project after the requested grant money runs out. You'll have to strategize with your colleagues what the most appropriate options are for your organization and this particular project. The potential revenue sources discussed in this chapter under "Budget Development Step 2: Identify Total Revenue" are good options to choose from.

If you suggest that once the prospective funder has put its seal of approval on the project, other grantmakers will follow suit, be sure to indicate what types of funders you intend to approach (see the types of funders listed in Chapter 4, or name specific funders you've already decided to approach). This will assure the funder that you have thought about what funding sources might be most suitable. If you suggest that you will reach out to individuals, be sure to indicate specific groups of people you will approach. This shows the funder that you have a plan. Avoid saying "We'll ask the community to fund this once the grant is over" without adding details that show you've thought your strategy through.

Tips from Funders

Experienced grantmakers offer the following budget pointers:

- Develop the budget for a proposal only after the proposed program has been carefully planned and all activities detailed.
- Devote the same care and deliberation to the budget as you devote to other parts of the proposal. Individuals experienced with budgeting can help, but decisions on time and cost can be made only by someone who thoroughly understands how the project is intended to work.
- Write a budget that can stand alone and accurately tell the whole story.
- Be aware of all pertinent financial regulations, those of your own organization and those of the funder.
- Keep a record of how you calculated all budget items (e.g., spreadsheets or worksheets used to develop the budget) so you can answer questions during review, negotiation, or project operation.
- Thoroughly document all budgeted expenses included in the application, either in the budget narrative or in appendixes.
- Make sure the items in your budget reflect the narrative text. Items in the budget that are not explained in the body of the proposal raise doubts in the minds of reviewers.
- Make sure your expense and revenue columns add up to the same total!
- Make sure the project budget is sufficient to perform the tasks described in the project description.
- Check to make sure that all budget items reflect your organization's values and are not at cross-purposes with the funder's goals. For example, if you say you care deeply about workers' rights, don't ask for funding for a conference held in a nonunion hotel. If the funder is intent on decreasing its carbon footprint, don't ask for things that use excessive fossil fuels.
- Include estimates from vendors if you request funds for capital expenditures, and make sure they aren't all the most expensive vendors. Funders want to know you sought out the best value for their dollars.
- Don't ask for more than you actually need. For example, don't ask for a $30,000 van if renting one for the occasions you need it during the year would cost only $5,000.

> A reviewer at a foundation was inclined to recommend funding a request regarding an environmental education program for young students until he got to the budget and saw very little in the line of curriculum and supplies, but a large line item for a new RV for the instructor, which hadn't been mentioned in the narrative!

Summary

The budget plays a critical role in the proposal: it tells the story of your project in numbers. Since the budget is often viewed independently, as a snapshot of the whole proposal, it must tell the same story as the narrative and serve as a summary of the entire project on its own. It must be free from inflated or unrealistic costs as reviewers can spot both.

When preparing your budget, hold conversations with everyone involved in the project to avoid hidden costs, and share budget worksheets with financial staff to make sure there are no negative implications from what you propose. Put your numbers in the funder's format, if requested, and double-check all your numbers to make sure revenue and expenses arrive at the same totals.

Budgets for public and private funders can vary greatly; public funders generally want much more detail. Keep your budget justification worksheets, audits, and other working documents ready to show funders who want a more comprehensive view of your financial landscape.

From the Funder's Corner

Frequent funder frustrations regarding budgets are:

- Lack of context: What the project will accomplish; what resources it takes to reach those goals; as well as time frame and scope of project
- Numbers don't match: Arithmetic; counting the same number twice or failing to include the cost; counting off-budget items
- Strange budget entries: Account names/groupings; questionable amounts, e.g., 10 percent of budget in miscellaneous.

—Ken Ristine

Key Terms

AUDIT: A formal examination of an organization's financial accounts, conducted by an external professional, to ensure the organization is managing its finances in accordance with generally accepted accounting practices (GAAP). An audit may also include an examination of the organization's compliance with applicable terms, laws, and regulations.

AUDITED FINANCIAL STATEMENT: A review and verification of an organization's financial statements by an accountant, according to generally accepted accounting principles (GAAP). Audited financial statements can assure funders that an organization's financial information is presented fairly.

AWARD: Financial or other assistance to accomplish a purpose. Awards include grants, contracts, and other agreements that provide money, or property in lieu of money, to eligible recipients.

BUDGET: A financial plan that estimates your income and expenses for a specific period of time (see also BUDGET PERIOD). Budgets may describe project or program activities or your entire organization's activities, and are primarily used to estimate and compare against actual financial results.

BUDGET JUSTIFICATION: An expanded version of your budget that clarifies for reviewers how the figures in the budget were calculated.

BUDGET NARRATIVE: A written explanation, in words, that helps anyone reading your numeric budgets understand what the numbers mean, how you arrived at them, and any implications that arise.

BUDGET PERIOD or **OPERATING PERIOD:** The interval of time, usually twelve months, into which the project period is divided for budgetary and funding purposes.

COMPILATION: A document created by an external financial professional that verifies the accuracy of an organization's financial information. Compilation and review processes are less rigorous than audits and may not reveal deeper problems.

COST-PLUS-FIXED-FEE CONTRACT: An award in which a funder provides reimbursement of allowable costs accrued by the grantee plus a predetermined fee agreed on by both parties (as opposed to a percentage of accrued costs). Because the fee is fixed, the funder is assured it will not swell.

COST-REIMBURSEMENT AWARD: An award in which the organization pays the full costs of the project as they are incurred, and the funder reimburses the organization based on receipts submitted.

COST-SHARING CONTRACT: An agreement by which part of the cost of a funded project is borne by the organization receiving the funds.

DIRECT COSTS: Costs directly associated with program delivery, research, or construction. General categories include, but are not limited to, salaries and wages, fringe benefits, supplies, travel, equipment, communication, and outside contractual services.

EMPLOYEE BENEFITS or **FRINGE BENEFITS:** Nonwage remuneration paid for by an individual's employer. Examples include FICA contributions, workers' compensation, tax withholding, and health insurance.

FEDERATED CAMPAIGN: A community-wide fundraising campaign, such as United Way, in which participants have the opportunity to support multiple nonprofits with one gift.

FISCAL YEAR: Any twelve-month period for which annual accounts are kept. The fiscal year for most universities is July 1 through June 30. The federal fiscal year is October 1 to September 30.

FIXED-PRICE CONTRACT: An award in which the grantseeker agrees to do the work for a specified amount of money, regardless of the time and cash actually spent.

FTE: Used to describe a staff position, it stands for full-time equivalent. For example, two half-time employees represent one FTE.

INDIRECT COSTS or **OPERATING COSTS** or **OVERHEAD** or **ADMINISTRATIVE COSTS:** The costs of administering the organization as a whole, so that the organization is in a position to implement the project. Utilities, general administrative expenses, and depreciation of equipment and facilities are some examples of indirect costs.

IN-KIND CONTRIBUTION or **GIFT IN KIND:** A nonmonetary donation of goods or services instead of dollars. Examples include volunteer time, donated space or transportation, or donations of goods, such as a copy machine, or services, such as the pro bono services of graphic designers.

LINE ITEM: A unit of information in a budget, shown on a separate line of its own.

OPERATING BUDGET: A budget that describes all the money your organization will raise and spend in one fiscal year, including all expenses, from staff to maintenance to insurance to printing, and all revenue, from grants and contracts to earned and contributed income.

PROJECT BUDGET: A budget that describes the income and expenses for your proposed project alone.

TOTAL PROJECT COSTS: The total direct and indirect costs your organization incurs to carry out a project.

13 ESTABLISHING YOUR QUALIFICATIONS

This chapter discusses how to assure funders that your organization has the experience, the people, and the systems in place to successfully implement the plans and projects you propose.

Grantmakers want assurances that if they fund a proposal, they can count on the recipient organizations to follow through on their promises. You can demonstrate evidence of your organization's capability and credibility in several different sections of your proposal, including organizational background (if funders ask for this section), project description, and qualifications. Wherever you put it, include sufficient detail to help the funder's reviewer or review panel understand your competitive advantage: the reason your organization, compared to others, is in an excellent position to tackle this problem.

Highlight Organizational Strengths

To highlight your organization's qualifications, include this information:

- How your organization's history, mission, and prior experience uniquely qualify it to address this problem or be selected for this project.
- What staff, whether permanent, temporary, or consulting, will be needed for the project; in what roles; and what relevant experience and professional backgrounds they have. If not all staff have yet been chosen, describe your planned selection process.
- What services or activities, if any, will be subcontracted, why, and to whom. Include the criteria used to choose the subcontractors, or the process you will use to select those not yet identified.
- What facilities and equipment will be needed for the project. Include those already possessed by the organization together with your plans for securing the remainder.
- What organizational relationships, e.g., advisory bodies, collaborators, elected officials, vendors, or consortium members, will enhance the project.
- What level of belief in the project's importance has been demonstrated by other community stakeholders, e.g., other funders, contributors of in-kind goods or services, volunteers, and endorsers. Include proof of funding and letters of endorsement.

- What internal systems are in place for administering the funds, once granted.
- How unique or special administrative issues will be resolved, e.g., decisions on copyright, patent, or ownership of items produced or purchased with grant funds.

History and Accomplishments

Most funders like to know about an organization's history and track record. However, just having been around a long time does not necessarily make your organization qualified to manage the proposed project, so be sure to include some distinctions along with your history. Any of the following might be a useful distinction to include:

- **Origins:** Perhaps your organization emerged from a unique set of circumstances that make it distinct from others. Perhaps it grew out of an incident, such as a pipeline explosion, the cruel killing of an animal, or the death of a child to drunk driving or anorexia. Perhaps all the founders had family members with the same health or mental health challenge, or two nonprofits merged, or state legislation called for the organization's creation.
- **Experience:** Perhaps your organization has tried related projects in the past, whether successful or not, that taught you lessons about how to improve your efforts.
- **Support:** Perhaps you've received financial support from multiple types of sources, in-kind contributions of goods or services, or significant commitments of time or advice from volunteers or experts.
- **Partnerships:** Perhaps your organization has invested the time necessary to build cooperative relationships with other organizations, agencies, or community groups.
- **Reputation:** Perhaps your organization has gained the respect of certain colleagues and associates, lawmakers, or the media.

Leadership

The importance of your organization's leadership may vary from one funder to the next. Long-established funders may prefer to fund organizations with a solid history and long list of accomplishments, organizations run by longtime staff and supported by carefully built alliances. But newer foundations, especially those created or led by entrepreneurs, may be more impressed by a founder with a vision and a handful of well-placed board members. A giving circle may put more value on a nonprofit organization's governance model than its history, or may be more impressed by a board made up of those being served than by a board of wealthy civic leaders. Federal funders of research grants may want to know only who the principal investigator is. The more you know about the funder and the funder's values, the easier it will be to establish credibility in your proposal.

Some funders ask pointed questions about an organization's leaders. Questions might include the following:

- Have they crafted a long-range or strategic plan for the organization?
- Were they instrumental in determining that this project was an organizational priority?
- Are they aware that this funding request is being submitted?
- Does the board, for a nonprofit, reflect the community or constituency served by the organization?

- How often does the board meet, and what percentage of members attend those meetings?
- Are board members genuinely engaged in the organization's governance?

Some funders insist that for an organization to qualify for funding, every board member must be a financial contributor. Many funders have realized that the questions they pose in their grant application forms or RFPs help drive organizations' behavior. By requiring organizations to jump through certain hoops to receive support, these funders help grantseeking organizations strengthen their infrastructure at both the organization and the project level. The effort you expend to adequately answer these questions about leadership is likely to help make your organization more competitive and more qualified for funding from all types of supporters.

Personnel

Review the funder's instructions to see what information is requested about personnel. Usually, these instructions are fairly general. If so, the specific Do's and Don'ts listed below may help.

- **Do** include the title, responsibilities, and percentage of time assigned to the project for each type of staff person. Sometimes this information can best be displayed in a table or organization chart.
- **Do** provide names and biographical sketches for all key staff. Proposals for large or complex projects or for research funding should include a full biography for the project director or principal investigator, including prior research and publications.
- **Do** tailor the biographies of key staff to emphasize experiences relevant to this project.
- **Do** briefly describe the selection process and criteria for key project positions that have not yet been filled.
- **Do** include ample justification for the use of consultants. Indicate the number of consultants and their responsibilities, and explain why these roles will not be filled through regular staff appointments. Include a background sketch for consultants who have already been identified.
- **Do** include, or be prepared to provide, letters agreeing to participation from any consultants or significant advisors mentioned by name in the proposal.
- **Do** mention the source of other compensation for key staff who will not be assigned full time to the project. Funders are wary of projects headed by part-time staff whose other sources of support are unknown.
- **Do** give a brief overview of the organizational and management structure of the project.
- **Do** include a description of any advisory bodies and the roles of their members.
- **Don't** include the names of well-known experts in the field and indicate that "they will be asked to participate once the project is funded."
- **Don't** pad biographies by referring to a "manuscript in progress."
- **Don't** request salaries for project directors that, when added to their other sources of compensation, total more than 100 percent of their salaries, unless you make this clear and explain it in the proposal. Most federal agencies simply do not allow this. Federal agencies demand documentation of other sources of income for key project staff, and increasingly, private foundations and corporations are also asking for written income verification.

- **Don't** propose inflated salaries for upper-echelon staff. The IRS Form 990, which itemizes your organization's current salary levels, is public information, accessible online for funders to check.

Infrastructure

Funders check to see that your organization is structurally able to support the proposed work. Things that might distinguish a strong organization from a less competitive one include the following:

Policies and procedures: Funders look for organizations that are prepared for issues that emerge in the middle of a project. Strong organizations have created standard processes for resolving such issues or have defined criteria, standards, or best practices that will help. You can demonstrate organizational strength if your organization has determined in advance what the chain of command is in case of an emergency, including who will speak to the press if the project makes the news, or how the project will proceed in the event of a natural or human disaster such as fire, theft, or embezzlement of funds.

Accounting systems: Funders look favorably on organizations that can manage money well. Nonprofits new to grantseeking may be unprepared to account for grant funds separately from other funds, or may not have data management systems sophisticated enough to track expenditures as precisely as a funder would wish. To strengthen your proposal, you can describe the capabilities of your current system, including the most recent upgrades.

Evaluation systems: You will be more competitive if you can prove that your proposed process for gathering statistical results has been agreed to by all parties who must participate, and that the proposed systems are feasible and cost-effective. Funders know that sometimes, especially among organizations, the people delivering the project's services may be reluctant to measure their work.

Communications systems: Funders appreciate knowing there is a written plan for disseminating periodic reports, with anticipated dates, expected information, and methods for communicating (e.g., phone, mail, or email). Indicating where else your organization plans to disseminate reports, such as to collaborators, other funders, elected officials, appropriate agencies, appropriate media, or professional associations, also shows forethought.

Prior work: One way to demonstrate capability to a funder is to show prior success. An organization that has curriculum developed or collaborators in place will be more appealing than one that's starting from scratch. If your organization is seeking grant money to expand a current program, show the funder how solid the current program is. If you seek support to expand your prevention education program from regional to national, let the funder know you've already developed materials and a geographic distribution map with contacts in your major markets.

With the emergence of several new, large private foundations in recent years, some nonprofits, lured by the promise of enormous grant awards, have discovered that they were structurally ill-equipped to absorb the large gifts they received. Trying to administer programs that suddenly trebled the size of their organizations resulted in unhealthy growth. They hired more staff than they could support with the current management, or didn't have systems in place to account for the money in a seamless way. When the grant funds ran out, they had to let go of staff, resulting in too much empty office space and the elimination of programs people had grown to count on.

Organizations must have a firm foundation beneath them to sustain the culture shift that is likely to accompany a major new program or project, so if your organization is stable, let the funder know. For more about strengthening your organization to be competitive among other grantseekers and successful at managing its work, see Chapter 1 and the further resources provided both at the back of this book and at the Getting Funded website, www.gettingfundedbook.com.

Facilities and Equipment

Provide in your proposal an adequate description of the facilities and major equipment needed for the project, identifying what your organization already has and what it is requesting funds to purchase, rent, or renovate. Funders prefer to see that an organization is, wherever possible, trying to build on existing facilities. Otherwise, the funder may have concerns about the time and cost that may be involved with arranging for the necessary facilities and equipment.

Other Assets

Whenever possible, emphasize in the qualifications section any unusual or outstanding facilities or equipment your organization already has, such as the following examples:

- Particularly well-equipped laboratories
- A large number of or specialized types of computers
- A large library or unusual materials collections
- Sophisticated or hard-to-secure laboratory equipment
- Outstanding materials production capabilities
- Advisory or consultative services, e.g., university-based evaluators or a survey research center
- Ready access to other organizations with unusual capabilities
- Research resources accessible to project staff

If facilities or equipment from other organizations are essential elements of the proposal, provide documentation that these will be made available.

And if any unusual facilities or equipment are to be used in the project, provide sufficient information to justify why they are being tried. Funders will want to know how such equipment will be developed and evaluated and what provisions will be made for alternatives should they turn out to be necessary to complete the project.

Address Weaknesses in Qualifications

Many proposals must find a way to demonstrate that the organization is capable and competitive while admitting to weaknesses in project design. Two common difficulties are addressed here.

Unfilled Project Leadership Positions

Most organizations must follow some type of open competition process when hiring staff for project positions, often in order to meet nondiscrimination and transparency requirements. This takes time. What to do if a funder's application requests that you enclose résumés for all project staff, when they haven't even been hired yet?

There are several ways that this problem has been handled by other grantseekers. The following examples describe some options. However, remember that you should first seek the advice of your human resources staff whenever you're planning a project that will involve hiring.

Example 1: A project director or principal investigator can be named from among those staff members in the organization who will be expected to have some responsibility for the funded project anyway. Most projects are designed with the expectation that a senior member of the organization's faculty or staff will provide informal supervision, even though this person's salary will not be charged to the project budget. By formally recognizing this already-presumed responsibility in your proposal or application, and including a percentage of the person's time in the salary requests, you can avoid the problem of having to submit a proposal that includes none of the names or backgrounds of key project staff. You may also choose to include a second leadership position, such as a co-director, assistant director, or senior research or development associate, to be hired to share administrative duties once the funds are committed.

Example 2: An existing staff member can be designated as a temporary or acting project director. You can present that person as the one responsible for the project until staff are found who meet the qualifications listed in the proposal. In some cases, the funder may want to approve your organization's selection of permanent project director before the project continues past this initial phase. The person designated acting project director may, at a later point, move to another position within the project or may be designated as the person in the organization to whom the permanent project director will report. In either case, the résumé and experience of this existing staff member can be included in the proposal to demonstrate project staff capability.

Example 3: If you know whom you wish to hire, but you cannot hire this person until funds are released upon approval of your project, make sure this is clearly specified in your proposal. Also provide evidence that the individual in question is willing to accept the position if the funds are received. It is also acceptable to employ someone as a consultant while writing a proposal to make certain that he or she will be satisfied with the role and responsibilities once an award is made.

These same approaches may be adapted to filling project positions other than that of the director. It's a good idea when possible, however, to identify as many of the project staff as possible prior to submitting your proposal. Not only will the funder consider it a plus if your project will not be delayed by hiring procedures, but demonstrating the existing capability and the prior experience in the field that is already available to your organization is also an important selling point.

Early Career Project Leaders

Some grantseekers know in advance that the project director's age, status in the organization, or lack of prior project management experience may place a proposal at a disadvantage. What can be done to increase your project's competitiveness in this case?

Again, there are several ways that this has been handled by others. Before implementing any of the ideas that follow, be sure to check with key leaders in your organization to confirm that the idea is legal and applicable to your situation.

Example 1: Submit your proposal to a funder that limits its awards to junior faculty members or beginning professionals. Some federal agencies and private foundations have "small grants" or "young investigators" programs explicitly designed for those who are not yet ready to apply for funds in direct competition with more experienced grantseekers.

Example 2: Send your proposal to funders that are more interested in the quality of the idea and the proposal than in the prior reputation of project staff. All funders want some assurance that the people doing the project are capable of doing what is proposed. But some funders are more likely than others to base their judgments more on personal impressions of the quality of the director and the proposal than on the extent and success of prior activities.

Example 3: Ask an experienced colleague to serve as project director or principal investigator, and ask the initiator of the project idea to take a less senior position. This is a time-honored approach used particularly in research proposals originated by junior faculty members. And it is an accepted practice as long as the person designated as project director has agreed to participate, is willing to assume the administrative and legal responsibilities, will actually play the role described in the proposal, and is not overburdened with other assignments. A variation on this approach is to have the more experienced person serve as co-director or co-investigator.

Example 4: Have a more experienced person serve as an active consultant to the project. Again, as long as the person named truly intends to play this role, most funders are willing to accept this practice.

Example 5: For beginning investigators with research proposals, include a brief biographical sketch of those who serve or served on your doctoral committee or supervised your postdoctoral research. Funders can judge the likely capability of a new investigator in part by the quality of his or her mentors. This same approach can be used by early career applicants in other fields who have previous experience working under someone well-known in the profession.

Summary

Present your organizational capability as if it were a résumé for the job that the grantmaker would, in essence, be hiring your organization to do by funding you. Illustrate clear alignment between the grantmaker's interests and your organization's skills, capacity, track record, and experience with the proposed work. Present clearly, honestly, and confidently your and your organization's ability to solve the problem identified in your need statement.

14 PREPARING SUPPLEMENTAL DOCUMENTS

This chapter describes supplemental materials that funders may ask for to support the major elements of your proposal.

Gather and Create Supplemental Documents

Funders may want particular information in addition to the proposal narrative and budget or budgets. In their guidelines or instructions, funders will include a list of other documents they require. Some may be legal documents, maps, drawings, or extra financial statements, while others are documents they'll use just to facilitate their review process.

Title Page, Transmittal Letter, or Cover Sheet

The TITLE PAGE, sometimes called a COVER SHEET or TRANSMITTAL LETTER, is like a resume for your application. Usually, directions on whether or not to include a title page are provided by the funder in the grant guidelines. There is no set format for title pages. A sample is provided in Figure 14.1. If not specified in the funder's guidelines, a title page normally includes the following information:

- The name of the organization submitting the application
- The title of the project
- The beginning and ending dates of the project
- The total project budget and the amount requested from this funder
- The names, contact information, and signatures of the project directors or principal investigators
- The name and signature of the person authorizing the proposal as approved by the applicant organization

An experienced proposal writer once joked that the most important choice in developing a successful project was a good title. A title that aptly describes the primary goal of the project in words that will be easily remembered and often repeated is a definite asset. Here are several Do's and Don'ts about choosing proposal titles:

- **Do make the title fit the funder.** A technical-sounding title might be appropriate for submission to the National Science Foundation or to one of the National Institutes of Health, but would be much less appropriate for a museum project submitted to a private foundation or a curriculum development project sent to a state education agency.

FIGURE 14.1 SAMPLE COVER SHEET FOR A STANDARD PROPOSAL

Common Application Form

Provide the following information in this order. For your convenience, you may choose to either copy and fill out this cover summary, or create your own using the headings listed below.

Funder applying to: _____ Date submitted: _____

Total proposed project/program budget: _____ Amount requested: _____

Program name: _____

Duration of project/program: from _____ to _____ When are funds needed? _____

Nature of request: __ capital __ project __ operating __ program __ endowment __ other

Organization information:

Name and address: _____

_____

Phone number: _____ TTY: _____ Fax number: _____

Email: _____ FEI number: _____ Date of incorporation: _____

Chief staff officer/title: _____ Phone number: _____

Contact person/title: _____ Phone number: _____

Board chairperson: _____ Date of organization's fiscal year: _____

Organization's total operating budget for past year: _____ and current year: _____

Has the governing board approved a policy which states that the organization does not discriminate as to age, race, religion, sex, or national origin?
❑ Yes ❑ No If yes, when? _____

Does the organization have federal tax exempt status? ❑ Yes ❑ No If no, please explain.

Has the organization's chief executive officer authorized this request? ❑ Yes ❑ No

An officer of the organization's governing body must sign this application.

The undersigned, an authorized officer of the organization, does herby certify that the information set forth in this grant application is true and correct, that the federal tax exemption determination letter attached hereto has not been revoked, and that the present operation of the organization and its current sources of support are not inconsistent with the organization's continuing tax exempt classification as set forth in such determination letter.

Signature: _____
Print name/title: _____
Date: _____

- **Do describe the purpose of the project.** Make sure the title gives reviewers a clear idea of what the project is about.
- **Do keep the title short.** Remember that most funders will have your proposal indexed or entered into some type of informational system that is probably searching for key words. Brevity helps. Reviewers in the throes of a decision-making meeting usually refer to proposals by shortened nicknames. Make it easy for them to remember yours.
- **Do use imagination and flair.** Select words that draw a picture in the mind of the reader, especially words people use in everyday conversation.
- **Don't use the name of the funder in the project title.** Some projects are named after a sole funder, but this is usually agreed upon after a decision has been made to fund a project, rather than at the initial stage of application.
- **Don't begin with "A Project to..."** This shows lack of imagination and adds unnecessary length.
- **Don't select a title that is likely to have been used by others.** One funder recalled receiving seventeen proposals called "New Beginnings." Sixteen were not funded.
- **Don't choose a title that might be considered comical if seen out of context.** Politicians have been known to skim the project titles listed in annual reports or government documents and criticize funders and organizations based on jargon-filled or flippant titles. And funders are sensitive to this possibility.

Executive Summary or Abstract

An EXECUTIVE SUMMARY, which is sometimes called an ABSTRACT, is an abbreviated version of your proposal—a snapshot that gives the reviewer the gist of your proposal at a glance. It should include your organization's name, mission, location, what your organization will do, who or what will be affected, and the anticipated outcome. Finish with a sentence that outlines the total organizational budget, the total project budget, and the requested grant amount so a reviewer can see the context and scale of your request.

Although the executive summary is one of the first sections in a proposal, you should write the executive summary last, after you've finished all the other sections, because

> *"We really wanted to fund this project, but the contact information page was not filled out. We didn't know whom to contact."*
>
> —Bank Trust Officer who manages family foundations

From the Funder's Corner

As a grantmaker, I often use websites to find basic contact information. While there are privacy issues, every site ought to at least provide an email address for the executive director and development director...even if the address is executivedirector@abc.org. And if you set up an email account in that name, make sure someone checks it.

There's an old saying, "You only have one chance to make a first impression." Most of the time your organization is making a first impression on potential supporters in ways and at times that you are not even aware of. —*Ken Ristine*

it is difficult to summarize a proposal effectively before all aspects have been clearly defined. The executive summary is typically no longer than one page. While most executive summaries are between 250 and 500 words, some funders request a summary of only one or two paragraphs.

Many grantseekers make the mistake of using the executive summary or abstract as an introduction rather than as a synopsis of the proposal.

Funders expect your executive summary to be a cogent summary of your proposed project. It must tell the entire story simply and clearly. It plays several important roles:

- Funders frequently use the executive summary to make the initial determination of whether a project is eligible for, or worthy of, further consideration. One experienced foundation executive says that in nine out of ten cases, she reads only the executive summary before deciding whether or not to reject a proposal or retain it for further analysis.
- Both public and private funders often copy proposals' executive summaries and circulate them separately to key funding officials who want to see a digest of all incoming projects.
- Reviewers may send the executive summary to advisors in their organization. For example, a corporate foundation will consult the local manager in the community that will be affected by a project. The local manager is often provided with the executive summary alone unless the proposed project is extensive or complex.
- Program managers within the grantseeking organization can circulate their executive summaries to others within their organizations who should know about a project but do not need to read the entire proposal.

Most federal agencies, many state funding sources, and an increasing number of private funders now provide preprinted executive summary or abstract pages that must be included with your proposal. These forms, usually available online, call for details such as the location of the project, the number of project participants, budget information and other sources of funds, and assurances that your organization has complied with various regulations.

If no format is specified, the executive summary should do the following:

- Briefly describe the problem that will be addressed
- Indicate whether your organization has been funded by this funder before
- Give a quick overview of your proposed solution, the time frame, the groups who will be affected, and the short-term and long-term outcomes of your project
- Present a concise description of your project's significance and ways the new knowledge will be shared
- Say why your organization and its staff are especially qualified to conduct the project
- Clearly state the amount requested and any other funders who are involved
- Include the requested amount, in the context of your project budget
- Show how the project's outcomes are consistent with the funder's goals

Proof of Compliance with Government Regulations

Federal and state funding applications require a plethora of forms to document that your organization is in compliance with government regulations on such issues as nondiscrimination, protection of human or animal research subjects, and protection of the public. In some cases, compliance must be established *before* you can submit the full proposal. Prior approval is normally documented by entering on the proposal's title page the number or numbers assigned to the organization by the funder for each compliance requirement. Go to the Getting Funded website, www.gettingfundedbook.com, to see sample copies of assurances and compliance forms.

Some public agencies will accept proposals from organizations whose compliance processes are still under review. The agencies signal this by indicating that you may enter the word "pending" in the space for the organization's documentation number. Some funders require that the process be finished prior to receipt of the grant, and others, by the end of the project's grant cycle. Renewal funds are seldom granted without compliance.

> It is common to focus too much of the executive summary on organizational background and need rather than the proposed project and the change to be brought about by achieving the outcomes. About a quarter of the executive summary should be about the problem, need, or opportunity, and the rest should be about what you will do and what difference it will make.

Proof of Nonprofit Tax Status

The most common attachment requested by private grantmakers is a copy of the LETTER OF DETERMINATION from the IRS that indicates that your organization is tax-exempt, as defined by section 501(c)(3) of the Internal Revenue Code. Funders need to know that your organization is not a private foundation as defined under section 509(a), since these organizations are not allowed to receive funds from other private foundations.

If your organization is a nonprofit, you should include a copy of your organization's determination letter in all funding applications, unless your organization is a public agency, such as a federal or state agency, a public school or university, or a federally recognized tribe, all of which have different IRS determinations but are still eligible for grants. Before you submit your documents, check your IRS determination letter to make sure these things are clear:

> Familiarize yourself with compliance requirements well in advance of the application deadline. The applicant organization, not the project director or proposal writer, is responsible for establishing compliance procedures or internal review processes, and the process often takes weeks or months to finalize. If you need these approvals, allow your organization plenty of time to prepare for and meet such institution-wide requirements.

- **The determination is current and has not lapsed.** The IRS sometimes offers new organizations a preliminary ruling of nonprofit eligibility, with an expiration date by which the organization must get a permanent designation. Make sure your determination letter has not expired.
- **The organization name is current and has not changed.** Organizations that change their names must renew their tax-exempt status by filing certain information by a specified date. Reestablishing 501(c)(3) status, handled by the IRS's regional offices, can take several months to complete. Funders may pledge a grant to an organization whose filing has lapsed, but they cannot distribute the funds until the 501(c)(3) status is reinstated.
- **There is no confusion about which organization has been granted tax-exempt status.** Organizations without official tax-exempt status sometimes apply for grants under the umbrella of a larger nonprofit, whose name appears on the determination letter. If you are applying under the aegis of another organization, make sure you clearly explain the relationship.
- **The photocopied letter of determination is legible.**

You may also be asked to include business licenses and proof of status as a non-profit corporation in the state in which your organization was incorporated. Incorporation certificates are in addition to and do not take the place of the IRS determination letter.

Board of Directors List

Many funders will ask who serves on your organization's board of directors. Apart from wanting to see if anyone at the funder's office knows anyone on your board, funders want to know why each individual was chosen to help govern your organization. You may want to indicate these things:

> Most funders eliminate applications based on the inclusion or omission of specific attachments.

- Where board members work, especially if there are certain employers in your community who would lend credibility to a board
- Where board members live, especially if you're proving that your organization is led by statewide leaders, not just people in the largest city or the state capitol
- Board members' areas of expertise, assuming they were asked to share that wisdom to shape your organization's finances, communication, legislative relations, or program development
- Board members' relationship to your organization's mission, whether as parent, client, student, patient, patron, expert in your field, or representative of a member organization
- What constituency board members represent, which indicates that they provide access to—or provide partnership with—cooperating organizations
- What percent of the board attends regular board meetings and financially supports your organization on an annual basis

The type of affiliations you include in your board of directors list will depend on what your organization values and what might appeal to the funder you are approaching. Look for clues in the funder's guidelines, in the RFP, and in printed and online materials about the funder. (For more about presenting your board of directors, see the resources on the Getting Funded website, www.gettingfundedbook.com.)

> One nonprofit organization demonstrates how its board reflects the community it serves by identifying the company affiliation and position of each board member, while an ecumenical religious group lists the religious denominations of their board members. Funders of social service agencies and community health clinics often look for a representative of the organization's clients or patients on the board roster.

Financial Statement and IRS Form 990

Some funders require that you include a copy of your organization's most recent financial statements, audited or reviewed by an outside professional. Some require a full audit for you to be eligible for funding. Others simply want to see that an external expert has reviewed your finances recently, so you can submit a less stringent *review* or *compilation*. (Check with your organization's financial staff or a certified public accountant to determine which will be best.) Information provided by the audit may help answer questions about your organizational budget.

Nonprofit organizations should be prepared to include their most recent annual IRS Form 990 (Return of Organization Exempt from Income Tax). Form 990 lists key financial information about an organization, including revenue, expenses, and salaries of organization leaders. Many funders will request your current organiza-

A reviewer on a government panel had trouble interpreting a proposal's budget, so she looked for the audit to make sense of the numbers, but no audit had been submitted. The organization was urged to get an audit done quickly, but the executive director of the organization said he hadn't thought an audit was necessary because the organization's board president was the head of a local credit union. However, when the rush audit was submitted, it noted many discrepancies and concerns, which might not have come to light without the external review. Funders request audited financial statements to make sure an organization is financially sound and using ethical accounting practices.

tional budget and balance sheet as well. They want to see what your organization has projected for expenses and revenue for the year and how it is doing against projections. The IRS revised the Form 990 in 2009, and the current version reveals much more about an organization than the prior version did. You'll want to make sure that yours portrays your organization in the best possible light. (For more information about IRS Form 990, see IRS.gov.)

Organizational Chart

You may be asked to submit a chart illustrating the hierarchy or chain of command in your organization or institution. This shows funders who is accountable to whom, and where, in the scheme of things, your project fits. It also shows them how many people will be supporting the proposed project and in the context of what other activities. If you are submitting your proposal electronically, turn your organizational chart into a PDF file before uploading it.

Letters of Support or Endorsement

If your project can succeed only with the cooperation of other organizations or agencies, funders may ask for LETTERS OF SUPPORT or ENDORSEMENT from key people in those organizations. For instance, if your program is based in the court system, funders may want to know that the presiding judge thinks your organization is competent and cooperative. If your program depends on a reciprocal arrangement with a state agency, funders will want to see proof that the relationship is collegial and respectful. Letters of support verify that your organization has built strong, healthy relationships with others. If the funder does not require letters of support (and some funders don't want to receive any documents they haven't specifically requested), simply include in your proposal a list of agencies or institutions from which you have letters of support, and offer to share those letters if requested.

When you request a letter of support or endorsement, let your endorser know how to address the letter, what types of information you want included (it helps to include some sample wording), and when you need it. To be safe, specify a deadline well before your own proposal deadline. Ask endorsers to send their letters to you, not directly to the funder, unless the funder has directed otherwise. If an endorser has

"Part III of the Form 990 is what we like to call the 'marketing' section because it is an opportunity for you to tell potential funders all of your organization's great accomplishments during the prior year. Instead of writing a one-sentence program description, use all of the available space and include non-accounting examples, like the number of unpaid volunteers. Also, have your board review the content before filing."

—CPA at a well-known accounting firm

From the Funder's Corner

The Form 990 tells a story about how your organization is run. If it is filled out correctly, the form discloses how resources are spent between program, management and general, and fundraising. I encourage grantwriters to look at their organization's Form 990 and make sure it is correct. I've run across information which, on the surface, was quite misleading because the Form 990 was filled out incorrectly. With GuideStar and other resources on the web, this information is out there and will be read. You need to be sure that the Form 990 is representing your organization correctly. —*Ken Ristine*

a particularly close relationship with the funder, you might suggest sending the funder a separate message (by phone, mail, or email) in addition to the formal letter of support that you attach to your proposal. Do not submit a form letter as a letter of support.

Memo of Understanding

A MEMO OF UNDERSTANDING or MOU is a legal, contractual document that outlines roles, responsibilities, and budget details among collaborators. It is drafted by the leaders of collaborating organizations before the proposal is submitted and is finalized after the notification of award. An MOU for a collaborative project will document in-kind or shared personnel, equipment, or space. If you need an MOU, it is advisable to have a legal review of the document.

Estimates and Bids from Vendors

If you're requesting money for any single capital expenditure that costs more than $500, you may be required to submit estimates from three potential vendors so the funder can see that you've shopped around and that the numbers proposed in your budget reflect reality. Funders request three estimates because if you include only one estimate, it will not be clear how that bid relates to prices from other suppliers in your area. Keep vendor bids in your proposal file so that they are easily at hand should a funder ask to see them before deciding whether to fund your proposal.

Summary

Pay close attention to funders' guidelines to determine which additional documents are to be included with your proposal, and follow the instructions meticulously. Failure to do so may eliminate your proposal from consideration even before it's been reviewed. Start gathering the requested documents early in the process, as some, especially those with legal implications, may take a long time to secure. Submit only those attachments requested by the funder unless you have written permission to submit additional information.

> Securing a letter of support from another organization can take weeks or months, so *plan ahead*.

> "*Foundations are unimpressed by name dropping. Letters of endorsement in glittering generalities by dignitaries and celebrities do little good. Foundations know that most likely, these persons have never seen, let alone studied, the proposals and that the letter may have been written by one of their staff members. The kinds of endorsements that do count are statements from current and potential cooperating institutions.*"
>
> —Guidelines of the M.J. Murdock Charitable Trust

Key Terms

ABSTRACT or **EXECUTIVE SUMMARY:** A synopsis of the full proposal. Some grantmakers provide an online form to complete, while others do not specify the format. Length varies by funder, from one to two paragraphs to one to two pages.

ATTACHMENT: A supplementary document requested by funders to support and augment elements in the main proposal or to verify organizational status. Common attachments are an organization's 501(c)(3) letter of determination, board of directors list, organizational chart, and copies of contracts, maps, construction drawings, and audited financial statements.

COVER SHEET or **TITLE PAGE** or **TRANSMITTAL LETTER:** A form, usually dictated by the funder, that accompanies a grant proposal upon submission and includes the name of the grantseeker, the title of the project, the start and end dates of the project, the total expected project cost, the amount being requested of the funder, and names, signatures, and contact information of those at the organization who are authorizing the proposal. Often required by government funders.

FORM 990: Internal Revenue Service form filed annually by public charities, listing assets, receipts, expenditures and compensation of officers.

LETTER OF DETERMINATION: A document issued by the IRS stating an organization's tax-exempt status.

LETTER OF ENDORSEMENT: A letter from someone who is familiar with your organization and who can specifically cite why you are qualified to do the proposed project, why it matters, and how it is anticipated in the community. The most effective letters demonstrate real familiarity rather than general endorsement.

LETTER OF SUPPORT: A letter from a stakeholder or other person who wants to endorse the grantseeking organization and the proposed project. Examples include a letter from a parent who supports the plan for new playground equipment, or a letter from a mayor who supports the renovation of a historic building. See also letter of endorsement.

MEMORANDUM OF UNDERSTANDING (MOU): A written contract between private grantmaker and funded organization that constrains how the organization may use the funds and establishes reporting or expenditure requirements. May also be a binding contract between two or more partner organizations.

ORGANIZATIONAL CHART: A graphic representation of the key positions in an organization that illustrates the chain of command and the relationships among the different positions.

15 CRAFTING LETTERS OF INQUIRY

This chapter is a guide to careful composition of a letter of inquiry. Some private foundations, though not all, use letters of inquiry to determine which proposals merit further review. If your letter of inquiry passes the first review, you will be invited to submit a full proposal. This invitation is a necessary step forward, but does not imply that you will get the grant. The best way to write an effective letter of inquiry is to first complete your full proposal, including any necessary revisions to project design, outcome statements, and evaluation plans. Then craft your letter of inquiry, using the suggestions in this chapter to make it as compelling as possible.

Understand the Role of the Letter of Inquiry

Many grantmakers require a letter of inquiry before they will accept a full proposal. These letters help funders quickly screen large numbers of requests to determine which projects they are interested in learning more about. Only upon determining interest will they request, or accept, a full proposal.

A strong letter of inquiry is a condensed version of your full proposal, a two- or three-page snapshot of what you propose, delivered in letter format. These letters are challenging to construct, as they must be explicit and clear, yet brief. Their job is to pitch an exciting, well-developed idea and entice a reviewer to say, "Tell me more."

Letters of inquiry are also called letters of interest, query letters, letters of intent, or LOIs. It's important that these letters make a strong initial impression. Reviewers often will determine within seconds whether they like an idea or not. In fact, some grantmakers have made funding decisions based on a query letter alone. Some funders assign clerical staff to screen LOIs. Others hire contract screeners to weed out the organizations that don't meet the funder's criteria, whether explicit or implicit. Still others have program officers or other staff members review and prioritize the letters, while some, especially family foundations, use trustees.

A reviewer's impression of your organization can hinge on how your letter looks on the page (white space is good), how readable it is (long words, long sentences, and long paragraphs are bad), and how clear and compelling it is. You have only seconds to capture a reviewer's attention, so you'll want to make it easy to see what's engaging about your project.

Write the Letter of Inquiry

Submitting a letter of inquiry is an opportunity to showcase your organization's capacity to carry out the proposed project. The letter should summarize and highlight the project's goals, objectives, and outcomes and demonstrate how well your proposal addresses the funder's priorities, considering the type of work you do, your geographic scope, the types of funders that have supported you in the past, and the dollar amount of your request.

Components of the Letter of Inquiry

A convincing letter of inquiry will answer these questions:

- **Who are you?** After clarifying that this document is a letter of inquiry, state the name, mission, and founding date of your organization. Then in one sentence, explain the purpose of the project, including the target population. For example, "We seek support to secure affordable housing for the schoolteachers on Eagle Island."
- **Why are you approaching this funder?** Make it clear that you understand the funder's priorities. Acknowledge the funder's behavior, guidelines, or goals, and mention why you think you're aligned with those.
- **What is the need, problem, or opportunity?** Present the need you plan to address, clearly and briefly. Include demographic and statistical evidence.
- **What is your plan?** List activities, methods, and timelines. Link your goals and objectives to the funder's priorities. Describe how your project addresses the need and demonstrates best practices. This part of the letter can be up to half of the total narrative.
- **Why should the funder support this project and your organization?** Emphasize your organization's capacity and commitment, as well as your staff members' qualifications. Name other organizations, agencies, or well-known individuals who agree with your statement of need and/or are working with you to address it.
- **How much does the project require, and how much are you asking for?** State the total cost of the project, the resources your organization is committing to it, and who else has already committed to support it. Specify the dollar amount you are requesting from the funder, and what you plan to use it for. Indicate who else is being approached for funding. Align the funding request with your goals and objectives, and briefly describe how the project will be continued after the grant ends.
- **What comes next?** Thank the funder for considering your proposal. Provide a name and contact information for the most appropriate person in your organization to answer questions about the project. Say whether the funder should anticipate your follow-up phone call. Have the most senior individual in your organization who is also connected with the proposal sign the letter in blue ink.

Tips for Writing the Letter of Inquiry

A compelling letter of inquiry will emerge from these tips on writing:

- **Keep it brief.**
- **Avoid big blocks of text.** Vary the length of your paragraphs. Draw the reader's eye to the most important things on the page by judiciously using bulleted lists, boldface type, italics, or underlining.

- **Avoid the words "we need."** Funders are concerned about the needs of your beneficiaries or the needs of the community, not the needs of the grantseeking organization. Your job is not to *have* needs, but to *meet* them.
- **Use active voice.** Avoid passive voice. Use "we will initiate," not "the program will be initiated."
- **Use action verbs.** Avoid "to be" constructions, e.g., is, are, was, or were. Rather than writing, "Our mission is to mobilize...," simply say, "We mobilize..." Rather than, "Our organization is called Old Pet Haven. It was founded in 1979. Our mission is to help prevent the unnecessary deaths of aging animals," use instead, "Old Pet Haven, founded in 1979, finds loving homes for aging pets, preventing unnecessary deaths."
- **Use verbs, not nouns.** Rather than writing, "We are in collaboration with...," simply say, "We collaborate with..."
- **Use simple, easily understood words.** Avoid jargon. Many reviewers have grown tired of overused words such as "at-risk" or anything ending with "-based."

The best practice for writing a letter of inquiry is to write your full proposal first, and then glean key information from the proposal to use in your letter. Writing a letter of inquiry before your project description and budget are fully developed will produce a half-baked product, and funders can taste the difference.

And it can't be said too often: connect the goals of your project or organization to the goals of the funder. Let the reader feel your enthusiasm and passion (without overdoing it). Write so that the problem, the need, flows into the solution, which then leads naturally to your request. And make sure the amount you are requesting can be located immediately on the page, perhaps making it boldface or putting it one type size bigger. Reviewers shouldn't have to search for the request.

Figures 15.1 and 15.2 exhibit fictional letters of inquiry—one to a private foundation, and one to a corporate giving program—that demonstrate all of the principles

From the Funder's Corner

First, remember that the goal of the letter is to sell the foundation on taking your project to the next step in their funding process. The focus of your letter is to talk about what you are trying to accomplish and why. The reason we (funders) ask for a letter rather than some sort of application form or a full proposal is that (1) application forms are very poor media for telling your story to educate and convince people of the importance of the needs/situation you want to address, and (2) your letter, ideally, summarizes a full proposal that you have written and that is available for you to use as reference if the letter prompts the funder to go to the next step in the process.

Second, if your letter is telling a compelling story, then as we come to the end of your letter, we are asking ourselves: "How much is this going to cost?" Answering that question is the entire purpose of your budget.

Again, since the letter is a summary of a full proposal, we are not looking for details. I specifically look for (1) the total amount/cost, (2) the broad-brush look at where you plan to raise the money (e.g., foundations, individual giving, government, or investment of organization reserves), and (3) how much are you asking of this foundation? All of these are subject, of course, to a general review of common sense. —*Ken Ristine*

discussed in this chapter. For more information on principles of effective writing or on researching funders' guidelines, past giving history, and priorities, see the Resources section or the Getting Funded website, www.gettingfundedbook.com.

Summary

A letter of inquiry is an abbreviated version of a full proposal. It offers grantmakers a brief synopsis of your idea so they can determine whether to invite a full proposal. A letter of inquiry should be roughly one-quarter about your organization and its fit with the funder, one-quarter about the need, one-quarter about the proposed work, and one-quarter about the budget. Funders who require these letters usually dictate the length and content, but most letters of intent are about two pages long. They should be printed on letterhead and signed by the grantseeking organization's most senior leader. A strong letter of inquiry will be visually inviting, easily absorbed, and potent.

FIGURE 15.1 SAMPLE LETTER OF INQUIRY TO A FOUNDATION

Dear [Name of Funder],

Thank you for all you have done for women and children in our region. We applaud your recent work with the Children's Advocacy Center and the award you received for your role in it. With this query letter, we invite your support of our related work.

The People's Law Center, founded in 1978, ensures equal access to the justice system for citizens who otherwise could not afford legal counsel. We serve about 1,250 families from our county each year, through:

- Information and referral services with our 800 number;
- Free legal clinics at county-wide, community-based venues;
- Sidewalk advocacy tables at a busy street corner on Saturday mornings; and
- Pro bono attorney services for those needing representation in court.

As with 24 of the 26 similar programs throughout our five-state region, the majority of our clients who need direct representation are women with children in domestic abuse situations, often complicated by other factors like poverty, unemployment, and housing issues. Since our county is predominantly rural, the number of attorneys available to take pro bono cases is small to begin with. And because these cases are time-consuming, emotionally draining, and complex, the pool of volunteer attorneys who are knowledgeable in family law and willing to take them shrinks each year.

Last year, a strategic planning process conducted by our board determined that our top priority for the coming year would be to launch an in-house legal program, with a full-time staff attorney, dedicated to family law cases. The program was designed by members of our board and staff, volunteer attorneys, judicial staff, colleagues from the local crisis center and battered women's shelter, and law enforcement personnel.

We anticipate that setting up and running this program for the first year will cost $85,000. In addition to the $5,000 we agree to absorb in our operating budget, we have garnered $30,000 from the local bar association, two churches, a service club, and three long-term individual donors.

Your guidelines state that your top priority is improving the lives of women and children in our region. Our program will provide direct representation to 50 domestic violence victims and their children in the next year. **We seek approval to submit a full proposal for a grant of $10,000 from your foundation.**

We intend to raise the remaining $40,000 from a start-up grant from United Way, two law firms, and the Apex Corporation. Funds to sustain the program will be generated by grants during the first two years, then from individual donors through mailed appeals, events, and personal solicitation.

If you have questions about our organization, our new program, or this request, please contact our Executive Director, Shelley Smith, at 555-123-4567. Thank you again for supporting families in our community. And thank you for your consideration.

Joshua Jordan
CHAIR, BOARD OF DIRECTORS
PEOPLE'S LAW CENTER

FIGURE 15.2 SAMPLE LETTER OF INQUIRY TO A CORPORATE GIVING PROGRAM

Dear [Name of Corporation],

Congratulations on your recent merger with Axis. We at the Community College thank the leaders of both companies for your past support of education in our region. We will soon gather 1,000 education supporters for a benefit concert, and we invite you to join us by becoming a corporate sponsor at the $5,000 level.

Our college has been providing affordable, accessible education to the students of our three-county area for 45 years. Eighty-eight percent of our graduates find employment in the area immediately upon completion of our two-year curriculum. Many of the employees and countless customers of your company are Community College alumni.

When the primary employer in the region closed its plant last year, scores of families who had dreamed that their children would be the first generation to attend college gave up hope. But the Community College isn't giving up hope. We're raising enough money in the next year to offer 100 scholarships to graduating seniors from local high schools.

One element of our fundraising strategy is to host a concert, featuring the well-known jazz singer Stella Raye, who graduated from the college in 1967. The concert will be May 6, in our campus auditorium. We expect the event to attract an audience that would be enthusiastic about your new product line.

To acknowledge your corporate sponsorship, we would be pleased to offer the following benefits to your company:

- Your name and logo on promotional posters in a three-county area
- Your name and logo on newspaper ads purchased four weeks prior to the concert
- Your name and logo on the front cover of the program at the concert
- Your name and logo on our website, with a link to yours
- Signage and table space in the lobby to display company literature
- Front-row-center tickets for you to distribute to eight guests
- An invitation to those eight guests to attend a backstage reception
- The opportunity for a company representative to introduce Ms. Raye on stage
- Acknowledgment in our college newsletter and our annual report

Your gift will ultimately affect the livelihood of hundreds of families among your employee and customer bases, hopefully anchoring some of our bright young people in the community. We hope that your abiding interest in the economic vitality of our region will encourage your participation in this effort to help educate the next generation of students. If you have questions about the college, the concert, or this request, please contact our Advancement Director, Sam Smith, at 333-555-1212. Thank you for your consideration.

Jean Worden,
PRESIDENT
COMMUNITY COLLEGE

16 REVIEWING & SUBMITTING YOUR PROPOSAL

This chapter sets out a process for multiple internal reviews of a proposal before submission. It also discusses how to ensure that your proposal gets submitted successfully.

First, before you send your proposal to anyone else, review the entire document yourself. This is your opportunity to compile information provided by a variety of people and make sure everything you need has been written and incorporated. Next, have several key people in your organization read the proposal. Include people who were part of your grantwriting team as well as any specific staff members that your organization has named as internal reviewers. Finally, if there are any outside organizations participating or collaborating with your organization, send the final draft of the proposal to the relevant contact people for their feedback. Remember that once you receive feedback, you will need additional time to make and double-check any additions, deletions, or revisions.

Check Your Work

When you read your entire proposal with an editor's eye, before you send it to others involved in the project for their review and feedback, take the time to make sure the proposal is a tight, coherent, readable final draft. If you notice any logic, content, or formatting issues, such as missing, incorrect, or inconsistent information or sections that squeeze too many words in with tiny font, now is the time to revise. The following suggestions can help:

- Read your proposal out loud to catch mistakes and over-lengthy passages.
- Read for spelling and grammar. Do not rely on spell-check alone.
- Check the final proposal against the funder's requirements and forms. Be sure to include everything that is required, and nothing that is not required.
- Have someone else edit the proposal as well. This could be someone inside your organization who has worked on the proposal, or who has written a successful proposal to this funder in the past. Or it could be a dispassionate person, inside or outside your organization, professional or volunteer, who can offer a fresh eye.

A state government funder reported that as many as 70 percent of the proposals submitted to them didn't make the initial screening cut because grantseekers did not follow the instructions in the RFP.

This is also your final chance to make the writing as powerful as possible. The following suggestions can help:

- Maintain a balance between conciseness and sufficient detail to effectively explain the project.
- Include statistics and other third-party verification that there is a need, problem, or opportunity, and that there are best practices or models that support your ideas.
- Be persuasive, but do not oversell your project. Promise only those outcomes and activities that you can definitely accomplish, given the requested resources.
- Ensure that the proposal flows logically from one section to another.
- Use storytelling to give reviewers an opportunity to connect on an emotional level to what they are reading.
- Include phrases from the funder's guidelines as signposts to help reviewers recognize where they are in your narrative.
- Guide reviewers to the most important parts of your proposal by using a table of contents, numbered pages, and clear headings and subheadings.
- Avoid lengthy introductory phrases that bury your most important points.
- Use language appropriate to the funder, explain technical phrases and terms, and avoid abbreviations and acronyms.
- Use charts, graphs, and photos to illustrate concepts from the narrative.
- Keep the type size readable and use sufficient margins, spacing, and white space to make the proposal inviting to the eye.

If you are reusing any material from a previous proposal, search each application thoroughly to make sure there is no reference to another grantmaker. Nothing says you don't pay attention to details like using someone else's name on a proposal requesting a relationship and funding.

A new program officer was being oriented on his first day at a major private foundation. His guide offered this piece of advice about reviewing proposals: "Ignore all adjectives"

The next step is to invite the most critical person you can recruit to review your proposal and offer feedback. Otherwise, you may commit one of the "seven deadly sins of proposal writing" outlined in Figure 16.1. These are the fatal flaws most frequently cited by funders and proposal reviewers.

Send the Proposal through Internal Review

Each organization has its own procedures and timelines that must be followed as proposals are developed, and many organizations require an internal review. Depending on the type of organization, the following people might be involved:

Program Director or Department Chair: The program director determines whether the proposal is consistent with the organization's program and budget priorities and the staff assignments of the program or department, and is responsible for ensuring the professional or scientific competence of the application.

FIGURE 16.1 THE SEVEN DEADLY SINS OF PROPOSAL WRITING

1. **The application doesn't have a clear focus.** The proposal doesn't concisely and compellingly convey what you want to do, why it is important, how it relates to the interests of the funder, and why your organization is the best qualified to carry it out. This is especially critical in the abstract or executive summary. A proposal can also look unclear if it is laced with jargon or isn't written clearly and directly.

2. **The presentation is sloppy.** An application with misspellings, typos, and poor grammar signals a sloppy mind and disrespect for the recipient. It is really important to correctly spell the name of the funder to which you are applying. One program officer recalled a proposal that spelled the name of her foundation seven different ways, apparently operating on the erroneous assumption that at least one of them would be right and the other six forgiven. Do not rely solely on spell check. Proofread carefully.

3. **The idea is unsound.** This is often a sin of commission—of simply biting off more than you can chew and promising far more than can reasonably be accomplished. Funders of research particularly cited "unrealistic plans" as something that quickly kills their interest in a proposal. But it can be a sin of omission, too—of simply failing to show how the project's proposed goals, procedures, and resources tie together in a coherent, creative, and manageable project. Ask a colleague to tell you if the internal logic of your project is adequately conveyed in the proposal. If not, focus on aligning all sections of your proposal.

4. **The proposal has an internal rather than an external focus.** Most funders give money to improve the lives of people, build better communities, advance society, create new knowledge, or for other external reasons. They seldom make awards because an organization needs to pay its staff, a faculty member cannot receive tenure without a funded project, or a group wants to upgrade its facilities. Unfortunately, every day, funders receive hundreds of proposals that are more focused on how the requested money will benefit the applicant than on a real commitment to the problem the grantmaker is trying to solve. Show reviewers that the project is not just about your organization, and that your work can help solve a larger problem in the community or the world.

5. **There are problems with the budget.** Experienced funders can quickly judge whether a budget is unrealistic (either too high or too low), is padded with nonessential expenses, or is "asking for the moon." Padded budgets can be taken as proof of inexperience or of disrespect. Ask for what you need. Remember, many reviewers look at the budget first as a way to decide whether they want to read the rest of the application.

6. **The instructions weren't followed.** Funders expect that you will be courteous and meticulous enough to answer all the questions they ask and to follow their instructions. You may feel there isn't much logic in their forms, but now is not the time to demonstrate your creativity by coming up with your own proposal format. Double-check that you have included all of the information requested. Stay within word and page limits. Omit irrelevant supplementary materials. Send the right number of copies. Not following the rules is one of the quickest ways to ensure your proposal isn't funded.

7. **The deadline was missed.** Good proposals take time to prepare, and your organization will have internal review steps that must be completed before the proposal can be submitted. Some programs require additional reviews at the state or regional level or, because of the nature of the project, expect approvals by professional committees of one kind or another. If you plot these out on a timeline and build in wiggle room for inevitable delays or last-minute negotiations, you should be okay. Missing a deadline is unacceptable to most funders, regardless of your excuse, so plan ahead. Be certain you know if it is a "postmark deadline" (the proposal to be stamped at the post office by a certain date) or a "receipt deadline" (the proposal to be mailed or submitted electronically to be in the hands of the grantmaker by a certain date). And don't forget to take time zones into account.

Division Director, Principal, or Dean: The division director reviews the proposal for alignment with the priorities of the division. The division director is also responsible for confirming availability of matching funds.

Staff of Budget Office: The budget office ensures that costs for all items have been identified correctly, that proposed salary levels and fringe benefit and indirect cost rates are appropriate, and that the budget totals are accurate.

Staff of Development Office: The development office ensures that this proposal is congruent with the long-term goals of development, as some organizations prioritize which proposals can be submitted simultaneously to a particular funder. Development offices will also make sure that promises of acknowledgments, communication, and stewardship correspond with department policies.

Internal Review Board: Organizations that have an Internal Review Board (IRB) must send each proposal for screening and approval. The IRB ensures that proposals comply with all relevant policies, protocols, and regulations, such as those dealing with protection of human or animal research subjects.

> Read your proposal out loud. You will discover the sentence that is so long you run out of air, or a choppy sentence that doesn't flow. Reading aloud will make it easier for you to catch problem areas and make revisions.

Executive Director, President, Superintendent, Governing Board: The executive director and other leaders provide final review and approval before a proposal is cleared for submission. This guarantees that the proposal has top-level priority and that the organization has agreed to fulfill all program and budget commitments made in the proposal. This level of approval normally results in a signature on a title page or transmittal letter.

Send the Proposal for External Review

If another organization's involvement is essential to your proposal, you will need to plan sufficient time for that organization to complete its own hierarchy of internal reviews. Some government departments require proposals to be reviewed at the state or regional level, particularly if state tax revenues or a regional allocation from a federal budget are involved. Some corporations and foundations require proposals to be reviewed by geographic committees before being sent to the central office.

Submit the Proposal

There are several ways to submit a proposal. The traditional method, mailing one or more hard copies to the funder, is quickly being replaced by various forms of electronic submission. Electronic submission can be as simple as emailing PDF files of your proposal to a funder, or as complex as filling out online templates and storing your draft and final proposal on a funder's server. Whatever the method, this step in the process is full of many details requiring special attention. The following suggestions will help you prepare to submit your proposal.

Most of the information you will need will be available from the funder's website, program announcement, RFP, or guidelines. When in doubt, contact the appropriate staff person. Always make sure your information is current: regulations, processes, and deadlines can change quickly and without notice.

- Reconfirm whether the funder wants proposals submitted electronically or on paper. If the funder wants hard copy, verify both the number of copies requested and the number of copies that must have original ink signatures. Check to see whether the funder has made requests about staples, paper clips, bindings, and covers, and find out whether photographs are permitted.

- Go over the guidelines or RFP to ensure that you have included all the requested items in the COVER LETTER, cover sheet, or transmittal letter. Do not rely on the cover sheet or transmittal letter to make an important point that is not repeated elsewhere in the body of the proposal, as this page is sometimes removed from the rest of the proposal as soon as the funder receives it.
- Confirm whether letters of endorsement are welcome. One experienced researcher lists, in a prominent place in the application, the names, affiliations, and contact information of "others who can provide perspective on this application." This allows her to diplomatically "drop names" in the proposal and make the point that individuals of influence and reputation are willing to stand behind her. But it leaves it up to the funder whether to request the letters. Never include anyone's name unless you have received permission in advance and for that particular proposal.
- Ask either your contact at the funder or someone who's been funded by this funder before whether it would help or harm your proposal to have someone from your board contact known colleagues at the funder.

Electronic Submission

Funders are moving quickly from paper applications to ELECTRONIC SUBMISSION. Some funders accept proposals that are simply emailed rather than mailed, while other funders require that you upload your document to their server. Many of these funders require you to house your application on their website while you're drafting it, as they want to watch what is being developed in order to predict the volume in each GRANT DOCKET or help grantseekers whom they select for assistance. Most funders who require electronic submission have created locked, online templates you must fill in to qualify.

Timelines for Electronic Submission

If the funder requires electronic submission, be sure to register in the online system early and practice the process for uploading and submitting. Read the guidelines carefully, and follow them closely. The process for registering and submitting proposals electronically may take several days, so don't wait until the last minute. If you build time into your plan for possible delays, you won't get caught sweating as the deadline approaches. Federal funders may accept requests to submit a proposal on paper instead of electronically, but often require a two-week lead time.

With electronic submission in particular, plan to finish and submit your proposal a week or more ahead of the deadline. Disaster can strike a funder's website when large numbers of grantseekers who have worked right up to the deadline all upload their documents at the same time. An overloaded computer system either freezes or accepts each document in the order received, which in either case delays receipt of some proposals until after the deadline.

A corporate funder disclosed that, "Eager grantseekers sometimes ask a powerful person inside the company to submit their proposal, assuming it will carry more weight. But we set up a specific submission process for a reason, and when people try to circumvent that process, it just makes us mad." She suggested that the influential corporate employee simply send a separate message endorsing the applicant.

During one federal funding cycle, the end-of-the-year rush of organizations submitting applications caused the computer program used by Grants.gov to interpret all DUNS numbers as viruses and kick all applications out of the computer system. Grantseekers who didn't check to make sure their applications were fully submitted lost out on that round of funding. Get an online receipt so that you know that your proposal was received.

Writing for Electronic Submission

The templates you may be required to use in some online processes will force you to be concise and exact with your writing. Word limits for each section are fixed, which makes it essential that your need statements be compelling and your stories carefully crafted for maximum impact. You will have to make choices about what the funder really needs to know. Unnecessary words such as adjectives should be the first words cut, and then you will have to keep cutting. Persuasive writing sparkles as it guides the reader along a clear path of rock-solid reasoning. (As you winnow your narrative down to its essence, you can keep an electronic file of the bits you cut out for use in other contexts.)

With electronic submission, computer programs scan your application for key words to qualify your proposal for the next stage of review. Cross-check your proposal with the language and requirements in the RFP, with the funder's stated values and priorities, and with electronic submission guidelines.

Formatting for Electronic Submission

The software programs for electronic applications are still under development and therefore can be difficult to manage. Aside from basic navigation and other ease-of-use issues, the biggest challenge is the limited space you are given to offer a compelling case and solid plan.

Electronic submission templates often establish a maximum number of words, spaces, or characters that can be included in each section of your proposal. Some templates count punctuation as two or even three spaces. Some assign specific counts for each letter. If you try to shoehorn in extra words, spaces, and punctuation, the program will either reject the whole section or cut off the end of your proposal, even in midsentence, once the limit is reached. Plan to leave a buffer of extra word or character counts in each section so you don't have to keep refashioning your proposal again and again. This kind of preparation can be very time-consuming.

It's often helpful to copy the template out of the funder's website and paste it into a word processing program. Then you can work on your draft without the encumbrances of the template, while constantly tracking word, space, and character count. Working in a word processing program also helps you avoid potential trouble caused by attempts to relocate blocks of text in the online application.

Use only basic punctuation such as periods, commas, semicolons, colons, dashes, parentheses, and apostrophes. Do not use boldface, italics, bullets, or any other non-text characters, because they will cause your formatting to come apart. Only if you can upload your whole proposal as a PDF file will the formatting hold. If you have to fill in discrete boxes for each question in the funder's application, there will be no way to keep the formatting consistent.

Troubleshooting Electronic Submission

If the bugs haven't been worked out of the funder's system, it can take much longer than you predicted to submit your proposal. This is particularly true for Grants.gov, the federal government gateway for federal funding opportunities and applications. The good news about Grants.gov is that it has tutorial and troubleshooting sections to guide you through the search and submission processes. There is also a section on Grants.gov devoted to tracking the latest software problems so that you can act accordingly. You can also talk to a customer service representative if necessary, and their service is very good. Check to see if the funder you're submitting to has a troubleshooting section.

Save a copy of the final submission from the "print view" feature of your word processing software, as well as a blank copy of the application.

Some electronic applications require a password to open the file containing your proposal. The passwords can change every year, so save these passwords somewhere accessible in case you are away when others might need them.

Summary

Once you have a final draft of your proposal, it's important to have several parties review it before you turn it in to the funder. After your proposal has cleared your internal review checklists, prepare carefully for submission. Start early if the funder requires electronic submission, as there are many potential obstacles. Be especially mindful of the funder's directions about submission, as small oversights or mistakes could get your proposal ejected from the process without review.

Key Terms

COVER LETTER: A letter that accompanies a proposal submitted to a private funder, and is usually less formal and prescribed than a title page or cover sheet for a government funder.

ELECTRONIC SUBMISSION: Turning in an application for funding online, usually through a formal process on the funder's website.

GRANT DOCKET: A calendar that indicates when pending proposals will be reviewed.

17 INVESTING IN ONGOING RELATIONSHIPS

This chapter covers how proposals are reviewed by funders, what steps to take if your proposal isn't selected for funding, and what happens over the life of the grant and beyond if your proposal does get funded.

Review by the Funder

Some funders review proposals making decisions as each is received, but this is rare. Most funders have deadlines for periodic grant dockets, and once the proposals have been received, a formal screening process begins.

The Internet has helped make review processes much more transparent. Many funders' websites disclose the step-by-step process as well as details on the criteria used to judge applications. Web addresses are in constant flux, but a web search of the name of the funder followed by the words "grant review process" can uncover current information.

While the processes of government agencies, foundations, and corporations vary, there are some common elements. The steps below are typical of most funders.

Step 1: Proposal Screened

The initial screening is often done by administrative staff members who weed out proposals that don't fit the basic specifications of the funder.

- Did the application arrive by the deadline?
- Is the organization eligible? Does the organization have the appropriate tax status or credentials?
- Does the organization fit within the geographic scope of the funder?
- Did the organization follow instructions about format, font, and margins, as well as number of copies and attachments?

Even given these minimal requirements, corporate funders and foundations say that well over half of the applications they receive are immediately rejected because they do not match their guidelines. Many government funders now have electronic screening processes where computers check for certain key words, eliminating proposals that don't include them.

This preliminary step usually takes thirty to forty-five days to occur. At its conclusion, organizations are usually sent a notification that their proposal has been rejected or that it has been received and assigned a processing number. The organization is then expected to refer to that number in any subsequent communications about the proposal.

Step 2: Proposals Considered

Proposals worthy of further consideration get additional reviews. This could be an internal process among program staff or leaders inside the funder, or an external process, which could be carried out through a written and/or in-person review by a group of outside experts, an advisory body, or the funder's representative in the community where the grantseeking organization is based. The reviewers usually read and score proposals on their own and then meet as a panel to discuss and give further consideration to those grant applications that have survived.

The reviewers, who usually have close ties to the funding source, may be employees of the corporation, members of the service club or professional association, or friends and family of the foundation's original donor. In the case of government funders, reviewers may be professional staff (program officers), hired experts, or community members with mastery of some aspect of that field.

As an example, an arts commission that funds facilities may choose to include among the reviewers people who are familiar with all the performance venues in the region; people who run sound and light at events; producers or directors of concerts, plays, and exhibitions; and people who understand nonprofit boards or finances.

A federal grantmaker who funds medical research might include among the reviewers practicing scientists and academics who are experts in that field, members of the public who have been affected by the disease or condition being researched, people in the private sector who deal with related pharmaceuticals, or representatives from professional associations in the field.

Having various perspectives on the subject represented on a review panel enriches the conversation about what's compelling or persuasive about each proposal and grantseeking organization. Especially in government review panels, it's a best practice for the panel to reflect the cultural makeup of the constituency affected by the grant to avoid any question of discrimination.

Most governmental sources now furnish the names and affiliations of their reviewers, although they may not tell you on which specific panel each individual serves. Government funders also typically tell you to which panel the proposal has been assigned, based on your proposal's title and abstract. This is another reason for careful title writing. If you are assigned to what you think is an inappropriate panel, you can call and ask for a change prior to further review.

As your grant proposal progresses through the grantmaker's review process, the proposal and your organization may be more deeply considered and explored through one of these common methods used by reviewers.

An on-site visit: While these are becoming increasingly rare, some funders insist on making site visits. They are looking for indications that what was reported in the proposal is consistent with what they see in person. They also hope to get a sense of the health and atmosphere of the workplace, meet people in the leadership (both on staff and in governing roles), talk with the program staff who would implement the project and the accountants who understand the finances best, and see the types of people, animals, or property that might benefit from the project. Funders often ask more probing questions about items in the proposal that they found confusing or intriguing. Most of all, they learn more about the grantseeking organization through having conversations than through simply reading text.

A telephone or email interview: These are conducted by a staff person or representative of the grantmaker, again to ask clarifying questions and get a better feel for the organization and its capacity to successfully complete the project.

A financial and/or legal review: Some federal agencies have separate staff who do cost analyses to ensure that the proposed expenditures are allowable and reasonable.

An executive review: Top officials in the agency, members of the foundation's board, or a company's contribution committee may review the entire proposal or its abstract to see if they concur with staff and/or reviewer recommendations.

An informal check-in: Many funders will confer informally with colleagues to see if others have heard of or funded the organization. Grantseekers may not realize how often funders compare notes, but it happens frequently enough that you should assume it is going to occur. This offers a persuasive reason to maintain good relations with prior funders.

As you can see from the proposal review methods outlined above, different grantmakers require different amounts of time for review. Many can take the better part of a year, so check each funder's schedule when doing your *initial* research and build the review interval into your proposal development timeline.

Step 3: Criteria Applied

Some decision-making processes are less formal and prescribed. In less sophisticated organizations, such as professional associations, churches, or family foundations, proposals might be discussed by the group, with decisions made by consensus or by majority vote. Some decisions get made simply because one person with influence encourages the others to adopt his or her point of view. In one family foundation, a sibling reported that they funded whatever they could all agree on. In a church group, they might decide to fund projects that manifest their core principles, whether stated in the guidelines or not. In a corporate setting, decisions might reflect unarticulated priorities too.

On the more rigorous end of the spectrum, government agencies usually describe the criteria quite clearly and indicate how much weight will be given to each section. You can find this information on their websites, in the program announcement, in the RFP, or in the guidelines. Many foundations and corporations are doing likewise.

A first-time federal reviewer was surprised to realize that not only was she required to score each section using an assigned point spread per question, she then had to write a paragraph justifying her score. Since the money being granted was public funds, it was incumbent on the funder to produce the rationale for every decision, in case a rejected applicant wanted a justification for their score.

In every review process, some proposals are so well-crafted that they rise to the top of everyone's list, while some are so bad that everyone agrees to eliminate them with little or no discussion. Reviewers and program officers ultimately spend most of their time comparing the applications in the middle. Among those, less concrete things like reputation and strength of leadership can be deciding factors. Funders who are risk averse may give priority to well-known organizations or to those they have funded in the past.

The volunteer members of a county agency's review panel had spent several days as a group discussing eighty proposals they had read prior to meeting. They had also done thirty-minute interviews with key staff from each of the grantseeking organizations. After determining their final recommendations, which were to go to the County Council for approval, a county staff person said, "We just need to make sure that every member of the County Council is getting funding for a group in his or her district." Thankfully, that was the case, but that criterion was news to the reviewers!

Examples of Review Criteria: Community Foundation

Appropriateness: How well does the project to be funded by this proposal meet the foundation's grant guidelines?

Significance: If the project does meet grant guidelines, how significant is the issue or opportunity to the community, and how meaningful will the project's outcome be? Is evidence offered to substantiate the problem described?

Capacity: How capable does this organization appear to be in carrying out the proposed project successfully?

- Does the organization have a credible record of performance with the issue addressed by this proposal?
- Does the organization's staff have experience working with the issue, populations, and services involved?
- Does the organization have sufficient staff to carry out the project?
- Does the organization have sufficient stability to carry out the project?
- Is the project's budget appropriate for the level and types of activities proposed?

Method: Given the project's proposed outcomes, does the plan of action seem appropriate, and will it be effective in achieving its goals?

- Does the plan of action give a clear enough picture of how the project will proceed?
- Does the plan of action clearly relate to the stated problem or opportunity?
- If this is a new program, is there a credible basis for the plan of action?

Clarity: Are the problem statement, plan of action, and proposed outcomes stated clearly so that reviewers can fully understand what is involved in the project? When finished reading the proposal, will reviewers understand why the project matters and what will happen if it is funded?

Examples of Review Criteria: National Science Foundation

Intellectual merit: What is the intellectual merit of the proposed activity?

- How important is the proposed activity to advancing knowledge and understanding within its own field or across different fields?
- How well qualified is the proposer (individual or team) to conduct the project?
- To what extent does the proposed activity suggest and explore creative and original concepts?

- How well conceived and organized is the proposed activity? Is there sufficient access to resources?

Broader impact: What are the broader impacts of the proposed activity?

- How well does the activity promote teaching, training, and learning?
- How well does the proposed activity augment the participation of underrepresented groups and promote diversity (e.g., ethnic, geographic, sex, gender, and disability diversity)?
- To what extent will it enhance the infrastructure for research and education, e.g., facilities, instrumentation, networks, and partnerships?
- Will the results be disseminated broadly to advance scientific and technological understanding?
- What may be the benefits of the proposed activity to society?

Examples of Review Criteria: National Institutes of Health (*Unsolicited Research Grants and Other Applications*)

Significance: Does this study address an important problem? If the aims of the application are achieved, how will scientific knowledge be advanced? What will be the effect of these studies on the concepts or methods that drive this field?

Approach: Are the conceptual framework, design, methods, and analyses adequately developed, well integrated, and appropriate to the aims of the project? Does the grantseeker acknowledge potential problem areas and consider alternative tactics?

Innovation: Does the project employ novel concepts, approaches, or methods? Are the aims original and innovative? Does the project challenge existing paradigms or develop new methodologies or technologies?

Investigator: Is the investigator appropriately trained and well suited to carry out this work? Is the work proposed appropriate to the experience level of the principal investigator and other researchers (if any)?

Environment: Does the scientific environment in which the work will be done contribute to the probability of success? Do the proposed experiments take advantage of unique features of the scientific environment or employ useful collaborative arrangements? Is there evidence of institutional support?

While the review criteria are intended for use primarily with unsolicited research project proposals, to the extent reasonable they will also form the basis of the review of solicited proposals and non-research activities.

In addition, in accordance with NIH policy, all applications will also be reviewed with respect to the following:

- The adequacy of plans for promoting diversity in terms of sex, gender, ethnicity, and other attributes of participants, as appropriate for the scientific goals of the research. Plans for the recruitment and retention of subjects will also be evaluated.
- The reasonableness of the budget and duration in relation to the proposed research.
- The adequacy of the protections for humans, animals, and the environment, to the extent they may be adversely affected by the project proposed in the application.

Step 4: Decision Made

Applications typically finish the review process in one of these categories:

- **Approved:** The proposal is worthy of support as proposed.
- **Approved, but for less than requested:** The funder is willing to support a part of the proposal. If this happens, you should always scale back what you've promised this funder you will accomplish.
- **Provisionally approved:** Some element of the project or its budget needs to be clarified or modified before a grant will be awarded.
- **Disapproved:** Not fundable at this time.
- **Deferred:** Consideration postponed until the next round of review. This is often done if the funder's budget fluctuates for some reason.

Step 5: Notification Delivered

Government Funders

All government agencies will eventually notify you whether your proposal has been approved, rejected, or held for further discussion. You may receive funding notification in several ways. With federal agencies, an announcement that you are to receive an award may first be sent to you by members of your congressional delegation. As a courtesy to those who approve their annual budgets, most federal agencies tell members of Congress of an award they plan to make at least 24 hours before the notice is sent to the applicant organization. This allows your politicians to give you the good news first. Or, you may simply get an official NOTICE OF GRANT AWARD (NGA).

Never start spending money just because you hear that your application is successful. Until you've received an official confirmation of expenditure authority from a government agency (a signed NGA) and have been notified how to request a draw on the award, any expenditure may be disallowed. Instructions for how to access the funds are typically described in a PAYEE'S GUIDE that arrives close to the award date. This document contains information and instructions to follow so that you can request funds through the federal Grant Administration and Payment System.

And remember, the principal investigator or project director is not the official award recipient. While that person may be the one receiving the notification, the application is submitted and the award received on behalf of the organization. So the payee on the check must first deposit the funds, and then those monies must be spent according to the policies and procedures of the applicant organization. It is here that your earlier consultations with the internal legal staff and business office of your organization will pay off. If they are familiar with the project, steps like getting signatures on contracts and setting up accounts will be done quickly. But if you have not involved these offices previously, your project start may be delayed for months while internal issues get resolved.

Private Funders

With private foundations and corporations, you may or may not receive formal notification of the outcome of your application, especially if the answer is no. Smaller private funders who do not have professional staff often do not bother to communicate with those they don't intend to support. If you have not received word after several months, contact the funder to check.

Foundations and corporations that have approved a grant normally send a letter pledging a certain sum toward the project or organization and indicating that the actual check will be furnished at some later date, or according to some type of payment schedule, or after the grantseeking organization has met certain CONTIN-GENCIES, such as raising the remainder of the money needed for the project or furnishing further information.

All corporations and foundations will ask you either to sign a form or to send them a letter specifying that you agree to use their money in a certain way and promising it will not be spent on the types of activities that may be prohibited by law, such as partisan lobbying. This agreement may need to be furnished before money is released. Provide the requested form or letter and keep a copy for your own files. Larger grantmakers now keep automated records of who has and has not responded, and your organization may be prohibited from receiving additional awards until the form or letter is received.

Negotiations

You may be asked to negotiate further before receiving a final award announcement and/or check. These negotiations are typically one of three kinds:

Fiscal Negotiations

In an effort to spread their money further, many funders will offer to give you less than you originally requested. *Do not agree to this without doing a commensurate scaling down of the scope of your project.*

Substantive Negotiations

Some program officers at funding agencies will ask that you make significant changes in what you propose to do or how you plan to do it. Listen carefully, because highly experienced funders can sometimes help you avoid major problems by adjusting your plans at the outset of the project. But sometimes these requested changes are capricious or based on the funder's inexperience. *Do not agree to changes that will so significantly alter your project that it is no longer of interest or worth to you.*

In some government programs, if there is a significant change to a proposal, a program officer may contact the prospective grantee to make a counteroffer before issuing the grant award. The grantseeker can accept or reject the changes and the funding offer. These offers are usually subject to further negotiation.

Legal Negotiations

Most often, this involves executing some type of written contract that will constrain how you are to use the funds and establish reporting or expenditure requirements. Foundations and corporations tend to call these documents LETTERS OF AGREEMENT or MEMORANDUMS OF UNDERSTANDING. In some federal agencies, this negotiation is called a POST-AWARD PERFORMANCE CONFERENCE. This initial one-time discussion takes place shortly after an award date. Its purpose is to establish a mutual understanding of the specific outcomes that are expected and to establish measures for assessing the project's progress and results. It also clarifies how monitoring and communication will take place.

In many federal programs, a grantee indicates acceptance of the terms of an award by requesting funds from the grant payment system. These terms will have been spelled out in the NGA. If you cannot accept the terms, the grant will be voided. Typically, they are not subject to appeal.

All funders have rules about how much variation you are permitted in spending the money differently than specified in the original budget. Be certain that during the negotiation phase you are clear about those rules. If not, expenditures that exceed permissible variations may be disallowed later. This can be financially, and sometimes legally, disastrous.

Disapproval

Funders tend to reject proposals for one or more of the following reasons:

- The project simply doesn't match their priorities or guidelines.
- The need for or importance of the project wasn't substantiated.
- The proposed methods appeared unsound or unfeasible.
- The competence of the applicant organization was questionable.
- The project budget was either unclear, unrealistic, or inappropriate.
- The proposal was poorly written.

Even a well-written proposal cannot hide basic flaws in concept or planning, but a poorly written one can result in a good project being disapproved.

The only people who never get rejected are those who don't submit proposals. In fact, some individuals and organizations with the best ideas get turned down the most often because they are "ahead of the curve" in their thinking. Few people are fortunate enough to receive a significant grant in any highly competitive field on their very first try. So, give yourself a day to wallow in grief and self-pity, and then get busy deciding how your application can be made stronger and whether you should resubmit it to the same source or look for other potential funders.

Resubmission

If your proposal is rejected, contact the funder to find out why. Explain that you want to improve your next application or would appreciate insights into what elements of the proposal could be strengthened. Under no circumstances should you challenge a decision or try to persuade funders to change their mind. Find out if you should reapply. Reviewers may have really wanted to fund your idea, but couldn't during that cycle because some other proposal was simply more urgent.

Secure copies of review comments, if available, and study them carefully. Based on that feedback, you can judge whether the idea is still worth pursuing or whether you might as well move on to another project or funder.

Renewal

A similar challenge faces organizations whose proposal is successful, particularly if support is secured for only one year at a time. Ask in advance if the funder would entertain a request for multiple-year support. It takes just as much effort to write a request for a one-year $50,000 proposal as it does to write a three-year $150,000 proposal.

More commonly, however, you are faced with submitting a request for renewal before the first year of the funded project is even half over. Usually, this is done in accordance with well-established procedures of the funder and, in most cases, will involve both a progress report on the current project and the presentation of the next year's operation and budget. The re-funding document is seldom as lengthy as the original application, but still requires careful thought. It also takes time, so it is important that you plan for this. Additionally, you will want to plan the project's evaluation so that data useful in this renewal application is produced early.

Typically, funders have separate pots of money for first-time grants and renewal grants. If budgets start to get tight, however, different funders will make different decisions about whether to give priority to renewal grants or new grants. So stay in touch with your funders even after receiving your first award.

Continuity

In many cases, grantmakers will commit to only a one-year grant and will expect you to find other sources of support to continue a project. You should think through how to do this at the outset of the project, because, normally, your plans for continuing the project will be an essential piece of information requested in the original proposal. Sustainability has become a priority with both private and government funders. Your ability to demonstrate the potential longevity of your project is a key element in how competitive your proposal will be.

There are several key lessons to share here:

- Do not promise that a project will be supported in the future by your own organization's budget unless this commitment has actually been made by the appropriate leaders and is substantiated in your application in some definite way. Public school districts, particularly, have a reputation for promising to use their own funds to continue innovations and, unfortunately, seldom doing so. Most grantmakers know this and consider such undocumented promises in an application as evidence of either lack of candor or inexperience.
- Realize that the principal staff on the currently funded project will need to be heavily involved in the development of applications for continued support even if the proposal document is being written by someone else. Plan for staff time accordingly. Consider the overworked project director, 150 percent of whose time has already been promised and who must now repeat the entire process of determining appropriate grant sources, writing abstracts or letters of inquiry, and submitting additional applications.
- If possible, include some resources in the budget of the first award that can help you secure funding for continuation. This may involve such things as travel funds to visit other prospective grantmakers or appearances at professional events that can help you document the significance of your work in future applications.
- Keep attuned to new needs or ideas produced in one project that can be explored in follow-up proposals. Being able to show how a future project is building on a previous one will often enhance your chances with new funders. They like to be associated with success.

All these concerns may be rather overwhelming to the person who has just completed a proposal and has vowed never to do another one (or at least not immediately). But writing proposals can be like eating potato chips: it's difficult to stop at one. One mark of a good project is how it prompts exciting new ideas that are worthy of external support. Once you have realized that the proposal preparation process is similar from application to application, subsequent proposals will go much more smoothly.

Recognition and Good Stewardship

It's easy to neglect your relationship with a funder, once the money is in hand. But there are three big reasons to invest in that relationship after being funded:

- You made a deal with your funders that you would deliver something if they funded you, so you need to follow through on that promise.

- They are more likely to fund you again if they feel like their first grant was appreciated, acknowledged, and worthwhile.
- Funders talk to one another, and if you take good care of them, they will let other potential funders know you are worth investing in.

There are two aspects of relationship-building with funders after you've been funded:

- **Recognition,** which includes public acknowledgment of their support
- **Stewardship,** which involves maintaining a relationship with them throughout and beyond the grant cycle, so they can see how their money is being used, what impact it's making, and how much you value them. Stewardship takes place between just you and your funders: it is not public, unless they choose to publicize something you've shared with them.

Publicly recognize your funders.

As you consider the following list of ways you might recognize funders for their support of your work, keep in mind that some methods may not be appropriate to the situation. For example, while some funders will appreciate your using their logo on your organization's letterhead, others will constrain the use of their trademarks. When in doubt, check with the funder about their preferences.

Here are some ways to publicly recognize or acknowledge funding from a funder or sponsor:

- Seek media coverage about their support of your work with a news release, or share the information with a reporter who covers your field, just to let them know. Send a copy of that communication to the funder so they know about it.

    Many government funders require that you include their logo on your materials and in your electronic presence so that taxpayers see evidence of their taxes at work in their communities.

- Include the funder's name and/or logo in your communications with stakeholders.
- Add an acknowledgment or logo on your letterhead or in the email signature block of relevant staff members.
- Provide an avenue for the funder to communicate with your constituents with a display table at an event or by inserting their brochures or flyers in packets for event participants.
- Send an email or postal mail message to your mailing list
- Include a photo or a feature story about your funders in your newsletter or on your website, and include links to their websites.
- Let funders offer samples of their products or give away an item or a coded coupon.
- Use something with a funder's brand on it at your event, e.g. pens, pads of paper, magnets, cups, or thumb drives.
- Have the master of ceremonies make an announcement acknowledging funders' support at an event, or offer funders the opportunity to have a representative say a few words to the audience.

    A family foundation had funded an organization to create a computer lab in a rural community where no one had Internet access. When a program officer from the foundation dropped in at the lab once on her way through town, she was thrilled to see a piece of white paper taped to the wall above the computers that read, "This computer lab sponsored by Stone Soup."

- Ask if there's someplace your funders would like you to acknowledge their support, such as in the trade publication for their industry or a niche newspaper.

A statewide alliance focusing on kids had a group of youngsters press their painted hands all over a long piece of brightly colored butcher paper, which they used to decorate the walls of their conference room. On it the kids had written, "Thank you to...," including the names of all the corporate sponsors of their annual event. The sponsors loved it because a lot of people saw it throughout the year, the organization didn't spend a lot of money on it, and it reflected the organization's mission and constituency.

Other placement options for a sponsor or funder acknowledgment or logo include the following:

- In marketing materials, e.g., posters, flyers, or ads for the funded project
- On the invitations and printed programs for your organization's events
- On signage at events: offer to hang funders' banners or display their names on an easel where people can see them as they enter, or include funders in an electronic slideshow
- In a sidebar of your e-newsletter or on your website, with a link to theirs
- In your annual report
- On the cover of handouts used in workshops or trainings sponsored by the funder
- On the wall at your office

An organization that was holding a conference took over a whole hotel and arranged with the hotel to have the room keys feature the name of the conference and the sponsor's logo for the duration of the conference.

As you plan your acknowledgment, have a conversation with the leaders of your organization about what types of recognition reflect your organization's brand and values. If you work with impressionable young people, you may want to be careful about how you deal with logos around them. One school determined that they wouldn't accept a grant from an athletic shoe company because the contract specified that the company's logo be painted on a wall at the school. You don't want your constituents to feel like you're compromising your values because there are logos and corporate representatives everywhere. And make sure you're not spending too much money on recognition—funders don't like to see precious resources spent on plaques or etched crystal paperweights that don't mean anything to them.

A nonprofit organization that prepares people emerging from homelessness to work in the restaurant world decorates a prominent wall of their restaurant with large, colorfully decorated dinner plates, each bearing the name and logo of a funder. The funders love the plates because they're mission related, inexpensive, and visible to hundreds of diners.

Steward your funder relationships.

Here are some ways to help funders feel like it was a good idea to fund you:

- Call as soon as you get notification to express your genuine delight—funders seldom get to experience the excitement an organization feels as it gets the good news.

- Send a handwritten note on a card, thanking them for their thoughtful deliberation process.
- Send a formal thank-you on letterhead, assuring them you will follow through on promised activity and keep them informed.
- Have the person responsible for using the funds, the program director or principal investigator, send a note a short while later, saying, "My staff is so excited to be launching this project, now that we have your support. We'll share stories as the project unfolds."
- Have someone who has participated in the funded activity—perhaps a volunteer, a client, or a staff person—share how the work is actually going and how that relates to the promised outcomes.
- Invite one or more representatives from the funder to come take a tour of the space where their money is being spent, e.g., a forest, a neighborhood, a lab, or backstage, so they can see the impact themselves and talk to people involved in the work. If they are too far away to come, make a brief video to capture the outcomes of their money at work, and send it to them electronically.
- Have people who have experienced the effects of the funded activity share those stories in their own words—in a letter, a card or postcard, an email, or a brief video.
- Send several one- to two-sentence quotes from beneficiaries arranged on a one-page flyer.
- Invite an appropriate person from the funder to participate in a focus group with other donors, funders, or experts where they're asked for their opinions about a meaty topic.
- If the funder has substantive material to share with your stakeholders, invite a representative to write a story for your newsletter, website, or blog or to speak in a classroom or meeting.
- Invite a few people from the funder as guests to a mission-related gathering you hold, e.g., a concert, a graduation, an open house, or a gala, and make sure a person of stature in your organization greets and attends to these guests the whole time. Give them tickets that they can share with people they're trying to cultivate or thank. Take a photo of them participating and send it to them later with a note.
- Take photos that illustrate how the grant funds are being used and suggest that funders share the pictures through their own websites, annual reports, or branded communiqués. That way, they can look good to their own stakeholders with your help.
- If you invite staff members from the funder to lunch, use the time to ask their opinions about what's going on in your field or share some exciting developments that no one else knows yet.

"We loved your thank-yous and continued attention! We're not used to hearing from people unless they want something."

—Head of Philanthropy for a chain of grocery stores

"When we gave tickets to our concert to the Corporate Contributions Officer, we assumed he would attend with his wife and their close friends. What we discovered was that he wanted to use the tickets as a benefit to the company's Employee of the Year and her husband, and a potential new customer they were wooing."

—President of a community college

- Share periodic updates by phone, email, or hard copy, whether the funder asks for them or not. Include challenges and delays too, so the program officers know exactly what's going on. No one wants surprises at the end of the grant cycle, and they may learn something from your challenges that can help other grantees avoid similar problems.
- Even after the grant cycle is over and the money is all spent, continue to provide updates on how the funder's support continues to make a difference. This is so unusual, it will be noted and shared with others.
- If the funding produces an end product that can be shared, offer to take it to the funder so all their staff members can experience it—perhaps some students showing the staff what they've learned about science or the environment, or some performers sharing a snippet of their singing, dancing, or acting.
- Offer to document the results of the funded project in a way that the funder can share with other grantees or others in the field.

Reporting

The most important thing you can do to invest in relationships with your funders is capture, measure, and report the impact of their funding. The results are what they paid for and that's what they want most of all. At a minimum you should submit a full written report at the end of the grant cycle explaining how the money was spent and what the outcomes were. Savvy grantseekers communicate more frequently with funders after the award, checking in every few months to let them know how the project is progressing, and sharing both successes and lessons learned along the way.

The best reports will include ending data compared to benchmark data, anecdotal reports of impact, and quotes from staff and beneficiaries. Share graphic representations of changes resulting from the funding, such as photos or other visual evidence of outcomes, and a full report on how the money was spent. Funders will be glad to have quotes, statistics, and photos to use in their own communications, which justify to their own members or employees their investment in your work.

> *"Grantwriters are always talking about how they want to build a relationship with us as they prepare to ask us for money. Once we award them the money, that's when we want the relationship to heat up, and that's when they seem to lose interest in us."*
>
> —Trustee for a family foundation

Summary

Funders can take anywhere from a day to a year to review your proposal and make a decision about whether to fund you. It is best not to contact them, unless you have news that might affect their decision. Once they decide, you may have to negotiate terms with them, and set up systems for getting paid and submitting reports. Go to the Getting Funded website, www.gettingfundedbook.com, for updated information.

Your relationship with a funder doesn't end when you get the check, although that's how it often feels to the funder. How you tend the relationship after you get funded has a huge impact on how funders perceive you and how they speak about you to others. Prove how important their relationship is by acknowledging their support intentionally and strategically, communicating with them often about how things are going and what you're learning, and helping them see the effect of their support so they can see what a wise investment they made by funding you.

Key Terms

CONTINGENCY: A condition imposed by a grantmaker that must be met before funds will be released to the grantseeking organization. Contingencies can include a requirement that your organization raise the remainder of the money needed for the project or furnish further information.

FUNDING OFFER: The amount of money, which can be more or less than the requested amount, that a funder offers a grantseeker.

LETTER OF AGREEMENT or MEMORANDUM OF UNDERSTANDING (MOU): A written contract between private grantmaker and funded organization that constrains how the organization may use the funds and establishes reporting or expenditure requirements. May also be a binding contract between two or more partner organizations.

NOTICE OF GRANT AWARD (NGA): A contract between federal grantmaker and funded organization that details how funds may be used and establishes expenditure requirements. The NGA is the confirmation of expenditure authority provided once the grant has been awarded.

PAYEE'S GUIDE: Instructions for how to access funds awarded by a federal agency. This term is specific to government grants.

POST-AWARD PERFORMANCE CONFERENCE: An initial, one-time discussion between government grantmaker and funded organization. It takes place shortly after the award date, and its purpose is to establish a mutual understanding of the specific outcomes that are expected and to set measures for assessing the project's progress and results. It also clarifies how monitoring and communication will take place.

APPENDIXES

APPENDIX A   PROPOSAL DEVELOPMENT CHECKLIST

Chapter 1: Ensuring Organizational Readiness

Have you done the following:

- ❑ Figured out if your organization is eligible to apply?
- ❑ Made sure your board is behind this effort?
- ❑ Crafted a strong, clear mission statement?
- ❑ Developed a strategic plan?
- ❑ Clarified who your primary stakeholders are?
- ❑ Researched the best strategy for addressing this problem?
- ❑ Determined what you think you can accomplish?
- ❑ Nailed down what differentiates your organization from others?
- ❑ Identified others who might cooperate with you on the project?
- ❑ Assessed your organization's reputation and addressed any negative perceptions?
- ❑ Enumerated a budget for the project that fits your organizational budget?
- ❑ Secured the buy-in of board, staff, and volunteers needed for the project?
- ❑ Assessed the infrastructure (e.g., equipment, systems) you will need to succeed?

Chapter 2: Defining the Need

Have you done the following:

- ❑ Determined how you know this need or opportunity exists?
- ❑ Corroborated the need with proof from others?
- ❑ Identified who else is doing similar work and what they're experiencing?
- ❑ Defined precisely who is affected?
- ❑ Ascertained the scope of the need and what part of it you can address?
- ❑ Identified the root cause of the need?
- ❑ Articulated what would happen if you didn't address this need or opportunity?

Chapter 3: Designing Your Project

Have you done the following:

- ❑ Articulated why this need is relevant to your community?
- ❑ Identified how this need relates to your organization's mission and work?
- ❑ Nailed down why this need or opportunity is relevant to this funder?
- ❑ Stated why now is the time to address this need?
- ❑ Confirmed that your organization has the capacity to implement the project?
- ❑ Narrowed down which methods you will use to carry out the project?
- ❑ Determined exactly what you think you can change with this work?

Chapter 5: Deciding How to Fund Your Project

Have you done the following:

- ❑ Figured out the most appropriate type of support to request?
- ❑ Decided whether to respond to an RFP or initiate your own proposal?

Chapter 6: Finding a Suitable Funding Match

Have you done the following:

- ❑ Researched which kinds of funding sources might be most suitable for this project?
- ❑ Sought out potential sources from among your organization's existing relationships (e.g., those you serve; your vendors, board, staff, volunteers, elected officials, partners; previous funders)?
- ❑ Screened prospective funders to prioritize those with the most common ground?
- ❑ Gathered information on these funders' guidelines, deadlines, compliance requirements, and legal and financial expectations to make sure your organization is eligible?
- ❑ Looked beyond the funders' guidelines for more information (e.g., annual reports, IRS Forms 990, websites; other people's experiences) that might help determine a good fit?

❑ Checked to make sure others in your institution aren't planning to approach the same funder?

Chapter 7: Making a Good First Impression
Have you done the following:

❑ Done your homework to see how the funder prefers to be approached?

❑ Combed through the funder's guidelines or instructions for clues about how to connect?

❑ Written a letter of inquiry if requested, according to the funder's instructions?

❑ Cultivated a relationship by offering value before asking for money?

Chapter 8: Preparing to Write
Have you done the following:

❑ Met with other key players in the project to discuss the project?

❑ Gathered a team of colleagues who will participate in and support the proposal-writing process?

❑ Created a timeline for developing the proposal?

❑ Started the process for getting compliance documents signed?

❑ Made a list of all the requirements in the funder's guidelines?

❑ Developed an outline of the major points to make in each proposal section?

❑ Identified the sections where input is needed from others and given them clear instructions on what you need, with deadlines?

❑ Secured early approvals from legal and financial staff?

❑ Identified those who might write letters of support or endorsement?

❑ Collected previous proposals, statistics, quotes, stories, photos, budgets, plans, and lists of board members, advisors, and key staff, with bios, so they're ready when you need them?

❑ Registered for electronic submission if appropriate and walked through the process?

❑ Scheduled uninterrupted time for writing, and blocked out your calendar near the deadline?

Chapter 9: Composing the Need Statement
Have you done the following:

❑ Prepared to answer why the need or opportunity is significant and timely?

❑ Pulled together statistics that make your case about the scope of the need?

❑ Determined what costs result from the need existing?

❑ Documented promising strategies for addressing the need?

❑ Calculated what potential barriers have exacerbated the need?

❑ Made sure your need statement doesn't describe too difficult a problem to solve?

❑ Refrained from calling the problem the absence of what you propose?

❑ Attributed the need to someone or something outside your organization, not to your organization itself?

❑ Crafted a need statement that can be the basis for every other section of the proposal?

Chapter 10: Writing the Project Description
Have you done the following:

❑ Captured your project in a logic model framework?

❑ Named clear goals and objectives that your project hopes to achieve?

❑ Devised clear, measurable outcomes that represent the change you seek?

❑ Made a convincing case for why you chose the strategy you will employ?

❑ Described the demographic profile of those who will benefit from the project?

❑ Named the key players who will be responsible for implementing the project?

❑ Illustrated graphically your plan for how the project will unfold?

❑ Clarified how you will share your findings and help others replicate your project?

❑ Demonstrated a clear plan for sustaining the project after this grant?

❑ Strategized how you might acknowledge the funder?

❑ Aligned the project description with other major elements of the proposal?

❑ Come up with a succinct and engaging introduction to your project?

Chapter 11: Designing an Evaluation Plan
Have you done the following:

- ❑ Decided precisely what you intend to measure?
- ❑ Determined what information to collect and from whom?
- ❑ Ensured that you will have access to that data and those people when necessary?
- ❑ Strategized how and by whom data will be collected and analyzed?
- ❑ Decided whether any outside evaluators will be involved and identified them?
- ❑ Come up with a timeline for data analysis and reporting?
- ❑ Established a baseline to measure against?
- ❑ Created a budget for the evaluation process?

Chapter 12: Developing the Project Budget
Have you done the following:

- ❑ Ascertained what internal guidelines your organization may have about budgets?
- ❑ Researched what the funder expects to get and in what format?
- ❑ Agreed on which elements of the budget your organization will contribute to the project?
- ❑ Identified all the costs associated with the project and which are direct costs and indirect costs?
- ❑ Captured and valued any in-kind contributions that will affect the budget?
- ❑ Arranged the budget (1) by category, (2) by time, and (3) by source, with justifications?
- ❑ Assembled your organizational budget, audited financial statement, and plan for future funding?
- ❑ Resolved how much to ask for and for what, and what you will do if less is awarded?
- ❑ Had others outside the project review the budget to see what questions are raised?

Chapter 13: Establishing Your Qualifications
Have you done the following:

- ❑ Demonstrated that your organization's experience and background positions it well for this project?
- ❑ Shown that the people who govern your organization are capable and paying attention?
- ❑ Included reassuring information about the staff who will implement the project?

- ❑ Discussed how you will go about securing appropriate staff upon funding?
- ❑ Proven that you have infrastructure and systems in place to enable the project?

Chapter 14: Preparing Supplemental Documents
Have you done the following:

- ❑ Followed instructions carefully as you filled out the cover sheet?
- ❑ Developed a title for the proposal that captures its essence?
- ❑ Written a compelling cover letter that invites further attention?
- ❑ Produced an executive summary or abstract that engages as it enlightens?
- ❑ Gotten signatures on all assurances and compliance forms?
- ❑ Included a legible copy of your IRS tax determination letter?
- ❑ Located a copy of your most recent IRS Form 990 and financial statements?
- ❑ Included a list of board members, advisors, partners, and so forth?
- ❑ Received letters of support and memos of understanding from partners in the project?
- ❑ Included an organizational chart, if requested?
- ❑ Prepared estimates from vendors, if items or services will be purchased?
- ❑ Looked over the RFP or guidelines one more time to make sure you have included everything requested?

Chapter 16: Reviewing and Submitting Your Proposal
Have you done the following:

- ❑ Subjected your proposal to review by several other colleagues?
- ❑ Checked to make sure you didn't commit any of the seven deadly sins of proposal writing?
- ❑ Combed the instructions one last time to ensure that you have complied with every request?
- ❑ Examined your electronic document to make sure every section fits in the space allowed?
- ❑ Arranged for early submission, whether electronic or hard copy, to make sure the application arrives well before the deadline?
- ❑ Verified that the proposal was received in time?

Hiring a freelance grantwriter can be a cost-effective solution for organizations that don't have the staff capacity to create competitive grant proposals. The right freelance grantwriter, with experience in the field, can expertly guide an organization through the proposal development process.

Using an outside grantwriter in no way diminishes an organization's need to prepare for and support the creation of the proposal. While an outside grantwriter can greatly assist the process, the bulk of the work of proposal preparation and development will still fall on organization staff. Grantwriters, whether internal or external to the organization, do not work in a vacuum. It is not only unrealistic to hand a list of proposal requirements to a freelance grantwriter and expect that person to "take it away" and write a proposal, it is also irresponsible. And it sets both your proposal and the freelance grantwriter up to fail. As discussed throughout this book, quality proposals are a result of the coordinated efforts of people at many levels of your organization. Indeed, the proposal process itself should be seen as a dynamic force for organizational self-reflection and growth.

Qualifications

If you are planning to seek outside grantwriting expertise, you should first consider all the factors addressed in Chapter 1 to make sure your organization is prepared for the proposal development process. If your organization is prepared, and you have determined it's best to hire outside help, here are a few questions to ask about a potential freelance grantwriter:

- Does the freelance grantwriter's résumé reflect sufficient knowledge and experience of grantwriting? How long has this person been writing proposals? For what types of organizations? What types of proposals?
- Does the freelance grantwriter have experience with your research area, knowledge base, service type, client population, and geographic region?

- If the freelance grantwriter is not familiar with your organization's work, or if your organization has unique aspects that few outsiders are likely to be familiar with, does the freelance grantwriter have transferable skills?
- Is there a match between the freelance grantwriter's experience and the skill level needed for your proposal?
- Has the freelance grantwriter had experience with proposals of similar size and scope?
- Is the freelance grantwriter capable of working closely with the individual staff members who will be helping compile and present the required information?
- Can the freelance grantwriter communicate clearly and respectfully to obtain information and support from people at all levels of your organization?
- Does the freelance grantwriter's work style (e.g., organizational skills, demeanor, approach to deadlines) fit with your organization's practices and culture?
- Does the freelance grantwriter share the vision of your organization?
- Do the freelance grantwriter's writing samples indicate the ability to create a compelling case for funding?
- How does the freelance grantwriter charge? By the hour? By the project? Can the freelance grantwriter provide an estimate in advance of how much the total cost of grantwriting services might be?

Expectations

Always ask for clarification about what the freelance grantwriter will do for your organization if hired, and how. Not all freelance grantwriters operate the same way, but there are some generally agreed-upon guidelines.

Freelance grantwriters *do*:

- Require that your organization be ready to write grants, or at least be willing to work hard to get there
- Work for rates by the hour or by the project
- Research funding sources and help make an organization's project sound appealing to funders

Freelance contractors *don't*:

- Take deferred payment or work on commission (i.e., for a percentage of the amount granted)
- Work pro bono, unless it is their own idea
- Write for individuals, with few exceptions

Costs

Individual freelancers estimate costs and bid for projects in different ways. Some prefer to charge an hourly rate so that they get paid no matter how long a project takes. This relieves them of risk in case there are unforeseen factors that prolong the project. Other freelancers will bid the cost of a particular project on a flat fee, or project rate. Many organizations like project rates because it gives them a fixed cost they can plan on for a particular proposal.

There are many variables that affect the cost of a grantwriting project. Some of these include:

- **The organization's level of preparedness:** Can the organization's staff provide information to the freelance grantwriter quickly and accurately? Will the freelance grantwriter need to create background documents, such as a case statement, lists of prior grants, or budget documents, for the organization? Grantwriting often exposes gaps in organizational readiness or program design that will have to be addressed to compete successfully for the grant. Experienced freelance grantwriters can help with this preparation, but the work will increase time and expense.
- **The organization's experience with grant-seeking:** Is there an archive of information or past successful proposals from which to pull data? Are there finance staff from the organization available to work with the freelance grantwriter? Has the organization already made sure that its outcomes are tied to its program activities and budget? The more information the organization has ready, the faster a freelance

grantwriter can complete a proposal.

- **The grantwriter's experience with the organization's sector:** The time it will take to complete a proposal will vary depending on how familiar the freelance grantwriter is with the organization's sector (e.g., housing, economic development, land conservation, dance) and the organization's beneficiaries.
- **The complexity of the proposal:** There is a great difference between submitting a proposal to a small family foundation and responding to a federal RFP. Some foundation proposals are four or five pages long and might take a freelance grantwriter fifteen to twenty-five hours to prepare, while a proposal to a federal agency or national foundation may take a freelance grantwriter more than a hundred hours to complete.
- **The level of familiarity with the funder:** If either the grantseeking organization or the freelance grantwriter has previous experience approaching the funder, and understands the nuances of the funder's guidelines, preferences, and culture or knows the funder's staff well, it should take less time to craft the proposal.

Freelance grantwriters who are also grants consultants have deeper and broader expertise. These and other experienced grantwriters will provide more value, and therefore charge more. Their experience may save money in the long run, however, as they can work more quickly and more adeptly than less experienced freelance grantwriters.

If your organization decides to bring in an outside grantwriter, do not underestimate the time it will take to coordinate the freelancer's work with that of others within your organization.

As with all forms of hiring, cost should be only one variable in selecting a freelance grantwriter. Other factors such as skill, experience, compatibility, and availability should also carry weight when making a choice to hire someone.

Ethics of Payment

When your organization hires a freelance grantwriter, you can negotiate either an hourly rate or a project fee. Compensation based on a percentage of a grant award is never ethical, and in some cases is illegal. A frequent question is, Can our organization hire a grantwriter for a percentage or commission of the grants awarded? The answer, simply, is no. Commissions are considered unethical by almost all professional organizations and funders. They are also a bad idea for both the grantseeking organization and the freelance grantwriter.

Funders frown upon percentage fees, and many will not fund an organization if they find out it pays contractors on this basis. Funders seldom allow fees

From the Funder's Corner

A funder's main concern about fundraiser compensation lies in the answer to this question: What would charitable fundraising look like if it were a standard practice to pay fundraisers on commission? Public confidence and support of organizations would be undermined. —*Ken Ristine*

for freelance grantwriters to be included in the project budget, and hiding the cost in another line item is dishonest. Furthermore, it is illegal to pay a grantwriter out of federal and federal flow-through grants.

The Association of Fundraising Professionals' Code of Ethical Principles and Standards of Professional Practice states that members are not to accept payment based on percentages of funds received.[1]

An organization may ask, Why should we pay the grantwriter if we didn't get the grant? How is that fair?

Proposals succeed or fail for a number of reasons, most of which are out of the grantwriter's control. Among these are the following:

- The strength of the project, including its feasibility, budget, and ability to meet a clear community need
- The match between the project and the funder's interests
- The organization's reputation, track record, and financial history

- The relationships, including how well the funder knows and trusts the grantseeking organization's board and staff
- The competition, including how many other requests the funder has received and from whom
- The timing and availability of funds, including how much money the funder has available in this funding cycle and whether some of the money has been set aside for other organizations

The quality and persuasiveness of a proposal can be shaped by the grantwriter, yet even the most beautifully written proposal will fail if other factors are not in its favor.

Many small organizations, just starting out, have wondered, How are we supposed to pay a freelance grantwriter if we don't have any money?

If an organization doesn't have any money, it is not ready to apply for grants. Grants should never be an organization's first dollar. New organizations need to raise funds from individuals first, approaching people who believe in the organization or the cause and are willing to make a contribution to get it started. For more information, go to the Getting Funded website, www.gettingfundedbook.com.

1. "Members shall not accept compensation or enter into a contract that is based on a percentage of contributions, nor shall members accept finder's fees or contingent fees. Business members must refrain from receiving compensation from the third parties derived from products or services for a client without disclosing that third-party compensation to the client (for example, volume rebates from vendors to business members)." *Code of Ethical Principles and Standards of Professional Practice*, © 1964, Association of Fundraising Professionals (AFP), all rights reserved. Reprinted with permission from the Association of Fundraising Professionals.

SYLLABUS FOR A NINE-SESSION COURSE

The following syllabus offers suggestions for classroom exercises and homework assignments to help students work through all sections of a proposal. By the end of the nine sessions, students will have a completed draft of a proposal. Further suggestions for assignments and classroom exercises are included on page 220.

Session 1

Content

- Where grants fit in an organization's overall fundraising strategy ("Principles of Successful Grantseeking")
- What is included in the proposal development process ("Diagram of the Proposal Development Process")
- How to determine organizational readiness (Chapter 1)

Classroom Exercises

- Ask students who they think are the key people who should be involved at each stage of the proposal development process (people both internal and external to their organizations).
- Invite students to imagine that they are giving away their own money, and ask them what they would want to know about grantseeking organizations and what would make one organization more appealing than its competitors. Use this discussion to show the relationship between grantseeking and topics of organizational readiness.

Assignments

- Read "Principles of Effective Grantseeking" and Chapters 1, 2, and 3.
- Assess your organization's level of readiness to seek grants by referring to the information in Chapter 1 and the questions in the "Checklist for Assessing Organizational Readiness" checklist

(Fig. 1.1). List which aspects of your organization are grant-ready, and which aspects require attention.
- Draft your organization's background in two paragraphs.

Session 2

Content

- Why and how to conduct a needs assessment (Chapter 2)
- How to use logic models; how to distinguish between outputs and outcomes (Chapter 3)

Classroom Exercises

- Review assignments; answer questions that emerge from the assigned reading.
- Discuss with students the distinction between organization needs and community needs, and ask students to practice describing both types of needs using examples from their organizations.
- Ask students how they might go about discovering and proving the need for ideas their organizations would like to get funded to do. What could they gather from their own organizations, and what other people or organizations might have experience with, or statistics about, the problem or opportunity? How might they conduct a needs assessment if there were no statistics available?
- Have students list the types of work their organizations do and practice articulating that work as outputs and as outcomes.
- Have students write down a so-that chain for two activities their organizations engage in, and see which items are outputs and which are outcomes or goals.

Assignments

- Read Chapters 4, 5, and 6.
- Locate statistics, or sources of statistics, to corroborate the need you hope to address.
- Draft a statement of need for your organization.
- Draft a logic model for your organization that reflects the need.

Session 3

Content

- What types of funders exist and where and how to look for them (Chapters 4 and 5)
- How to discern which funders are good matches for your organization (Chapter 6)

Classroom Exercises

- Review assignments; answer questions that emerge from the assigned reading.
- Discuss the sources of statistics students discovered for corroborating need.
- Have students form small groups and edit and revise their need statements and outcome statements; debrief as a class.
- After discussing different types of funders, have students brainstorm which types might be most appropriate for the organizations represented in the class.
- Have students return to their small groups and discuss how different types of funders (e.g., government, corporate, family foundation, trade union) might have different motivations and priorities.
- Make a list of grantseeking organizations and a corresponding list of grantmakers who funded them. Bring copies of the lists to class and have students match grantseeker to grantmaker, using the criteria listed in "Look for Common Ground" in Chapter 6. Or print the names of the funders on sheets of paper that can be taped to the walls of the classroom, so students can get up and walk around as they look for potential matches. (You'll find a generic version of this exercise on the Getting Funded website, www.gettingfundedbook.com.)

Assignments

- Read Chapters 7, 8, 9, and 10.
- Research funders and identify a few worth pursuing, including justifications for why they would be a good fit.
- Identify five opportunities to cultivate a relationship with a potential funder.

Note to Instructors: Contact your favorite online grant search resource and ask if your students can have temporary access for a few days at no cost. Most sources will comply.

Session 4

Content

- How to prepare to write a proposal (Chapter 8)
- How to write need statements and project descriptions (Chapters 9 and 10)

Classroom Exercises

- Review assignments; answer questions that emerge from the assigned reading.
- In small groups, have students discuss who belongs on a project description planning team and how to engage those individuals in the process.
- Give students time to draft their project descriptions in class, then discuss.

Assignments

- Read Chapters 11, 13, 14, and 15.
- Revise your need statement.
- Write a draft project description.

Session 5

Content

- What is evaluation (Chapter 11)
- What are qualifications (Chapter 13)
- What supplemental documents are required (Chapter 14)

Classroom Exercises

- Review assignments; answer questions that emerge from the assigned reading.
- Have students form small groups to review their statements of need and project descriptions, then have students share the results of their conversations with the whole class.
- Have students brainstorm what they could evaluate and how to align that with need and outcomes.
- Have students return to their small groups to discuss what it would take to get others in their organizations to support the evaluation process.
- Have students practice writing the opening lines of a letter of inquiry.

Assignments

- Read Chapter 12.
- Draft more finalized proposal sections on organizational background and qualifications.
- Draft more finalized proposal section on evaluation.

Session 6

Content

- How to create a project budget (Chapter 12)
- How to determine how much to ask for (Chapter 12)
- How to plan for future funding (Chapter 12)
- How to respond to a reduced award (Chapter 12)

Classroom Exercises

- Review assignments; answer questions that emerge from the assigned reading.
- Have students work in pairs to list possible income and expense items in a generic organizational budget, not including specific project-related costs.
- Have students brainstorm how to determine the costs of a project with others in the organization.
- Bring actual budgets from real proposals and have students try to figure out as much as they can about the organizations by looking at nothing but their budgets. Have students first work alone, and then in small groups.
- Have students practice pulling project costs out of a larger organizational budget.
- Have students brainstorm about how to deal with questions about future funding.

Assignments

- Read Chapter 16.
- Draft a budget to accompany your proposal, including budget justification worksheets.
- Draft a plan for sustaining your project beyond this grant.
- Draft an answer to the question about what you would do if awarded a smaller amount.

Session 7

Content

- How to conduct an internal review (Chapter 16)
- How to write an executive summary (Chapters 8 and 14)
- When and how to write letters of inquiry (Chapter 15)

Classroom Exercises

- Review assignments; answer questions that emerge from the assigned reading.
- Have students critique each other's budget drafts.
- Have students practice writing an executive summary in class.

- Have students practice writing a letter of inquiry in class, then review one another's letters.

Assignments

- Read Chapter 17.
- Finalize your entire proposal, including support documents and a letter of inquiry. Bring enough copies for a group review at next class, plus one copy to turn in. Use either "The Seven Deadly Sins of Proposal Writing" (Fig. 16.1) or the "Proposal Development Checklist" in Appendix A to review.

Session 8

Content

- What makes a proposal work: students and professional grantwriters critique proposals

Classroom Exercises

- Answer questions that emerge from the assigned reading.
- Have students critique one another's letters of inquiry in small groups; debrief as a class.
- Have students form small groups, each including a guest grantwriter, and review one another's proposals.
- Reconvene as a large group and ask the guest grantwriters to share patterns, strengths, and opportunities for growth they identified in students' proposals, then share tips, tricks, lessons learned, and pet peeves from their own experiences.

Assignments

- Finalize your proposal, incorporating feedback from the group and class discussion.
- Draft a cultivation and stewardship plan for a particular funder.

Session 9

Content

- What happens after submission (Chapter 17)
- How to steward a relationship with a funder after getting a grant (Chapter 17)
- Funders' perspectives: invite a guest panel of grantmakers, preferably one person from a government funder, one person from a corporation, one person from a foundation, and one person from a community-based group, such as public foundation or service club

Classroom Exercises

- Have students work in pairs to brainstorm ways to cultivate a relationship with a funder before applying for a grant; debrief as a class.
- Have students turn in final proposals with budgets.
- Review cultivation and stewardship plans.
- Discuss what to do in the event of rejection.
- Have students work in pairs to brainstorm funder recognition tactics that don't cost much money and that align with their organization's current activities, mission, and culture.
- Welcome the panel of guest funders.
- Celebrate the successful completion of class with treats.

SYLLABUS FOR A ONE-DAY WORKSHOP

This syllabus offers suggestions for how to structure a one-day workshop to present key information about grantseeking and grantwriting.

Morning—Part I

List elements of standard applications and discuss lengths and formats, then cover the three most important areas, listed below:

Need: Review the importance of need, then ask students:

- How they could determine and corroborate need
- Where they could look for statistics
- Whom they could gather information from, if no research had been done
- How they could determine who else is doing similar work
- How they could distinguish their organization or their work from others'

Project description: Review goals, objectives, outputs, and outcomes, then have students practice differentiating between outputs and outcomes in their own work.

Evaluation: Review the importance of evaluation, then have students explore:

- What types of things could be tracked and measured
- How to determine a baseline and a target

Morning—Part II

- Review types of grant sources and the distinctions among them.
- Break students into groups and ask them to pretend they are different types of funders to see how their motivations, questions, and answers might vary.
- Bring guidelines from government, corporate, and foundation funders and review them to explore matches with organizations students represent. Stress the importance of finding the best fit between project goals and funder goals.

Afternoon—Part I

- Review how to write a letter of inquiry.
- Have students practice writing an LOI, then have them form small groups to critique what they wrote.

Afternoon—Part II

- Provide a brief overview of budgets.
- Have students work in pairs to come up with revenues and expenses categories, then show students how budgets are usually formatted.
- Have groups of students study sample budgets to see what they can tell from the numbers.
- Describe the entire proposal process, time frame, and key players involved in each stage.
- List common challenges, and how to address them:
  - How much money to request
  - How to respond if a funder offers a reduced award
  - How to answer questions about future funding
  - How to get others in their organizations to cooperate in the proposal development process
- Answer final questions from students.

MORE CLASSROOM EXERCISES AND ASSIGNMENTS

The following list includes optional assignments and classroom exercises that instructors can use to enhance classroom instruction and textbook review.

Part I: Know Your Organization and Field

- Have students share their own experience of any of the trends mentioned in the book's introduction.
- Have students form small groups to discuss their own organizations' preparedness and what role they see themselves playing in the grantseeking process.
- Have students locate statistics from government sources that prove the need they intend to address.
- Have students identify three ways of addressing a need, then find information that might help them decide which method would be most appropriate.
- Have students research who else is working on the issue within the same geographic scope.
- Have students form small groups to discuss which stakeholders (internal and external) should be included either in their own proposal idea or in a generic example posed by the instructor.
- Ask students to articulate why it matters whether a proposal is solicited or unsolicited.
- Assign students to identify and bring to class a request for proposal (RFP) they have found using the Internet. Examine these and see how they differ.
- Ask students to explain the difference between a grant and a contract.

Part II: Know the Funders

- Have students locate four different funders and explore how responses to them might differ.
- Have students form four or five small groups and have each group represent a type of funder (e.g., government, corporate, family foundation, service club). Have the groups compile lists of questions they would put on an application form, then discuss what would constitute

a compelling answer, depending on the type of funder they represent. (Consider having one foundation that is old and established, and another foundation that is edgy and entrepreneurial.) Ask students to share and discuss their impressions with the whole class.

Part III: Write and Submit a Competitive Proposal

- Assign students to develop an outline of a proposal, indicating the main points to be covered in each section and identifying which parts will require input from other sources.
- Have students develop a timeline for steps in developing their proposal.
- Have students write a paragraph describing a need they wish to address, then break into small groups to read one another's statements and determine whether they describe internal, organizational needs or external, community needs.
- Ask students to list organizations or agencies they might include in a needs assessment or focus group to clarify the extent of the need they hope to address.
- Present students with a sample statement of need. Have students draft a plan of action to address the need, matching the scope of the need with the scope of the proposed solution and its desired outcomes.
- Have students form small groups. Give each group several one-paragraph project descriptions, and have the group draft a goal, an objective, an outcome, and an output related to each. Have them share their answers with the class.
- Have students draft a two-paragraph plan for dissemination of results, including anticipated audiences.
- Assign students to research three Internet sites with particularly useful guidance on evaluation and to report to the whole class on their favorite.
- Assign teams of students to create a program logic model for a project suggested by the instructor, and discuss how each team's answers compare.
- Have students submit a paragraph describing a particular evaluation problem they're experiencing as they write their proposal. Have one or two professional evaluators attend class and offer options for resolving the difficulties.

- Assign students to come to class having prioritized three methods of evaluation for their project with an assessment of which option is most useful, easiest, least expensive, and most appropriate for that organization. Discuss students' choices with the full class.
- Assign students to research a funder that accepts proposals that include indirect costs, and determine which costs in their organization's budget would be in that category.
- Pass out several IRS Forms 990 and have students analyze them in small groups. (You can find Forms 990 online at www.guidestar.org.)
- Have students create a three-year budget for a start-up project, with the hope that the project will remain in place after the initial grant, and show which costs might be incurred in each phase of implementation.
- Have students create a budget (a mock one or one tied to their proposal) with multiple sources of revenue (including in-kind contributions of services and goods), some from the grant-seeking organization and some from external sources.
- Invite students to write a paragraph asserting why an emerging organization with little experience is qualified to carry out a project.
- Have each student bring a roster of a board of directors, including members' bios or backgrounds, to see what reviewers might be able to tell about that organization from their board list.
- Have students prepare a letter of inquiry for a specific project tailored to (1) a government funder, (2) a staffed private foundation, (3) a corporate giving officer, and (4) a professional association.
- Have students search the Internet for information on why proposals get rejected, then share their findings with their fellow students.
- Invite students to make a list of ten ways to thank a funder without spending much money and ten ways to keep the funder informed and engaged after the grant has been awarded.

The more that students can apply the concepts in this book to real experiences, the more they'll learn. Have fun teaching to diverse learning styles with interactive class sessions and interesting assignments!

GLOSSARY

ABSTRACT: A synopsis of the full proposal. Some grant-makers provide an online form to complete, while others do not specify the format. Length varies by funder, from one to two paragraphs to one to two pages. Also called EXECUTIVE SUMMARY.

ACTIVITY: A specific step that will be taken so that an organization's methods or tactics work.

ACTIVITIES STATEMENT: A statement of the specific tasks and timelines that will be used to reach the project's goals.

ADMINISTRATIVE COSTS: See INDIRECT COSTS.

APPROACH: The course of action you engage in to effect change. Also called STRATEGY.

ATTACHMENT: A supplementary document requested by funders to support and augment elements in the main proposal or to verify organizational status. Common attachments are an organization's 501(c)(3) letter of determination, board of directors list, organizational chart, and copies of contracts, maps, construction drawings, and audited financial statements.

AUDIT: A formal examination of an organization's financial accounts, conducted by an external professional, to ensure the organization is managing its finances in accordance with generally accepted accounting practices (GAAP). An audit may also include an examination of the organization's compliance with applicable terms, laws, and regulations.

AUDITED FINANCIAL STATEMENT: A review and verification of an organization's financial statements by an accountant, according to generally accepted accounting principles (GAAP). Audited financial statements can assure funders that an organization's financial information is presented fairly.

AWARD: Financial or other assistance to accomplish a purpose. Awards include grants, contracts, and other agreements that provide money, or property in lieu of money, to eligible recipients.

BENCHMARK EVALUATION: A type of evaluation that compares measurements taken after a project is underway with benchmark assessments, which are measurements taken before the work began, or at intervals during it.

BUDGET: A financial plan that estimates your income and expenses for a specific period of time (see also BUDGET PERIOD). Budgets may describe project or program activities or your entire organization's activities, and are primarily used to estimate and compare against actual financial results.

BUDGET JUSTIFICATION: An expanded version of your budget that clarifies for reviewers how the figures in the budget were calculated.

BUDGET NARRATIVE: A written explanation, in words, that helps anyone reading your numeric budgets understand what the numbers mean, how you arrived at them, and any implications that arise.

BUDGET PERIOD: The interval of time, usually twelve months, into which the project period is divided for budgetary and funding purposes. Also called OPERATING PERIOD.

CAPACITY-BUILDING GRANT: An investment in an organization's ability to function more effectively, scale up, or become more self-sustaining. This type of grant often pays for strategic planning, technology planning, leadership development or training, fundraising training, or development of an earned-income stream. Sometimes capacity-building grants pay for new staff or new systems, such as a donor database. Also called TECHNICAL ASSISTANCE GRANT.

CAPITAL CONTRIBUTION: Funding that helps an organization secure land, build or remodel facilities, or acquire equipment. Also called CAPITAL GRANT.

CASE STATEMENT: An internal document that collects and distills all the data you've collected on your proposed project so that everything you need to communicate with supporters—from volunteers and collaborators to government agencies, private grantmaking organizations, the media, and individual donors—is available in one document.

CENTRAL CONTRACTOR REGISTRATION (CCR): All grantseekers who wish to submit a proposal to the federal government must first register with CCR in order to use the online portal Grants.gov. Go online to www.bpn.gov/ccr for details. See also DUNS NUMBER.

CHALLENGE GRANT: Money provided by a funder as an incentive for others to contribute. Usually, recipients of challenge grants must raise a specified amount of contributions from others before the grant money will be awarded. See also MATCHING GRANT.

COLLABORATOR: One of the people or groups with common goals, and shared or complementary interests, assets, and professional skills, that work cooperatively for the community's benefit.

COMMUNITY FOUNDATION: A foundation formed to encourage people from a particular geographic community to contribute cash, appreciated stocks, real estate, or other assets to a pooled fund. Community foundations use the interest generated by the pooled assets to provide grants to organizations in their community; they also administer donor-advised funds, in which contributions to the foundation can be directed to organizations of the donor's choice. See also PUBLIC FOUNDATION.

COMPANY-SPONSORED CORPORATE FOUNDATION: See CORPORATE FOUNDATION.

COMPILATION: A document created by an external financial professional that verifies the accuracy of an organization's financial information. Compilation and review processes are less rigorous than audits and may not reveal deeper problems.

CONTINGENCY: A condition imposed by a grantmaker that must be met before funds will be released to the grantseeking organization. Contingencies can include a requirement that your organization raise the remainder of the money needed for the project or furnish further information.

CONTINUATION AWARD: A grant or contract that renews support of a previously funded project. Most continuation awards must be reviewed and reapproved; they may or may not require a complete proposal at each approval period, depending on the funder. Also called CONTINUING SUPPORT.

CONTRACT: An award for a project solicited through an RFP (request for proposal). The funder will have already identified the need and the expected outcomes, selected an acceptable cost range, and estimated the time required to complete the proposal.

CONTRIBUTED INCOME: Money generated by an organization by asking individuals, organizations, or small businesses to make charitable gifts. Compare to EARNED INCOME AND GRANTED INCOME.

CONTRIBUTION IN KIND: See IN-KIND CONTRIBUTION.

CORPORATE FOUNDATION: A legally independent grantmaking organization with close ties to the corporation that provides its funds. Corporate foundations must publicly disclose grantmaking activities and grant a certain percentage of assets each year. Also called COMPANY-SPONSORED CORPORATE FOUNDATION. Compare to CORPORATE GIVING PROGRAM.

CORPORATE GIVING PROGRAM: A program that makes corporate gifts, derived from corporate profits, outside the construct of a corporate foundation. Corporate giving programs may also be called corporate social responsibility departments; they usually work closely with the company's marketing, community relations, and public relations departments. Compare to CORPORATE FOUNDATION.

COST-PLUS-FIXED-FEE CONTRACT: An award in which a funder provides reimbursement of allowable costs accrued by the grantee plus a predetermined fee agreed on by both parties (as opposed to a percentage of accrued costs). Because the fee is fixed, the funder is assured it will not swell.

COST-REIMBURSEMENT AWARD: An award in which the organization pays the full costs of the project as they are incurred, and the funder reimburses the organization based on receipts submitted. Compare to FIXED-PRICE CONTRACT.

COST-SHARING CONTRACT: An agreement by which part of the cost of a funded project is borne by the organization receiving the funds. See also MATCHING FUNDS.

COVER LETTER: A letter that accompanies a proposal submitted to a private funder, and is usually less formal and prescribed than a title page or cover sheet for a government funder. Compare to COVER SHEET.

COVER SHEET: A form, usually dictated by the funder, that accompanies a grant proposal upon submission and includes the name of the grantseeker, the title of the project, the start and end dates of the project, the total expected project cost, the amount being requested of the funder, and names, signatures, and contact information of those at the organization who are authorizing the proposal. Often required by government funders. Also called TITLE PAGE or TRANSMITTAL LETTER.

DEMONSTRATION GRANT: See PILOT GRANT.

DEMONSTRATION PROJECT: See PILOT PROJECT.

DIRECT COSTS: Costs directly associated with program delivery, research, or construction. General categories include, but are not limited to, salaries and wages, fringe benefits, supplies, travel, equipment, communication, and outside contractual services. Also called DISSEMINATION: The process of sharing the lessons learned and the knowledge and results gained by doing a project, usually through a conference presentation, website posting, journal article, or other peer information exchange.

DUNS NUMBER: An organizational identification number necessary to apply for federal grants. Federal funders use the nine-digit DUNS (Data Universal Number System) numbers to track applicants. Grantseekers can obtain a DUNS number for free through Dun & Bradstreet or Central Contractor Registration.

EARNED INCOME: Money generated by an organization through sales of products or fees for services. Examples include tuition, fees, concert tickets, conference registration, books or how-to videos, adventure travel to habitat preserved by the organization, or contracted transportation for clients with disabilities. Compare to CONTRIBUTED INCOME AND GRANTED INCOME.

ELECTRONIC SUBMISSION: Turning in an application for funding online, usually through a formal process on the funder's website.

EMPLOYEE BENEFITS: Nonwage remuneration paid for by an individual's employer. Examples include FICA contributions, workers' compensation, tax withholding, and health insurance. Also called FRINGE BENEFITS.

EMPLOYEE GIFT MATCHING: A program in which a company matches, often dollar for dollar up to a maximum amount, the contributions its employees make to nonprofits of their own choice (sometimes restricted to particular fields).

EMPLOYEE GIVING GROUP: A group of company employees that collects contributions from co-workers and then determines among the group whom to fund. While the money being granted is not corporate funds, companies often encourage employee giving by supporting the process with space and staff.

ENDOWMENT: Money that an organization puts into restricted, conservative investments so that the interest earned can pay for program or operating expenses.

EXECUTIVE SUMMARY: See ABSTRACT.

EXTERNALLY FUNDED PROJECT: See SPONSORED PROJECT.

FAMILY FOUNDATION: A private foundation funded by a family. Usually, family members set the grantmaking priorities and make the funding decisions. See also PRIVATE FOUNDATION.

FEDERATED CAMPAIGN: A community-wide fundraising campaign, such as United Way, in which participants have the opportunity to support multiple nonprofits with one gift.

FELLOWSHIP: Funding awarded to organizations or institutions that then offer financial support to students. Also called SCHOLARSHIP or INTERNSHIP.

FISCAL YEAR: Any twelve-month period for which annual accounts are kept. The fiscal year for most universities is July 1 through June 30. The federal fiscal year is October 1 to September 30.

FIXED-PRICE CONTRACT: An award in which the grantseeker agrees to do the work for a specified amount of money, regardless of the time and cash actually spent. Compare to COST-REIMBURSEMENT AWARD.

FORM 990: Internal Revenue Service form filed annually by public charities, listing assets, receipts, expenditures and compensation of officers. See also FORM 990-PF.

FORM 990-PF: Internal Revenue Service form filed annually by private foundations, listing assets, receipts, expenditures, compensation of officers, and all grants made during the year. See also FORM 990.

FORMATIVE EVALUATION: A type of evaluation that measures progress against goals as a project takes form. It judges the effectiveness of the project while it is being implemented. Formative evaluation focuses on the success of the *process*, as distinct from the end product. Compare to SUMMATIVE EVALUATION.

FRINGE BENEFITS: See EMPLOYEE BENEFITS.

FTE: Used to describe a staff position, it stands for full-time equivalent. For example, two half-time employees represent one FTE.

FULL PROPOSAL: A proposal that is detailed and from five to two hundred pages long. Most often, grantmakers provide a template and explicit instructions that they want grantseekers to follow.

FUNDER: The agency, foundation, or individual that gives the award or grant. Also called GRANTMAKER.

FUNDING CYCLE: The period during which a funder accepts proposals and awards funding. Some funders have many cycles in a year, while others have only one.

FUNDING OFFER: The amount of money, which can be more or less than the requested amount, that a funder offers a grantseeker.

GANTT CHART: A type of bar chart that illustrates a project schedule.

GENERAL PURPOSE GRANT: See OPERATING GRANT.

GIFT IN KIND: See IN-KIND CONTRIBUTION.

GIVING CIRCLE: A group of individuals who pool their financial resources to make a joint contribution that will have greater impact than one person's gift could.

GOAL: One of the overarching targets you hope to achieve through the proposed work.

GOAL STATEMENT: A broad description of the intended results of your project.

GOVERNMENT FUNDER: A funder that makes grants, derived from taxes, to support the priorities of its jurisdiction, whether that be federal, state, or local. Also called GOVERNMENT GRANTMAKER.

GRANT: An award of financial support, equipment, or other assistance, based on a proposal written in the format and to the guidelines required by the funder. A grant does not have to be paid back to the funder.

GRANT DOCKET: A calendar that indicates when pending proposals will be reviewed.

GRANTED INCOME: Revenue generated by awards from grantmakers.

GRANTEE: The agency or organization that receives the award or grant.

GRANTMAKER: The agency, foundation, or individual that gives the award or grant. Also called FUNDER.

GRANTSEEKER: The agency or organization that is looking for funding or grants of any type.

GRANTWRITER: The person who writes and assembles the proposal on behalf of a grantseeking organization. May be a hired consultant or on staff at the grantseeking organization.

GUIDELINES: A funder's description of what it hopes to accomplish by giving money, as well as a description of who may apply and instructions and rules for how proposals must be assembled and submitted.

HARD DATA: See QUANTITATIVE INFORMATION.

IMPACT EVALUATION: See OUTCOME EVALUATION.

INDEPENDENT FOUNDATION: See PRIVATE FOUNDATION.

INDIRECT COSTS: The costs of administering the organization as a whole, so that the organization is in a position to implement the project. Utilities, general administrative expenses, and depreciation of equipment and facilities are some examples of indirect costs. Also called OPERATING COSTS or OVERHEAD or ADMINISTRATIVE COSTS.

INFRASTRUCTURE: The buildings, equipment, systems, and policies that make an organizational functional.

IN-KIND CONTRIBUTION: A nonmonetary donation of goods or services instead of dollars. Examples include volunteer time, donated space or transportation, or donations of goods, such as a copy machine, or services, such as the pro bono services of graphic designers. Also called CONTRIBUTION IN KIND or GIFT IN KIND.

LETTER OF AGREEMENT: See MEMORANDUM OF UNDERSTANDING (MOU).

LETTER OF COMMITMENT: A binding contract between the grantseeking organization and other organizations that have a memorandum of understanding (MOU) or other agreement to collaborate on the project. The letter of commitment states each party's intent to work together and stipulates roles and responsibilities, benchmark dates, and the goals that each party will strive to achieve.

LETTER OF DETERMINATION: A document issued by the IRS stating an organization's tax-exempt status.

LETTER OF ENDORSEMENT: A letter from someone who is familiar with your organization and who can specifically cite why you are qualified to do the proposed project, why it matters, and how it is anticipated in the community. The most effective letters demonstrate real familiarity rather than general endorsement. See also LETTER OF SUPPORT.

LETTER OF INQUIRY (LOI): A one- to three-page synopsis of the full proposal in business letter format, used as a first step to get an invitation to submit a full proposal. Grantmakers use LOIs to quickly determine which organizations and projects interest them most. Also called LETTER OF INTENT or LETTER OF INTEREST or QUERY LETTER.

LETTER OF SUPPORT: A letter from a stakeholder or other person who wants to endorse the grantseeking organization and the proposed project. Examples include a letter from a parent who supports the plan for new playground equipment, or a letter from a mayor who supports the renovation of a historic building. See also LETTER OF ENDORSEMENT.

LINE ITEM: A unit of information in a budget, shown on a separate line of its own.

LOAN GUARANTEE: A form of assistance in which a grantmaker uses its good reputation to help an organization secure a loan. In case of default, the grantmaker must reflect the loan in its accounts as if the amount had been granted.

LOGIC MODEL: A graphic representation of a project that shows the relationships between what you propose to do and the results you will achieve.

MATCHING FUNDS: Funds raised by the grantseeking organization and contributed to the project in the amount required by a grantmaker as a condition for receiving a contract, grant, or award. See also COST-SHARING CONTRACT.

MATCHING GRANT: Money provided by a funder as an incentive for others to contribute. Usually, the grant funds will match other contributions dollar-for-dollar up to a particular amount. See also CHALLENGE GRANT.

MEMORANDUM OF UNDERSTANDING (MOU): A written contract between private grantmaker and funded organization that constrains how the organization may use the funds and establishes reporting or expenditure requirements. May also be a binding contract between two or more partner organizations. Also called LETTER OF AGREEMENT. See also NOTICE OF GRANT AWARD (NGA).

METHOD: The way that an organization implements a project and/or evaluates the results of a project, including the steps taken to achieve project outcomes. Methods may also be called TACTICS OR PROCEDURES OR TECHNIQUES.

NARRATIVE: A proposal narrative is the word-based description of the project, as distinct from charts, photos, and budgets. A budget narrative is the word-based explanation of the numeric information provided in the budget itself.

NEED: The situation your work will affect, or the reason you plan to undertake the proposed project. May also be referred to as the PROBLEM or the OPPORTUNITY.

NEED STATEMENT: The section of the proposal that answers the question, What is the problem (or opportunity) that warrants attention? This is the section that identifies the problem, who else agrees it's a problem, and what data lead you to believe that. Also called PROBLEM STATEMENT or OPPORTUNITY STATEMENT or STATEMENT OF NEED.

NOTICE OF GRANT AWARD (NGA): A contract between federal grantmaker and funded organization that details how funds may be used and establishes expenditure requirements. The NGA is the confirmation of expenditure authority provided once the grant has been awarded. See also MEMORANDUM OF UNDERSTANDING (MOU).

OBJECTIVE: A specific, measurable indication that you are making progress toward your goal. There are at least four types of objectives: behavioral, performance, product, and process.

OBJECTIVE STATEMENT: A specific statement that describes a specific and measurable result that your project will accomplish.

OPERATING BUDGET: A budget that describes all the money your organization will raise and spend in one fiscal year, including all expenses, from staff to maintenance to insurance to printing, and all revenue, from grants and contracts to earned and contributed income.

OPERATING COSTS: The costs of administering the organization as a whole, so that the organization is in a position to implement the project. Utilities, general administrative expenses, and depreciation of equipment and facilities are some examples of operating costs. Also called INDIRECT COSTS or OVERHEAD or ADMINISTRATIVE COSTS.

OPERATING FOUNDATION: A type of public foundation that is usually aligned with an institution, such as a university or hospital, and was created to sustain that institution.

OPERATING GRANT: A grant that supports an organization's operating costs. Also called GENERAL PURPOSE GRANT. See also OPERATING COSTS. Compare to PROJECT GRANT.

OPERATING PERIOD: See BUDGET PERIOD.

OPPORTUNITY: See NEED.

OPPORTUNITY STATEMENT: See NEED STATEMENT.

ORGANIZATIONAL CHART: A graphic representation of the key positions in an organization that illustrates the chain of command and the relationships among the different positions.

OUTCOME: A specific, measurable change in decision making, knowledge, attitude, or behavior resulting from your project's outputs.

OUTCOME EVALUATION: A type of summative evaluation that looks at what has *changed* among individuals, groups, the community, or the knowledge base as a result of a project. It provides data to assess the larger consequence of what a project has achieved. Also called IMPACT EVALUATION.

OUTCOME STATEMENT: A narrative description of the project's outcomes: what will change in the lives of individuals, groups, animals, the environment, or the community as a result of the project. It should be stated in measurable terms. See also OUTCOME.

OUTPUT: A quantifiable item or unit of service resulting from the activities you propose.

OVERHEAD: See OPERATING COSTS.

PARTNER: A contractually bound party that works closely with another party with specified rights and responsibilities.

PAYEE'S GUIDE: Instructions for how to access funds awarded by a federal agency. This term is specific to government grants.

PERT CHART: A project management tool used to schedule, organize, and coordinate tasks within a project.

PILOT GRANT: Specific financial support for a demonstration project or pilot project, which aims to show the effectiveness of a model or approach that could later be replicated by the grantee or others using funds from elsewhere. Also called DEMONSTRATION GRANT. See also PILOT PROJECT.

PILOT PROJECT: Project that aims to show the effectiveness of a model or approach that could be replicated by others. Also called DEMONSTRATION PROJECT. Pilot projects are often funded by a specific type of grant called a PILOT GRANT or DEMONSTRATION GRANT.

POST-AWARD PERFORMANCE CONFERENCE: An initial, one-time discussion between government grantmaker and funded organization. It takes place shortly after the award date, and its purpose is to establish a mutual understanding of the specific outcomes that are expected and to set measures for assessing the project's progress and results. It also clarifies how monitoring and communication will take place.

PRINCIPAL INVESTIGATOR (PI): The person in charge of, and responsible for, an experiment or research project.

PRIVATE FOUNDATION: A private grantmaking organization that is usually funded by a single source,

such as an individual, a family, or a business. This category includes FAMILY FOUNDATIONS and COMPANY-SPONSORED CORPORATE FOUNDATIONS.

PROBLEM: See NEED.

PROBLEM STATEMENT: See NEED STATEMENT.

PROGRAM GRANT: A grant that supports the costs of a particular activity, as distinct from an operating grant, which supports the whole organization. See also PROJECT GRANT. Compare to OPERATING GRANT.

PROGRAM-RELATED INVESTMENTS: Very low-interest loans from foundations for program-specific purposes such as economic development, low-income housing, or minority enterprise encouragement.

PROJECT BUDGET: A budget that describes the income and expenses for your proposed project alone.

PROJECT GRANT: A grant that supports the costs of a particular activity, as distinct from an operating grant, which supports the whole organization. A fairly limited initiative in terms of scope and duration is usually called a project. Activities with wider scope or longer duration are usually called programs. See also PROGRAM GRANT. Compare to OPERATING GRANT.

PUBLIC FOUNDATION: A charitable foundation that raises money from the public to be granted to worthy applicants. Public foundations should not be confused with government funders, which are public funding sources. This category includes OPERATING FOUNDATIONS and COMMUNITY FOUNDATIONS and other public foundations.

QUALITATIVE INFORMATION: Information that is subjective and less than concrete, often referred to as SOFT DATA. Examples include anecdotes or quotes; responses from participants in surveys, interviews, or focus groups; observations made by a professional; or changed perceptions, attitudes, or behaviors reported by the target audience.

QUANTITATIVE INFORMATION: Information that is concrete and objective, often referred to as HARD DATA. Examples include test scores, the number of animals who were adopted, or the number of "bed nights" in a shelter. Data must be properly cited, up to date, and from a verifiable and well-regarded source.

QUERY LETTER: See LETTER OF INQUIRY.

REPLICATION: An event in which another organization uses your project as a model to do their own, similar project.

REQUEST FOR PROPOSAL (RFP): The notice released by funders to invite grantseekers to submit a proposal.

SEED MONEY: Funding that helps launch a new initiative or new organization. Also called **START-UP MONEY.**

SMART RULE: A list of recommended characteristics for goals: Specific, Measurable, Achievable, Realistic, and Time-bound.

SOFT DATA: See **QUALITATIVE INFORMATION.**

SOLE-SOURCE OFFERING: An RFP in which the funder intends to give the grant or contract to a preselected recipient.

SOLICITED PROPOSAL: A proposal submitted in response to an invitation initiated by the grantmaker. The funder contacts preselected organizations and invites them to submit a proposal for a specific kind of project or constituency that the funder has already identified as a funding priority. Compare to **UNSOLICITED PROPOSAL.**

SO-THAT CHAIN: An exercise that helps identify project outputs and outcomes. Either individually or in groups, participants write down a series of phrases describing what activity will be undertaken and why, followed by the prompt "so that." Participants continue this pattern to home in on definable objectives and a clear goal for the proposed activity.

SPONSORED PROJECT: A specific activity or program that is financed by funds from a source outside the organization. Also called **EXTERNALLY FUNDED PROJECT.**

STAKEHOLDER: One of the people or organizations touched by the situation you hope to affect. Internal stakeholders might include staff, board members, and volunteers, as well as the people or groups you serve, such as clients, audiences, or students. External stakeholders might include cooperating agencies and organizations, elected officials, local planners and policy makers, individual donors, and people and groups tangentially affected by the issue.

START-UP MONEY: See **SEED MONEY.**

STATEMENT OF NEED: See **NEED STATEMENT.**

STRATEGY: The course of action you engage in to effect change. Also called **APPROACH.**

SUMMATIVE EVALUATION: A type of evaluation that measures and reports what was achieved by the end of your project. Summative evaluation focuses on the *product*. It judges the effectiveness of the project after it has been implemented. Compare to **FORMATIVE EVALUATION.**

SUSTAINABILITY: A project's ability to continue after the grant funds end.

TACTIC: See **METHOD.**

TECHNICAL ASSISTANCE GRANT: See **CAPACITY-BUILDING GRANT.**

TITLE PAGE: See **COVER SHEET.**

TOTAL PROJECT COSTS: The total direct and indirect costs your organization incurs to carry out a project.

TRANSMITTAL LETTER: See **COVER SHEET.**

UNSOLICITED PROPOSAL: A funding request submitted as part of a competitive process that is open to any organization that fits the funder's guidelines. Compare to **SOLICITED PROPOSAL.**

RESOURCES AND REFERENCES

This section lists resources the authors have found valuable in their grantwriting and consulting careers as well as in the writing of this book. It is not exhaustive; it is intended to provide a starting place for readers as they pursue the research, planning, project development, and proposal writing activities discussed in this book. The list is arranged by topic, approximating the order in which these topics are addressed in the book.

All online resources listed here were as up-to-date as possible at the time of printing. For an expanded and regularly updated list of online and off-line resources for grantseekers, please see the Getting Funded website at www.gettingfundedbook.com.

Public libraries provide a wealth of information and should always be considered as a resource for grantseekers. You will find regularly updated information not only about nonprofit and fundraising topics but also about more general topics such as statistical and economic data. Many libraries provide free access to authoritative general databases that can be searched for information about individuals, organizations, and businesses. Librarians are experts in finding information and want to help, so be sure to ask them how to find what you are looking for.

The Cooperating Collections of the Foundation Center, free funding information centers located in libraries, community foundations, and other nonprofit resource centers, provide publications, grants databases, and other supplementary materials and services for grantseekers. The Foundation Center Cooperating Collections' websites are often particularly good sources of nonprofit information. An example of such a site can be found at the Redmond Library, in the King County Library System, www. kcls.org/philanthropy. To find a Cooperating Collections location near you, visit http://foundationcenter. org/collections/.

Organizational Readiness and Capacity

Tools that define and assess organizational capacity can help organizations identify their unique capacity-building needs and guide the development of plans to address them.

Organizational Capacity Assessment Tool

www.caseygrants.org/pages/resources/resources_ downloadassessment.asp
A self-assessment instrument provided by the Marguerite Casey Foundation to help nonprofits identify capacity strengths and challenges and establish capacity-building goals. Available for free download.

Publications

The Best of the Board Café: Hands-on Solutions for Nonprofit Boards. 2nd ed. Jan Masaoka. Saint Paul, MN: Amherst H. Wilder Foundation Publishing Center (in partnership with CompassPoint Nonprofit Services)/Fieldstone Alliance, 2009.

Boards on Fire! Inspiring Leaders to Raise Money Joyfully. Susan Howlett. Seattle: Word & Raby, 2010.

Capacity Building for Nonprofits: New Directions for Philanthropic Fundraising. David J. Kinsey, J. Russell Raker II, and Lilya D. Wagner, eds. San Francisco: Jossey-Bass, 2003.

Designing and Managing Programs: An Effectiveness-Based Approach. 3rd ed. Peter M. Kettner, Robert M. Moroney, and Lawrence L. Martin. Thousand Oaks, CA: Sage Publications, 2007.

Effective Capacity Building in Nonprofit Organizations. Prepared for Venture Philanthropy Partners by McKinsey & Company, 2005. The full report, including a capacity assessment grid, is available for free download at www.vppartners. org/learning/reports/capacity/assessment.pdf

The Five Life Stages of Nonprofit Organizations: Where You Are, Where You're Going and What to Expect When You Get There. Judith Sharken Simon. Saint Paul, MN: Amherst H. Wilder Foundation Publishing Center/Fieldstone Alliance, 2001.

Fundraising for Social Change. 6th ed. Kim Klein. San Francisco: Jossey-Bass, 2011.

The Jossey-Bass Handbook of Nonprofit Leadership and Management. 3rd ed. David O. Renz and Robert D. Herman. San Francisco: Jossey-Bass, 2010.

Nonprofit Consulting Essentials: What Nonprofits and Consultants Need to Know. Penelope Cagney and Alliance for Nonprofit Management. San Francisco: Jossey-Bass, 2010.

The Nonprofit Development Companion: A Workbook for Fundraising Success. Brydon M. DeWitt. Hoboken, NJ: John Wiley & Sons, 2010.

The Nonprofit Marketing Guide: High-Impact, Low-Cost Ways to Build Support for Your Good Cause. Kivi Leroux Miller. San Francisco: Jossey-Bass, 2010.

Selling Social Change (Without Selling Out): Earned Income Strategies for Nonprofits. Andy Robinson. San Francisco: Jossey-Bass, 2002.

Statistics and Facts

You can find statistics and resources to help you corroborate and assess the need for your work in the online resources listed below. Also check local sources, including your chamber of commerce, United Way, the state demographer, city planners, and other government departments related to your work.

American FactFinder

http://factfinder2.census.gov

This is one of the websites of the U.S. Census Bureau. If you're looking for a source that provides population, housing, and other demographic information, this site can provide detailed statistics.

The Annie E. Casey Foundation Knowledge Center

www.aecf.org/KnowledgeCenter.aspx

The Annie E. Casey Foundation has funded copious research on issues related to children and families. Search the foundation's Knowledge Center to see if there are statistics about your field.

Bureau of Labor Statistics

www.bls.gov/bls/other.htm

A web portal of the U.S. Department of Labor, this site provides links to principal federal statistical agencies and the corresponding statistical agencies of governments around the globe. Public policy information related to health care, retirement, wages, workplace safety, education and training, economic development, consumer spending, and other topics can be accessed through this website.

The Centers for Disease Control and Prevention

http://www.cdc.gov/datastatistics/

A portal for data and statistics from the Centers for Disease Control and Prevention that provides access to vital records, health statistics grouped by topic, and a wealth of tools, publications, and research study data. The CDC also hosts an archival site with a vast collection of statistical information regarding the health of U.S. citizens, the **National Center for Health Statistics**, on the CDC website at www.cdc.gov/nchs.

EconData.Net

www.econdata.net

An online gateway to regional economic data. The website offers a free, downloadable guide, *Socioeconomic Data for Understanding Your Regional Economy: A User's Guide,* that will be useful for anyone trying to make sense of the often arcane economic data that is available. Find the guide by clicking "User's Guide" in the navigation on the website. For a succinct list of other websites with regional economic data, click on "Ten Best Sites."

FedStats

www.fedstats.gov

Statistics from more than one hundred agencies. Information is grouped in various ways including by state, topic, and agency. Topics such as agriculture, education, occupations, and women are covered.

Institute of Education Sciences, National Center for Education Statistics

www.nces.ed.gov

This U.S. Department of Education agency website can provide essential data for writing proposals that address the educational needs of local communities and rural districts in the United States. Education statistics can also give another view into a community's economic development positioning. The site's "Data Tools" tab provides search engines dedicated to finding the data sources for colleges, public and private schools, and libraries.

National Center for Charitable Statistics

http://nccs.urban.org/

A national clearinghouse of data on the nonprofit sector in the United States. Look at the "NCCS Community Platform" and the annual nonprofit fundraising survey.

Population Reference Bureau

www.prb.org

The PRB website provides reports and statistics for nations and geographic regions worldwide. For North American nonprofits, the PRB's section on the North

American region contains a wide range of reports that will be of interest, including articles on Hispanic and Asian population growth, adult mortality and death trends, and data on poverty rates in America's midsize counties, small towns, and rural areas. Although the Population Reference Bureau is a fee-based membership group, access to the archive is free.

U.S. Census Bureau

www.census.gov/

Economic indicators, summarized census data and maps, and projected census information are just some of the types of information available through the U.S. Census Bureau's main website. Find more statistics at American FactFinder (see separate entry). Learn more about tracked and reported government expenditures in the *Consolidated Federal Funds Report,* an annual report from the U.S. Census Bureau. That report and related statistics can be found at www.census.gov/govs/cffr/

USA.gov

www.usa.gov

The government's official web portal about U.S. government information and services on the web.

Researching Funders
General Information

Big Online America

www.bigdatabase.com

A searchable online database from the same source as FoundationSearch (see the "Private Funders" section), though Big Online America has fewer search capabilities. This database includes U.S. and Canadian foundations, corporations, and government programs.

The Chronicle of Philanthropy

www.philanthropy.com/

The industry periodical for professionals in fundraising.

Economic Research Institute

www.eri-nonprofit-salaries.com/index.cfm

A website that provides IRS Form 990s.

Public Funders

Catalog of Federal Domestic Assistance

www.cfda.gov

A searchable database of information about all types of federal assistance programs.

Community of Science (COS)

www.cos.com

The Funding Opportunities Database at the COS website allows you to search in a variety of ways for grants associated with the National Institutes of Health (NIH), National Science Foundation (NSF), United States Department of Agriculture (USDA), Small Business Innovation Research (SBIR), and Medical Research Council (MRC).

Grants.gov

www.grants.gov

A single electronic entry point for accessing grants from all twenty-six federal grantmaking agencies. It provides a unified process for finding and applying for all federal grant opportunities.

USA.gov

www.usa.gov

Provides easy one-stop access to all online U.S. federal government resources, including government grants information.

U.S. Census Bureau, *Consolidated Federal Funds Report*

www.census.gov/govs/cffr

This annual report details government expenditures, including grant and contract awards.

Private Funders

Council on Foundations

www.cof.org

While the primary audience of the Council on Foundations is funders, the website has many resources for grantseekers as well, including information about the different types of private foundations. The Community Foundation Locator can help you discover community foundations in your area. Find it under "Resources" in the "Community Foundations" section of the website.

Forum of Regional Associations of Grantmakers

www.givingforum.org

The forum serves grantmakers, but many of the regional associations who belong maintain online, searchable databases that describe their members and are available to subscribers or through local libraries. Search the forum's website or try "regional association of grantmakers" + your state on your favorite search engine to find out whether there is a useful directory for your area.

Foundation Center

http://foundationcenter.org/

The Foundation Center conducts research and provides analysis, training, and resources on philanthropy in the United States and around the world. Located in New York, it maintains field office libraries in Atlanta, Cleveland, San Francisco, and Washington, DC, and supports Cooperating Collections in all fifty states, Puerto Rico, and several countries.

The Foundation Center website includes IRS Form 990s, statistics, and an excellent Frequently Asked Questions section on all aspects of nonprofit organizations and fundraising, including where to find sample proposals.

The "Nonprofit Collaboration Resources" section includes a database of real-life examples and resources on how nonprofits can collaborate. The website provides subscription access to the *Foundation Directory Online* and *FDO Professional* database, but the latter is also available for free at all Cooperating Collections.

A subsidiary website called **Glasspockets**, at http://glasspockets.org/, supports and promotes transparency and accountability in foundations and includes a directory of some large foundations with very detailed information about them.

FC Stats, the Foundation Center's Statistical Information Service at http://foundationcenter. org/findfunders/statistics/, is a free online service providing lists and tables of statistical information about U.S. private and community funders and their funding patterns.

Foundation Directory Online

http://fconline.foundationcenter.org

A searchable online database of foundations and corporate giving programs in the United States, compiled by the Foundation Center and updated weekly. It includes IRS Form 990s. Available by subscription at the Foundation Center website or free at Foundation Center Cooperating Collections (see above). Your local library system may also provide free access to this resource. *FDO Professional* is a more exhaustive version that costs more.

Foundations On-Line

www.foundations.org/page2.html

Extensive lists of foundation and corporate websites.

FoundationSearch

www.foundationsearch.com

A searchable online database of foundations and corporate giving programs, updated daily. Especially useful features include lists of funders' board members and their relationships with other boards, and the option to set up automatic updates on funders you've identified as good prospects.

Giving USA

www.givingusareports.org

Giving USA, a collaboration between the Giving USA Foundation and the Center on Philanthropy at Indiana University, conducts and publishes research on charitable giving in the United States.

GrantStation

www.grantstation.com/

An online funding resource that provides access to information on U.S., Canadian, and international grantmakers as well as state and federal grants and loans. Members receive a weekly electronic newsletter with national and regional grant opportunities and a monthly electronic newsletter with grant information for nonprofit organizations working internationally. Available by subscription and in some public libraries.

GuideStar

www.guidestar.org

GuideStar has a database of Forms 990 from grant-seeking organizations as well as of the Form 990-PFs that private foundations are required to file. In addition to grant research information, the website also has a wide range of information about philanthropy.

Needs Assessment

See the "Statistics and Facts" section.

Project Development and Logic Models

Designing and Managing Programs: An Effectiveness-Based Approach. 3rd ed. Peter M. Kettner, Robert M. Moroney, and Lawrence L. Martin. Thousand Oaks, CA: Sage Publications, 2007.

The Logical Framework Approach. AusGUIDElines: Australian Agency for International Development, Overseas Aid Program of the Australian Government. Commonwealth of Australia, 2000. Available for free download at http://portals. wi.wur.nl/files/docs/ppme/ausguidelines-logical%20framework%20approach.pdf

The Logic Model Guidebook: Better Strategies for Great Results. Lisa Wyatt Knowlton and Cynthia C. Phillips, eds. Thousand Oaks, CA: Sage Publications, 2009.

Outcomes for Success! Jane Reisman and Judith Clegg. Seattle: The Evaluation Forum, 2000. http://www.evaluationforum.com/publications/outcomes_for_success.html

Program Planning & Proposal Writing, Los Angeles, The Grantsmanship Center

W.K. Kellogg Foundation Logic Model Development Guide. Battle Creek, MI: W.K. Kellogg Foundation, 2004. Available for free download at http://www.wkkf.org/knowledge-center/resources/2006/02/WK-Kellogg-Foundation-Logic-Model-Development-Guide.aspx

Evaluation and Outcomes

Organizational Research Services

www.organizationalresearch.com/

This website offers a free downloadable version of Jane Reisman and Judith Clegg's original book, *Outcomes for Success!* as well as many other helpful publications.

Charting Impact

www.chartingimpact.org

A tool to help nonprofits tell the story of their impact to key stakeholders and the public with information about their plans and progress. Developed by BBB Wise Giving Alliance, GuideStar USA, and Independent Sector with the participation of nearly 200 nonprofit and philanthropic leaders, five questions are used to help your nonprofit consider and communicate your progress toward your impact.

Council on Foundations

www.cof.org

The Council on Foundations hosts an online evaluation network that offers resources. Search the website for "evaluation" for a list of documents. While intended for grantmakers, the publication *Evaluating Impact for Small Foundations: Useful Evaluation Terms, Tools & Resources* can help grantseekers understand how funders view the evaluation process. The publication is available at www.cof.org/files/Documents/Family_Foundations/Evaluation/Resource-List.pdf.

Tools and Resources for Assessing Social Impact (TRASI)

http://trasi.foundationcenter.org

A database produced by the Foundation Center in partnership with McKinsey & Company and with input from experts in the field on approaches to impact assessment, guidelines for creating and conducting an assessment, and tools for measuring social change.

Evaluation Checklists

www.wmich.edu/evalctr/checklists/

This website of the Evaluation Center at Western Michigan University is a compilation of checklists for conducting various aspects of an evaluation, with the goal of improving evaluation quality and consistency, and enhancing evaluation capacity. Written by evaluation experts, the website presents brief distillations of lessons learned from practice. Checklist categories include evaluation management, models, values and criteria, and meta-evaluation. At least thirty checklists are available, and the site is regularly updated.

The Evaluation Exchange

www.hfrp.org/evaluation/the-evaluation-exchange

A periodical on emerging strategies in evaluating child and family services. It is published by the Harvard Family Research Project, part of the Harvard Graduate School of Education, and subscriptions are free.

Professional Development Modules

www.oerl.sri.com

The professional development modules available at the Online Evaluation Resource Library offer self-guided training on a variety of evaluation topics, including evaluation design, methodological approaches and sampling, questionnaires, and interviews. Designed for novice and experienced evaluators, the modules present step-by-step strategies with scenarios and case studies for how strategies can be applied to specific evaluation projects.

Publications

"Data Collection Instruments for Evaluating Family Involvement." Helen Westmoreland, Suzanne Bouffard, Kelley O'Carroll, and Heidi Rosenberg. *FINE Newsletter*, Volume I, Issue 2 (Issue Topic: Family Involvement Policy), 2009. Cambridge, MA: Harvard Family Research Project. Avail-

able for free download at http://www.hfrp.org/
family-involvement/publications-resources/data-collection-instruments-for-evaluating-family-involvement

Designing Initiative Evaluation: A Systems-Oriented Framework for Evaluating Social Change Efforts. Battle Creek, MI: W.K. Kellogg Foundation, 2007. Available for free download at www.wkkf.org/knowledge-center/resources/2008/04/Designing-Initiative-Evaluation-A-Systems-Orientated-Framework-For-Evaluating-Social-Change-Efforts.aspx

Designing Projects and Project Evaluations Using the Logical Framework Approach. Bill Jackson, for the IUCN (World Conservation Union) Monitoring and Evaluation Initiative, 1997. Available for free download at http://cmsdata.iucn.org/downloads/logframepaper3.pdf

Effective Grant Writing and Program Evaluation for Human Service Professionals. Francis K. O. Yuen, Kenneth L. Terao, and Anna Marie Schmidt. Hoboken, NJ: John Wiley & Sons, 2009.

The End of Fundraising: Raise More Money by Selling Your Impact. Jason Saul. San Francisco: Jossey-Bass, 2011.

Evaluation: A Systematic Approach. 7th ed. Peter H. Rossi, Mark W. Lipsey, and Howard E. Freeman. Thousand Oaks, CA: Sage Publications, 2004.

Grantwriting Beyond the Basics, Book 3: Successful Program Evaluation. Michael K. Wells. Portland, OR: Portland State University Continuing Education Press, 2007.

Handbook of Practical Program Evaluation. 3rd ed. Joseph S. Wholey, Harry P. Hatry, and Kathryn E. Newcomer. San Francisco: Jossey-Bass, 2010.

Nonprofits and Evaluation: New Directions for Evaluation. No. 119. Joanne G. Carman and Kimberly A. Fredericks, eds. San Francisco: Jossey-Bass, 2008.

Mission Impact: Breakthrough Strategies for Nonprofits. Robert M. Sheehan, Jr. Hoboken, NJ: John Wiley & Sons, 2010.

Outcomes for Success! Jane Reisman and Judith Clegg. Seattle: The Evaluation Forum, 2000. This is an expanded edition of the original *Outcomes for Success!* series, which introduces readers to outcome-based evaluations and walks them through how to develop outcomes. Available at http://www.evaluationforum.com/publications/outcomes_for_success.html

Outcome Funding: A New Approach to Targeted Grantmaking. 3rd ed. Harold S. Williams, Arthur Y. Webb, and William J. Phillips. Rensselaerville, NY: Rensselaerville Institute, 1996. Read this to understand how funders integrate logic model paradigms into their work to fulfill their philanthropic mission.

Supporting Success: Improving Higher Education Outcomes for Students from Foster Care. Casey Family Programs. Updated December 2010. Available for free download at www.casey.org/Resources/Publications/SupportingSuccess.htm

Thinking about Program Evaluation. 2nd ed. Richard A. Berk and Peter Henry Rossi. Thousand Oaks, CA: Sage Publications, 1998.

Utilization-Focused Evaluation. 4th ed. Michael Quinn Patton. Thousand Oaks, CA: Sage Publications, 2008.

W.K. Kellogg Foundation Evaluation Handbook. Battle Creek, MI: W.K. Kellogg Foundation, 2010. Available for free download at www.wkkf.org/knowledge-center/resources/2010/W-K-Kellogg-Foundation-Evaluation-Handbook.aspx (or search the Kellogg Foundation website's "Knowledge Center" for "Evaluation Handbook"). This handbook provides a framework for thinking about evaluation as a relevant and useful program tool. It was written primarily for project directors who have direct responsibility for the ongoing evaluation of W.K. Kellogg Foundation–funded projects.

Budget

Government and Not-for-Profit Accounting: Concepts and Practices. 5th ed. Michael H. Granof and Saleha B. Khumawala. Hoboken, NJ: John Wiley & Sons, 2010.

Grantwriting Beyond the Basics, Book 2: Understanding Nonprofit Finances. Michael Wells. Portland, OR: Portland State University Continuing Education Press, 2006.

The Nonprofit Development Companion: A Workbook for Fundraising Success. Brydon M. DeWitt. Hoboken, NJ: John Wiley & Sons, 2011.

Not-for-Profit Budgeting and Financial Management. 4th ed. Edward J. McMillan. Hoboken, NJ: John Wiley & Sons, 2010.

The Simplified Guide to Not-for-Profit Accounting, Formation & Reporting. Laurence Scot. Hoboken, NJ: John Wiley & Sons, 2010.

Wiley Not-for-Profit GAAP 2011: Interpretation and Application of Generally Accepted Accounting Principles. Richard F. Larking and Marie DiTommaso. Hoboken, NJ: John Wiley & Sons, 2011.

Grant Community

There are several nationally active electronic mailing lists where one can post questions, read archives, and keep up with the national dialogue about grantseeking. In addition to the national resources listed below, search for local or regional chapters of the national organizations or for independent region-specific associations, such as the Puget Sound Grantwriters Association (www.grantwriters.org).

Ask colleagues if there are field-specific organizations or electronic mailing lists you could join. For example, in education alone there are several options. CRFNet (Corporate and Foundation Relations for Educational Institutions) is a free online discussion group focused on building partnerships between educational institutions and corporations and foundations. Fundraising professionals at universities have CASE (Council for Advancement and Support of Education), and those at community colleges have CRD (Council for Resource Development). There undoubtedly are similar organizations in your field.

Association of Fundraising Professionals
www.afpnet.org

Charity Channel
www.charitychannel.com

The Chronicle of Philanthropy
www.philanthropy.com

Grant Professionals Association
www.grantprofessionals.org

The Grantsmanship Center
www.tgci.com

General Information about Grantwriting

Achieving Excellence in Fundraising. 3rd ed. Eugene R. Tempel, Timothy L. Seiler, and Eva E. Aldrich, eds. San Francisco: Jossey-Bass, 2011.

Effective Grant Writing and Program Evaluation for Human Service Professionals. Francis K. O. Yuen, Kenneth L. Terao, and Anna Marie Schmidt. Hoboken, NJ: John Wiley & Sons, 2009.

The End of Fundraising: Raise More Money by Selling Your Impact. Jason Saul. San Francisco: Jossey-Bass, 2011.

Fundraising Principles and Practice. Adrian Sargeant and Jen Shang. San Francisco: Jossey-Bass, 2010.

Grant Writing in Higher Education: A Step-by-Step Guide. Kenneth T. Henson. Upper Saddle River, NJ: Allyn and Bacon (imprint of Pearson), 2003.

Grantwriting Beyond the Basics, Book 1: Proven Strategies Professionals Use to Make Their Proposals Work. Portland, OR: Portland State University Continuing Education Press, 2005.

Grassroots Grants: An Activist's Guide to Grantseeking. 2nd ed. Andy Robinson. San Francisco: Jossey-Bass, 2004.

Program Planning & Proposal Writing. Norton J. Kiritz. Los Angeles: The Grantsmanship Center, 1972.

Rural Philanthropy: Building Dialogue from Within. Rev. ed. Rachael Swierzewski. Washington, DC: National Committee for Responsive Philanthropy, 2007. Available for free download at www.ncrp.org/files/NCRP2007-Rural_Philanthropy_REVISEDEDITION_FINAL-Lowres.pdf

Storytelling for Grantseekers: A Guide to Creative Nonprofit Fundraising. Cheryl A. Clarke. San Francisco: Jossey-Bass, 2009.

"Thank You for Submitting Your Proposal": A Foundation Director Reveals What Happens Next. Martin Teitel. Medfield, MA: Emerson & Church Publishers, 2006.

Winning Grants Step by Step. 3rd ed. Mim Carlson and Tori O'Neal-McElrath. San Francisco: Jossey-Bass, 2008.

General Information About Writing

The Elements of Style. 4th ed. William Strunk and E.B. White. White Plains, NY: Pearson Longman, 1999.

Steps to Writing Well. Jean Wyrick. Boston: Wadsworth, Cengage Learning, 2010.

INDEX